MW00611310

The NEW GUIDEBOOK *for*

PASTORS

The NEW GUIDEBOOK *for* PASTORS

by JAMES W. BRYANT and MAC BRUNSON

B&H
PUBLISHING GROUP

Nashville, Tennessee

© 2007 by James W. Bryant and Donald McCall Brunson
All rights reserved
Printed in the United States of America

ISBN: 978-0-8054-4429-2

Published by B & H Publishing Group,
Nashville, Tennessee

Dewey Decimal Classification: 253
Subject Heading: CLERGY—GUIDEBOOKS
                 PASTORAL THEOLOGY

Unless otherwise designated, Scripture quotations are from the
Holman Christian Standard Bible,® copyright © 1999, 2000, 2002,
2003 by Holman Bible Publishers, Nashville, Tennessee; all rights
reserved. Other Bible versions quoted are KJV, King James Version;
NASB, New American Standard Bible®, copyright © The Lockman
Foundation 1960, 1962, 1963, 1968, 1971, 1972, 1973, 1975, 1977,
1995, used by permission; NIV, New International Version, copyright © 1973, 1978, 1984 by International Bible Society, used by
permission of Zondervan, all rights reserved; NKJV, New King James
Version, copyright © 1982 by Thomas Nelson, Inc., used by permission, all rights reserved.

09 10 11 12 13   17 16 15 14 13 12 11 10 9 8 7 6 5 4 3

Table of Contents

Preface and Acknowledgments

The idea of *The New Guidebook for Pastors* was germinated in a conversation two years ago with B & H Publishing Group about the possibility of revising and updating *Criswell's Guidebook for Pastors* by W. A. Criswell.[1] I had served as Dr. Criswell's minister of evangelism and church organization from 1968–1973. My wife, Ruby, and I had traveled with the Criswells during that time and remained good friends down through the years. I was in conversation with Mac Brunson, then pastor of the First Baptist Church of Dallas, about coauthoring the revision. As I talked with various people about the proposed revision, several said, "Why don't you and Mac write your own guidebook?" When I approached Mac, he was very enthusiastic about the idea of *The New Guidebook for Pastors*, telling me that he had been thinking the same thing himself. B & H Publishing Group was enthusiastic about the new direction.

Both Mac and I are indebted to our wives, Debbie Brunson and Ruby Bryant, for encouraging us and doing some proofreading along the way. Also, before Mac left Dallas to become pastor of the First Baptist Church of Jacksonville, Florida, his able administrative assistant, Sharron Kemp, was of great assistance to us both. She and her husband, George, moved to the church in Jacksonville to help Mac there. She has been a great help in completing this book. Thank you, Sharron!

Among the quotes and testimonies by other pastors and ministers in the book you will find frequent references to two world-famous pastors of the Dallas First Baptist Church who preceded Mac Brunson there—George W. Truett and W. A. Criswell. They, being dead, still speak. Thank you, Drs. Truett and Criswell, for your life messages, examples, and writings that still encourage pastors today. Thank you also to the other pastors, ministers, and evangelical leaders who contributed their testimonies at the beginning of the various chapters: Richard Wells, Joe Brown, Russell Moore, David Allen, Daniel Henderson, H. B. London, Wade Rials, Zig Ziglar, Bill Taylor, Scott Bryant, Sal Saberna, Johnny Hunt, Paige Patterson, Jim Henry, Steve Hunter, John Morgan, Jerry Johnson, Jerry Falwell, Steve Gaines, John Sullivan, and Jerry Vines.

Thanks also to our friends at B & H Publishing Group. Their professionalism blended with their personal touch has made this task delightful from the beginning. Thank you, Jimmy Draper, past president of LifeWay, the parent company of B & H, for encouraging us to go ahead with this book before you retired. Thank you, Len Goss, and all your associates who guided us through the process. By the way, unless otherwise indicated, all Scripture quotations are from the *Holman Christian Standard Bible*, published by Holman Bible Publishers, a subsidiary of B & H.

This book is unique in that I was Mac Brunson's pastor at Sagamore Hill Baptist Church in Fort Worth, Texas, when he was at Southwestern Baptist Theological Seminary in the early 1980s. Then he became my pastor at the First Baptist Church of Dallas when I returned to Dallas to teach at Criswell College in 2002. That alone gives an interesting intergenerational flavor to the book.

Our final and most profound thanks goes to God our Father, Christ our Savior, and the Holy Spirit, our blessed Comforter, who have guided us in this endeavor and will bless this book in the lives of countless pastors both now and until Jesus comes again. Praise be to God!

Jim Bryant
Senior Professor of Pastoral Theology
Criswell College
Dallas, Texas

Mac Brunson
Senior Pastor
First Baptist Church
Jacksonville, Florida

The New
Guidebook
for Pastors

TESTIMONY:
Introduction

C. Richard Wells
Senior Pastor, South Canyon Baptist Church,
Rapid City, South Dakota

Like so many others, I had a childhood "religious experience." My parents were regular church attenders and read the Bible at night, so it seemed natural for me and my brother to "join the church"—which I did at age nine on a "revival" Sunday, with a group of other boys. We were baptized that very night, but I, at least, had no idea why. Yet outwardly I was the quintessential Christian kid; I didn't rebel, I attended church every Sunday and even felt called to preach. But in my heart I was not even sure God existed.

Until—in the language of C. S. Lewis—God got me in checkmate. It's a long story. It begins with a buddy in the Navy who obviously knew God in a way I did not and whose witness ate away at my churchy façade.

Then six months after my discharge, I found myself pastor of a church—and the most miserable human being on earth. For weeks, I coped with prescription tranquilizers. Then came an invitation in the mail—to a conference at the First Baptist Church of Dallas. Miserable as I was, I jumped at the chance to get away, and thus moved into "check."

For each night, alone in the balcony, I heard W. A. Criswell preach the simple gospel truth that we must be born again, not just be religious. By week's end, I knew what was missing, and early the next week, I knelt in my study and gave my life to Jesus Christ.

That was more than thirty years ago. Twenty-one of those years I spent in the academic world, teaching future pastors, and now I have returned to the pastorate myself. There is much to be learned about being a pastor—much from books and much more in the crucible of congregational life. But without conversion, all our learning and experience come to nothing.

Introduction

Many books have been written in recent years on individual topics involved in pastoral ministry, but few have been written to encompass the entirety of that ministry. This is an attempt to be comprehensive and complete, recognizing that each chapter could be turned into a book. The bibliography at the end of the book will enable the serious pastor to pursue the topic of each chapter for himself. Hopefully, this book will be of value from the time a call to preach is experienced by a young man all the way throughout his lifetime of ministry, to retirement and beyond. It could be given as a gift from a pastor to a man whom he ordains to the gospel ministry. It could be used as a textbook in pastoral ministry classes in colleges and seminaries. Denominational leaders could give it as a gift when new pastors come under their care. It could be given by laypersons to pastors they love and for whom they care.

In surveying the existing books on pastoral ministry or pastoral theology, an interesting observation may be noted. The earlier books, before 1940, dealt mostly with what could be called the "spiritual" aspects of the Christian ministry. Beginning with Andrew Blackwood, the great Princeton professor of practical theology, whose books were used in countless seminaries, the shift was made from the personal to the practical.[1] The personal was addressed, but only briefly. Pastoral guidebooks became "how to" books. Certainly pastors need to know how to pastor their churches, but they first need to know how to be pastors. Being comes before doing. Pastoring is not so much a career as it is a calling.

Pastors need to remember that they are called first to serve the Lord and then to serve the church. The heart of the pastor's ministry is his preaching. But every pastor needs to remember that the man is as much the message as the words that he speaks. Like David, pastors need to develop integrity of heart as well as skillfulness of hand as God-called pastors (Ps. 78:72).

Since New Testament times instructions have been given to pastors about how to fulfill the ministry God has given them. Jesus gave both the Twelve (Matt. 10:5–15) and the seventy (Luke 10:1–12) practical instructions before He sent them out to minister. Paul wrote 1 Timothy, Titus, and 2 Timothy to those young pastors with very serious instructions. "Timothy, guard what has been entrusted to you" (1 Tim. 6:20). "Before God and Christ Jesus, who is going to judge the living and the dead, and by His appearing and His kingdom, I solemnly charge you" (2 Tim. 4:1). Peter directed instructions to pastors in his letters: "I exhort the elders among you" (1 Pet. 5:1).

Even in the Old Testament, instructions were given to the priests and Levites about how to fulfill their God-appointed ministries (see Lev. 8; 9; 22). In every era of church history pastoral supervisors and mentors wrote instructions to pastors under them. In the patristic period the great Athanasius, bishop of Alexandria, Egypt, in the fourth century, wrote "festal letters" to his pastors every Easter that included both doctrinal and practical instructions. He was not the only one of the Church Fathers to do so.

During the Reformation period Ulrich Zwingli, the first leader of the Reformed movement in Switzerland, wrote the first *Manual for Pastors* to come out of the Reformation. However, both of the other major leaders of the Reformation—Martin Luther and John Calvin—wrote instructions to pastors of Lutheran and Reformed churches. From England, Richard Baxter's *The Reformed Pastor*, a classic book written in the 1600s and last revised in 1829, is still in print today.[2]

The modern period abounded with books on "pastoral ministry" or "pastoral theology," as it was frequently called. In surveying books in theological libraries today, most such books on the Christian minister or the Christian ministry are more than a quarter of a century old. W. A. Criswell's *Guidebook for Pastors* was published in 1980.[3] So many things have changed in the world since then. The era in which the contemporary pastor serves is now clearly identified as the postmodern era. It is time for *The New Guidebook for Pastors*.

Some years ago one of the authors was invited by the Lutheran bishop of Dusseldorf to come to Germany and speak to his new pastors. The bishop had been converted to Christ long after he had become a Lutheran minister. When asked what he saw as the greatest need of his young, beginning pastors, he replied, "They need to be saved." In a private conversation with one of the young men, the author asked how he decided to become a minister. He shared that he was working in a trucking company and the work was very hard. He did not think he wanted to work that hard the rest of his life. He looked around at the various professions and decided that being a pastor in Germany would be easy. German Lutheran pastors have their salaries guaranteed by the government, whether or not anyone attends the churches they serve. So this young man decided to become a pastor. He had no personal conversion experience and no sense of a divine call. There is nothing in the Bible that even approaches such an idea of the pastorate.

Richard Baxter challenged the pastors to whom he wrote, "See that the work of grace be thoroughly wrought in your own souls."[4] One might think that being a pastor means that he is automatically a Christian. Such is just not the case. Jesus said very clearly that there will be many surprised preachers in the day of judgment who will say, "'Lord, Lord, didn't we prophesy in Your name, drive out demons in Your name, and do many miracles in Your name?' Then [Jesus] will announce to them, 'I never knew you! Depart from Me, you lawbreakers!'" (Matt. 7:22–23).

Every pastor should ask himself, "Am I really saved?" There are too many true stories of pastors who were spiritually lost and needed to be saved. John Wesley was an Anglican missionary to America before he returned to England and was saved in his famous Aldersgate experience.

It is not only essential that the pastor be a genuine, regenerated, born-again Christian, but that he also be a godly man. Richard Baxter pleaded with the pastors who read his book, "O, brethren, watch therefore over your own hearts; keep out lusts and passions and worldly inclinations; keep up the life of faith and love and zeal; be much at home, and be much with God.... Above all, be much in secret prayer and meditation."[5] You must be a Christian before doing anything for Christ. You must be a holy person before you can do holy works. You must *be* a pastor first, and then *do* the pastoring. Pastoral ministry should be a deeply spiritual ministry, involving who you are and not just what you do. The first item in a pastor's job description should be a spiritual item.

The pastor cannot lead his people any higher or any deeper than he has gone himself. This author's younger son asked him several years ago if he had a life-mission statement. I don't think I had ever been asked that question before. From the top of my head, but from the bottom of my heart, I blurted out the slogan that appeared on every church bulletin of the church I attended as a teenage boy: "To Know Christ and to Make Him Known."

The pastor's first goal should be to know Christ. Only as you know Him can you make Him known. The first part of that slogan has to do primarily with the spiritual, the second part primarily with the practical. The pastor does not want to be so heavenly minded that he is no earthly good, but neither does he want to preach to others and become disqualified himself (1 Cor. 9:27).

As you read through this book, you will discover that the individual chapters are distinct but integrally related. The first task of the pastor is to preach. But he cannot preach with power and conviction if he does not approach it as a divine assignment to which he has been called. Nor can he preach with power if he does not pray. His praying and his preaching will be enhanced or hindered by his family relationships. His preaching will not result in a church that is alive, happy, and growing unless he learns how to lead. It is more exciting to preach to a church full than to a church empty. It is also spiritual leadership, not preaching alone, that fills churches. The pastor's preaching should not be tacked on to the end of the worship service. It should be the integral high point and climax of the worship service.

Preaching and worship can be enhanced or hindered by technology or the lack of it. The preaching, especially the evangelistic invitation at the end of the sermon, is dependent for visible results on evangelism and missions during the week. Administering the ordinances, conducting weddings, and presiding over funerals should be made an integral part of preaching and not an interruption of it. Do you get the idea? All of pastoral ministry has direct implications for a pastor's preaching.

Just like life, pastoral ministry has a beginning, a middle, and an end. Finishing is as important as beginning. In fact, it is the beginning and the end that make sense of the middle. How you finish is often the way you will be remembered. The author's (Bryant) mother used to say that farm life was a hard life but a sweet life. The same is true of the pastor's life. Being a pastor is perhaps the highest and noblest calling a man can receive. From the outside it may be viewed as a great privilege, and it is. But from the inside it is a great responsibility that encompasses back-breaking, mind-bending, heart-rending work with serious accountability to God.

The pastorate is hard work, and the pastor should work hard. Done biblically, approached spiritually, pursued passionately, evaluated constantly, and studied intently, the pastorate can be the most satisfying and blessed calling any man could ever hope to pursue. Fred Swank, pastor of the same church for more than forty-two years,[6] often said that to move from the pastorate to the presidency of the United States would be a step downward. In a society that measures success by numbers, budgets, and buildings, not every pastor will move onward and upward to bigger and better things. For one thing, bigger is not always better.

Some pastors, like Jeremiah, would leave where they are if they could, but God has placed them in a specific place for His own purposes. Even dying cities and dying churches need pastors. Of all the awards a pastor might receive, none will be better than the WD award: "Well done, good and faithful slave! . . . Share your master's joy!" (Matt. 25:23). This award will not be given on the basis of numbers, budgets, or buildings. It will be awarded on the basis of faithfulness. Faithfulness is what makes Jesus happy. Ultimately, He is the one person every pastor should desire to please.

TESTIMONY:
The Pastor and His Call

Joe Brown
Senior Pastor, Hickory Grove Baptist Church,
Charlotte, North Carolina

Has God called you into ministry? Have you experienced a time when God was both personal and demanding enough to mention your name and tell you He has a plan for your life? Jeremiah 29:11 states that all of us were created by a God who has a plan and a purpose for our lives.

I remember vividly God calling me to preach—twice! The first time I heard the call but did not obey. The second time I answered God's call with complete obedience and without conditions. Since that time, I have seen God affirm His call upon my life in a thousand different ways.

For years, I have been hesitant to share my calling with anyone because it was so personal, powerful, and specific. I was fearful that God might call someone to ministry and, because the call was not as intense as mine was, he might dismiss it as wishful thinking.

If you are struggling with the call of God on your life, I urge you to continue reading this chapter. I regret that when God was calling me, I did not have this book at my disposal. If God has called you and you have accepted, you were called to a Person and not just to a plan. You have been called to be sold out to God. You have been called to die to yourself and to live for God. Obey His call!

CHAPTER 1

The Pastor and His Call

Outside of assurance of personal conversion to Christ, no other spiritual conviction will help a pastor in his journey more than a firm conviction that God has called him to preach. The pastorate is not so much a profession as it is a calling.[1] Young men often ask their pastors how they can know that God is calling them to preach and that they are not just following their own aspirations. The Bible has clear instructions on God's call and God's gifts that accompany this call.

The two primary passages that answer the question about one's call are Isaiah 6 and Jeremiah 1. Isaiah was an adult when God called him to be a prophet or spokesman for God. Jeremiah was a young man, probably a teenager. The entire Protestant approach to the ministry is built on the calls of Isaiah and Jeremiah.

The Call of Isaiah

We notice several things about the prophet Isaiah's call from the Lord.

A Definite Call

Isaiah was a volunteer, but only in response to the call of God. His call is recorded in Isaiah 6. It is so definite that it is dated "in the year that King Uzziah died" (Isa. 6:1). We know this was about 740 BC. Uzziah was the only king of Judah Isaiah had ever known. He ruled the southern kingdom of Judah for fifty-two years. It was a marvelous time for the nation. Uzziah was a righteous king who sought the Lord from the time he mounted the throne at sixteen years of age until the last few years of his reign (see 2 Chron. 26).

Uzziah was a great builder. He built up the kingdom of Judah economically, militarily, and spiritually. He built and fortified entire new cities. He was a military inventor. He invented devices to shoot multiple arrows at the same time and catapults to launch large stones toward the enemy. He loved the soil. He was an innovative farmer. He was greatly beloved by his people, Isaiah included.

But when the king was at the height of his popularity and strength, "he grew arrogant and it led to his own destruction" (2 Chron. 26:16). He took it upon himself to violate God's clear division between prophet, priest, and king. He went into the temple to burn incense before God as if he were a priest. A priest named Azariah, along with eighty others, followed Uzziah into the temple and confronted him: "Uzziah, you have no right to offer incense to the LORD—only the consecrated priests, the descendants of Aaron, have the right to offer incense. Leave the sanctuary" (2 Chron. 26:18).

Uzziah became furious. In the midst of that fury God struck him with leprosy, which broke out on his face that was red with rage. The priests picked him up and rushed him out of the temple. And he was glad to go. Uzziah was a leper until the day of his death. He lived alone in a house outside the city of Jerusalem until he died.

What a tragedy! Sometimes it takes a national tragedy like this to get the attention of someone whom God is calling to serve Him. In the year that King Uzziah died, Isaiah had his great, initial experience with and call from the Lord.

An Experience with God

The call to preach is first of all a call from and unto God. It is as real as one's initial experience of salvation. Isaiah "saw the Lord" (Isa. 6:1). There is a parallel between a man's conversion experience and his call to preach. Both are datable. Although much may happen leading up to the experiences, both are definite and datable experiences. You may not know the exact calendar date of either experience, but you should be able to describe approximately when, where, and under what circumstances both happened. If God has not called you to preach, you should have the integrity to leave the ministry. You can serve the Lord and even preach as a layperson, but you should not be a pastor unless you know for certain that God has called you to preach. This call will be tied to a great experience with God.

An Awesome Experience

The description of Isaiah's experience with God is awesome. Isaiah described the throne room of God, the angels, the voices, the physical feelings, the sounds, the sights, and the smells. It was that moving and that real. From this passage the famous hymn, "Holy, Holy, Holy" was written. All Christians are commanded by God, "Be holy because I, the LORD your God, am holy" (Lev. 19:2). In being called to preach, a man is singled out from among all of God's people to have a higher calling, a greater vision, a deeper experience with God. The call to preach is not to be taken lightly or presumptuously.

A Convicting Call

You would think that the closer a man comes to God, the cleaner and holier he will feel. In fact, just the opposite is true. No serious preacher of the gospel feels worthy of the call to preach. If he does, he is headed for destruction and disillusionment. The call to preach does not make us feel any more holy than the call to salvation does. The closer you get to God, the brighter the light is and the more you see yourself as sinful. Isaiah was convicted of his sinfulness, and he cried out, "Woe is me, for I am ruined, because I am a man of unclean lips and live among a people of unclean lips, and because my eyes have seen the King, the LORD of Hosts" (Isa. 6:5).

When a man sees God as He really is, he sees himself as he is. No man should feel worthy of being called to preach. Pastors are sinful. But in the call of God, their sin can be forgiven and purged. In Isaiah's great vision of God, an angel took a red-hot coal from the altar of incense and cauterized Isaiah's lips. He was made clean before God. Now he was ready for the call!

Volunteering for the Ministry

There is almost humor in Isaiah's call. He never felt worthy, but he did feel cleansed. And he heard God calling. The conversation in Isaiah 6 is reminiscent of the divine conversation among the Trinity in Genesis 1 when God said, "Let Us make man in Our image" (Gen. 1:26). Isaiah heard the same Trinity of God asking, "Who should I send? Who will go for Us?" (Isa. 6:8). Immediately Isaiah volunteered. He was the only man there in the vision, yet he jumped up and down and waved his hands, volunteering for God's service as a messenger of God. A call from God should be answered.

Isaiah answered God's call, and his ministry spanned more than sixty years. God used him mightily with several of Judah's kings. It was Isaiah who announced that Hezekiah would survive a terminal disease and live another fifteen years. It was Isaiah who announced the divine destruction of the Assyrian army when 185,000 soldiers besieging Jerusalem were killed by an angel in one night. It was Isaiah who announced the coming virgin birth of Christ (see Isa. 7:14). The second half of Isaiah is a prophecy of great comfort detailing the coming messianic kingdom of Christ. What a wonderful assignment Isaiah had. He was the court prophet to several kings.

The Call of Jeremiah

Jeremiah's call was quite different from Isaiah's. Isaiah was an adult; Jeremiah was a teenager. Isaiah was a volunteer prophet; Jeremiah was a reluctant prophet. Isaiah could hardly wait to get started preaching; Jeremiah did not want to preach. Yet Jeremiah's call teaches us that God plans before we are born what He wants us to do. God told Jeremiah, "I chose you before I formed you in the womb; I set you apart before you were born. I appointed you a prophet to the nations" (Jer. 1:5).

Reminiscent of Moses in Exodus 3–4, Jeremiah offered reason after reason for not answering God's call to preach. The primary reasons Jeremiah gave were his youth, his poor speaking ability, and his fear of standing before people. God brushed all these reasons aside and personally touched Jeremiah's mouth while saying, "Look, I have filled your mouth with My words" (Jer. 1:9). Isaiah had wanted to be a prophet; Jeremiah could not keep from it.

An Undeniable Call

Jeremiah could not keep from preaching even though he did not feel successful. After his first sermon the people wanted to kill him. It was the worst time possible to become a prophet. Jerusalem was under siege by the Babylonians. Jeremiah was trapped inside the city. Food was running out. Time was running out. Feelings were running wild. Jeremiah was put in prison not only to keep him from preaching the truth but also to keep him from being murdered by the rebellious people. When he wrote the book of Jeremiah, the king of Judah found out about it and burned it page by page. God told him to write it again and this time to hide it. Because Jeremiah preached the truth he was threatened, opposed, and imprisoned.

There was a point at which the prophet said, "That's it! I'm not going to preach anymore!" Many pastors have felt that way. If you are thinking about leaving the ministry, you need to read about how Jeremiah almost did so. He said, "If I say: I won't mention Him or speak any longer in His name, His message becomes a fire burning in my heart, shut up in my bones. I become tired of holding it in, and I cannot prevail" (Jer. 20:9).

When young men ask you how they can know for certain that God is calling them to preach and how they can know this is not just their own desire, tell them to stay out of the ministry *if they can*. The ministry is hard and even disappointing at times. Stay out of it if you can. *If you can't* stay out of the ministry, that may be the surest sign God is calling you to preach.

A Permanent Call

The call to preach is not dependent on being able to secure and keep a church. A distinction must be made between the call of God to a man to preach the gospel and the call of a local church to a man to become their pastor. The New Testament emphasizes a plurality of elders in the various churches, though only one elder seems to have been in charge. A young man, called to preach, may begin his ministry in a church by being a youth pastor or another church staff member. He may even begin as a volunteer, unpaid staff member.

Pastors in small as well as large churches would be wise to involve the men who surrender to preach as soon as possible. One way is to enlist them as unpaid staff members. Send them to school and involve them in the leadership of the church while they study. After they finish school, they may be called as staff members or pastors of other churches.

There may come a time when God's assignment takes a pastor out of the pastorate. A church may call a man to be its pastor, but God calls a man to preach. Taking an assignment beyond the local church does not take a man out of the gospel ministry. He may leave the pastorate, but he must not leave the ministry. Even of Israel as a nation it is said, "God's gracious gifts and calling are irrevocable" (Rom. 11:29). How much more so the call of God to preach the gospel of Jesus Christ! It is a permanent calling.

If a paid position in a local church is not available, a God-called preacher can become a bivocational pastor, earning his living in the secular world and making himself available to preach in prison, in nursing homes, in home Bible studies, or even on the street. Moving from the pastorate into theological education or into denominational work does not relieve the God-called preacher of his calling. Preach the Word. Many retired pastors become great blessings to local churches simply as Sunday school teachers. A pastor may retire from the pastorate, but he must not retire from the ministry.

Your Call

Now that we have discussed Isaiah's call and Jeremiah's call, let's focus on some questions about your own call.

When Will You Answer?

Many young men, perhaps as teenagers, receive a call from God to preach, but they do not answer. They may or may not go to college. If they do go to college, they may just begin working when they finish their studies. They marry and have children. Then, at an unexpected time, God reminds them of His call and they must answer. Like Jeremiah, they cannot keep from it. It would have been better if they had answered when they were first called.

But God doesn't limit His call to teenagers. Many men are called out of business to full-time Christian service when they are young adults or even older adults. They may feel like they are playing catch-up the rest of their lives. Genesis 12:1 seems to indicate that Abraham had not fully answered God's call on his life immediately when it came. Yet there came a time when he did answer the call. God still wanted him.

If God called you earlier in life to be a preacher and you did not answer, volunteer like Isaiah and see if God still wants you. He probably does.

How Will You Answer?

Whether your call to preach comes to you as a young man, as Jeremiah's call did, or whether it comes to you as an adult, as Isaiah's did, you need to answer. It is almost as if God taps you on the shoulder and you must turn around to see who it is and what He wants. The call may come while listening to a sermon. It may come during an invitation. It may come while you are reading your Bible or praying. It may come as you serve as a layperson in your church and suddenly realize that God has gifted you to serve Him full-time.

However and whenever your call comes from God, you need to answer personally and publicly. It is important to tell your pastor what is happening. If you are married, your wife will need great understanding and compassion. After all, you were not a preacher nor did you intend to be one when she married you. The two of you in prayer must agree that you are willing to answer God's call, no matter where it leads. If you have children old enough to understand, they need to be brought into the circle of prayer. The agreement of a husband and wife and family in a decision to answer God's call is powerful. A pastor's greatest affirmation along the way as he struggles with entering the ministry will come from his wife and family. Make sure they are involved.

Where Will You Answer?

Ask your pastor if you can become his unpaid assistant so he can help train you and guide you as you enter the ministry. Adopt the attitude of Abraham. Be willing to leave your comfort zone. God told Abraham, "Go out from your land, your relatives, and your father's house to the land that I will show you" (Gen. 12:1). He did not tell Abraham where that commitment would lead. Hebrews 11:8 declares, "By faith Abraham, when he was called, obeyed and went out to a place he was going to receive as an inheritance; he went out, not knowing where he was going."

That is what it is like to answer God's call. It may take you far from home, away from your friends, to a strange place that you may or may not enjoy. You make the commitment. God will make a way.

As much as anything, answering God's call is a step of faith. It is like enlisting in the military. You put your life and your future in someone else's hands. Matthew 28:18–20, frequently referred to as the Great Commission, gives that future a worldwide framework. The call is to make disciples of all nations. That is scary. But the reward of such a faith commitment is glorious. Jesus said, "Remember, I am with you always, to the end of the age" (Matt. 28:20). It is better to walk in the darkness with your hand in His hand than to walk in the light all alone.

In the Old Testament and New Testament alike, God promises to be with His servants as they follow Him. To Joshua He said, "Haven't I commanded you: be strong and courageous? Do not be afraid or discouraged, for the LORD your God is with you wherever you go" (Josh. 1:9). That is a good verse for every man who answers God's call to preach to claim as his own.

As a pastor you may not earn what you could if you were in business. But the Bible says to all believers, "Your life should be free from the love of money. Be satisfied with what you have, for He Himself has said, 'I will never leave you or forsake you.' Therefore, we may boldly say: 'The Lord is my helper; I will not be afraid. What can man do to me?'" (Heb. 13:5–6). After all, God and one man are a majority! Take a step of faith and obedience. You will never be sorry that you did, but you may forever regret it if you don't.

Rick Stanley, the stepbrother of Elvis Presley, said that Elvis told him shortly before he died that he was called to preach when he was fourteen years old and that he regretted he did not answer the call. One cannot help but wonder how different the life of Elvis and of the world would have been if he had answered that call. Nobody can answer God's call on your life but you. Answer it!

TESTIMONY:

The Pastor and His Preparation

Russell Moore

Senior Vice President for Academic Administration
and Dean of the School of Theology
Southern Baptist Theological Seminary, Louisville, Kentucky

An unprepared preacher is more dangerous than an unprepared Air Force pilot and more deadly than an unprepared cardiac surgeon. The preacher needs to know the Bible from cover to cover. He needs to know at least the English text and be able to see the nuances of the original Greek and Hebrew texts. He needs to see how the Scripture fits together and how it applies to theological and ethical questions. He needs to become conversant with the false ideologies and winds of doctrine that will capture some of the people to whom he preaches. He needs to know how to channel his natural giftedness, how to ward off distracting aspects of his personality, and how to present the gospel in order to get a hearing from both believers and the lost.

Not every preacher can go to college or seminary. Even so, in these perilous times the most effective ministries seem to start with a time of intense preparation, in a community of men training to preach, under the mentorship of godly Christian scholar-preachers.

An education is only the beginning of a life immersed in the Word of God. But preparation is crucial because we know there's something wicked out there; there are lives at stake; and only one sword will do. The call to preach is a call to prepare!

CHAPTER 2 | The Pastor and His Preparation

The pastor needs spiritual preparation as well as practical preparation for the ministry. His spiritual preparation begins long before he is born. As we saw in Jeremiah 1:5, God ordained Jeremiah as a prophet when He formed him in his mother's womb. Isaiah expressed the same thing in Isaiah 49:1. Before you were born, God knew what you would look like. He knew how tall you would be, your bone structure, and even your future (Ps. 139:13–16). No matter how privileged or underprivileged your childhood may have been, God knew that you were going to come to Christ and answer His call to preach. He knew that you were going to be a preacher. He determined everything, both positive and negative, that brought you to this moment. He has prepared you, and He is continuing to prepare you for the job He wants you to do.

The Pastor's Spiritual Preparation

In addition to the eternal plan of God in the past, God also provides spiritual preparation for the pastor in the present. Paul said, "For we are His creation—created in Christ Jesus for good works, which God prepared ahead of time so that we should walk in them" (Eph. 2:10). God has not only prepared us for our work, but He has also prepared our work for us. Realizing this is a step of faith every pastor needs to take. God has something for you to do. Salvation by grace through faith is the first preparation that God does in a preacher's life. At the moment of salvation, the pastor receives the Holy Spirit of God and of Christ. Romans 8:9 says, "Now if anyone does not have the Spirit of Christ, he is not His" (NKJV). The difference between a mere profession of faith in Christ and the possession of His eternal life is having the Holy Spirit inside.

We understand that denominations differ over the doctrine of the Holy Spirit, but we are going to take the following approach to the doctrine here. *Receiving* the Holy Spirit takes place at conversion, not in some subsequent experience. The baptism of the Holy Spirit occurs at salvation when a person receives the Holy Spirit. It is not a subsequent experience. The Bible is clear that those are not repeatable experiences. In fact, Hebrews 6:4–6 declares that a person can be saved only once. He cannot be saved a second time. You receive the Holy Spirit only one time. He never leaves you or forsakes you. This is the permanent *indwelling* of the Holy Spirit.

The *fullness* of the Holy Spirit is a repeatable event that results in an anointing power on those who are filled so they can witness for Christ and preach Him with boldness and effectiveness. The book of Acts points out nine times that certain people were filled with the Holy Spirit. Sometimes the same people were filled again and again.

Part of God's spiritual preparation of a man to preach is the fullness of the Holy Spirit. Having been born of the Spirit and now being indwelt by the Spirit, the man of God needs to be filled with the Holy Spirit in order to be effective in the work to which God calls him. Every preacher, before he stands to preach the gospel of Christ, should ask to be filled with the Holy Spirit for that assignment. Without the Holy Spirit, preaching will be dead. And dead sermons kill churches.

The Gifts of the Holy Spirit

When God calls a man to the ministry, He equips him for the ministry. Not only does God equip the pastor with the fullness of the Holy Spirit when prayed for, but He also gives pastors special, spiritual gifts—the gifts of the Holy Spirit. Although the subject of the gifts of the Holy Spirit applies to the entire body of Christ, it certainly is crucial for pastors. Your spiritual gift is part of your spiritual preparation. There are three primary passages on the gifts of the Holy Spirit in the New Testament: 1 Corinthians 12, Romans 12, and Ephesians 4.

For purposes of discussion, let's begin with 1 Corinthians 12:4 where Paul divides the gifts of the Holy Spirit into three categories.

(The word translated as "different" is the Greek word *katagoria*, from which we get our English word *categories*.) The three categories of gifts Paul labels as "ministries" (v. 5), "activities" (v. 6), and "manifestations" (v. 7). We will call these gifts *motivational* gifts, *ministry* gifts, and *manifestation* gifts.

The first category of gifts may be considered as primary, basic motivational gifts. Motivational gifts are called "grace gifts" (*charismata*) in Romans 12. This means that they are given at the time of your experience of grace in salvation, and they are spiritual abilities that should direct and motivate every Christian's service, but especially that of the pastor.

Finding Your Basic Motivational Spiritual Gift

Romans 12:6–8 itemizes seven different motivational gifts: prophecy (proclaiming the truth), service (meeting people's physical needs), teaching (clarifying the truth), exhorting (encouraging), giving (meeting people's financial needs), leading (meeting people's organizational needs), and mercy (meeting people's emotional needs). There is a principle of concentration woven throughout these verses leading to two implications, one very clear, and the other very probable. If we are commanded to concentrate on one of these gifts, the implication is that every Christian has *at least one* of these seven basic motivational gifts.

The probable implication is that each Christian has *only one* of the seven motivational gifts on which to concentrate. Just as persons receive natural abilities when they are born physically, so also they receive spiritual abilities when they are born again spiritually. The discovery of one's basic motivational gift is very liberating and enhancing, especially for a pastor.

Ephesians 4 personifies the gifts in gifted men that seem to be given by the risen Christ to the church at His ascension: apostles, prophets, evangelists, and pastor-teachers. First Corinthians 12:8–11 itemizes manifestation gifts, those gifts called out in others as each of us, especially pastors, exercises his motivational gifts.

Some people suggest that the list of gifts in Romans 12 represents the seven basic motivational gifts of which every Christian has at least one, and probably only one, since concentration implies singleness of mind. If this is true, every pastor needs to discover which one of the seven basic motivational gifts he has. As he concentrates on that gift, it will become the power by which he serves. He is commanded in the rest of the New Testament to practice all seven gifts, but only one of them will really motivate him. Once he discovers his motivational gift, he will become focused in his work.

If the seven gifts in Romans 12 represent severally and singly the power by which we serve, then the four personified gifts in Ephesians 4 represent the opportunities we have to serve. The motivational gift will never change throughout a pastor's entire ministry. His ministry gift may change, but the power by which he serves will never change. The opportunity to serve may change. A pastor may exercise his one motivational gift in different ministries during his lifetime of ministry. He may be an apostle, a missionary, or a church planter. Then he may become a prophet, proclaiming the truth with great power. He may become a pastor-teacher in a local church (the Greek construction indicates a hyphenated gift). Or he may become an evangelist. He may move from one ministry opportunity to another, but he will always approach that ministry according to his motivational gift.

Now let's put the three passages together in the life of a pastor. In the list of personified spiritual gifts in Ephesians 4, the office of pastor-teacher is listed. Every pastor ought to be a teacher. Not every teacher ought to be a pastor. The pastor may not have the motivational gift of teaching, but he must teach. This is implicit in the Great Commission, "Teaching them to observe everything I have commanded you" (Matt. 28:20).

Every God-called preacher is responsible to show his love for Jesus Christ by feeding and tending His sheep. This cannot be done without teaching the Word of God. Expository preaching through books of the Bible is a form of feeding and tending the sheep. The pastor feeds the people together and tends them separately. But both feeding and tending the sheep are to be done with the Word of God. Every pastor should be a teacher.

If a pastor's basic motivational gift is the gift of prophecy, this will affect the way he pursues his ministry. The gift of prophecy is not limited to prediction of the future, but it is primarily proclaiming the truth. Just like Elijah in the Old Testament and John the Baptist in the New Testament, the prophet of God thunders forth the message of God about the present and the future. Pastors with the gift of prophecy reach people for Christ from the pulpit.

If a pastor has the gift of service, he will emphasize meeting people's physical needs. But he must discipline himself to feed as well as tend the flock of God. A pastor's heart that has the gift of service will always be a heart of help. The pastor with this gift looks like one big heart with hands. God has gifted him to help meet people's physical needs. That is what fulfills him. He loves to help people. But he must not allow himself to neglect his responsibility to study, pray, preach, and teach. People need spiritual help above all. And they get this spiritual help through the teaching of the Word of God.

A pastor with the gift of service should always take his Bible with him when he goes out to help people. It is better to teach a person to fish than it is to bring him a fish. Sound biblical preaching will teach people to fish. If a pastor only rescues people physically and financially and not spiritually, he will have to do this over and over again. He may wear himself out if he spends all his time trying to meet the physical needs of his flock. But he refreshes himself in the Word and then refreshes his people.

The pastor who has the gift of exhorting often spends himself in counseling people. That is a great strength in a pastor, but he should counsel people with and according to the Word of God. Exhorters make wonderful preachers because they readily apply truth to life. But this application must come from the Word of God and not from counseling books. He must exhort his people with the Word of God. In fact, the more the pastor teaches his people the Word of God, the less counseling he will have to do. The Holy Spirit, through the Word, will counsel them.

The pastor who has the gift of giving often becomes financially blessed because of God's clear principle in Luke 6:38. If God blesses a pastor financially, he should be careful not to reflect that blessing in extravagance. Nor should he fall into the trap of operating as if money were the solution to all problems. Sometimes pastors who become independently wealthy offer to serve without pay. That is unscriptural. Both Jesus and Paul talk about a pastor working for his salary. If the pastor wants to give his salary back to the church, that is another matter, but he should never offer to serve without pay. The church would be misled into thinking that all pastors should do that, and this is wrong. He needs to look upon the Word of God as true riches and teach his people the whole counsel of God, not just what the Bible says about money.

The pastor who has the gift of leading is exceptional. All pastors should be leaders, but the spiritual gift of ruling or leading is a special gift that must be exercised with care. Note this interesting thing about the construction of Romans 12: Following the listing of the seven spiritual gifts in Romans 12:6–8, the next seven verses have a word of admonition about each of the seven gifts. Verse 14 is an admonition for those pastors who have the gift of leading or organizing: "Bless those who persecute you; bless and do not curse." People do not like to be organized. Rebellious people do not like to be led. A pastor who has the gift of leading should teach his people the Word of God.

When Adrian Rogers became pastor of Bellevue Baptist Church in Memphis, Tennessee, the church had been a strong deacon-led church for decades. One of his predecessors, R. G. Lee, had preferred a deacon-led church because he was often gone for preaching engagements. Ramsey Pollard, who followed Lee, was unable to change that procedure. Adrian Rogers believed in a strong pastor-and-staff-led church. When asked what he did to turn this around, he replied that he had the deacons meet only for an hour one Sunday afternoon a month. He took the first forty-five minutes and taught them what the Bible said about the role of deacons and left them only fifteen minutes to discuss business. According to Acts 6, they were to be assistants to the pastor, not an official board. He taught them the Word of God.

The pastor who has the gift of mercy had better have a lot of tears to shed because a lot of sad and moving things happen in a church. He is admonished in Romans 12:15 not to spend all of his time weeping with people but first rejoicing with them. If mercy is meeting people's emotional needs, they need to laugh as well as cry. In fact, the pastor who does not learn to laugh with his people will not be allowed to cry with them. You have to earn that right. Pastors with the gift of mercy have a wonderful hospital and funeral ministry. But they should cultivate ministries to families with new babies and relish family weddings as well. And they must discipline themselves not to turn aside from the study of the Word and prayer to meet people's emotional needs immediately.

Each motivational gift has its strengths and its vulnerabilities. That is why we need one another in the church. Only one person has all seven gifts—and that is Jesus. It is in the collective distribution of the gifts to various Christians that the likeness of Christ is realized in a church. Fellowship problems occur in a church when members are not taught to discover and function according to their respective spiritual gifts. It is important that the pastor discover which one of the seven gifts fulfills him. When he functions according to his spiritual gift, his ministry will have spiritual power.

Just like many blondes would like to be brunettes, many short people would like to be taller, and many tall people would like to be shorter, a pastor might prefer another spiritual gift than the one he has been given. Most pastors would choose the gift of prophecy, if they were allowed to do so. Pastors with this gift can preach people out of the pews down to the altar. But not every pastor has this gift. God makes the choice. All pastors need to discover, accept, cultivate, develop, and use the spiritual gifts that God has given them.

In the commentaries on the seven motivational gifts that are outlined in Romans 12:9–15, the characteristics and vulnerabilities of each gift are listed. Verse 9 relates to verse 6 and comments on the gift of prophecy. The pastor who has this gift must be sure to connect love with the exercise of his gift. If he is not careful and prayerful, with his sharp and convicting preaching he could leave broken and wounded hearers without giving them the balm of Gilead for their wounds.

Jesse Hendley, the scholar-evangelist who is now in heaven, had the gift of prophecy. He became known early in his ministry as "Hell Fire Hendley." After more than fifty years as an evangelist, he advised young prophets that they should never preach on hell if they could not do it with broken hearts. This is what verse 9 is driving at when it says, "Let love be without hypocrisy" (NKJV).

Note the admonition that follows: "Abhor what is evil. Cling to what is good." This reveals both a characteristic and a vulnerability of the gift of prophecy, or proclaiming the truth. Little sins bother the prophet. His preaching often lashes out at the little foxes that spoil the vine. However, if he allows little sins to enter his own life, he will be robbed of power in the pulpit. He will preach to others but become disqualified himself.

Verse 10 relates to the first part of verse 7, and it comments on the gift of service. Service rendered without love is empty. First Corinthians 13 makes this clear. If a pastor who has the gift of service renders it out of duty rather than love, he will burn himself out. Service rendered without love is vulnerable to the "appreciation trap." Many pastors with the gift of service want to be told they are appreciated all the time. This just doesn't happen. It comes down to the question of who you are serving. Are you serving the Lord or are you serving people?

It is the Lord who commands us to serve. Jesus reminds us in Luke 17:9 that servants should not expect to be complimented when they are doing what they have been commanded to do. Often congregations have no idea how much a pastor does, and he does not need to tell them. The One who needs to know does know. He is the One who will say some day, "Well done, good and faithful servant."

Verse 11 relates to the last part of verse 7, and it comments on the gift of teaching. The teacher is to be diligent; he is to work hard at learning so he can teach. The teacher must also have a passion for what he teaches. He is to be fervent in spirit. Some pastors who have the gift of teaching go down deeper, stay down longer, and come up dryer than you can imagine, and then they wonder why their sermons are so dull. How many church services start at eleven o'clock sharp and finish at twelve o'clock dull? The teacher should also remember that his first responsibility is to the Lord. This will keep him sharp and help him realize that his sermons don't have to please the people, but they must please the Lord.

Verse 12 relates to verse 8, and it gives an admonition to the exhorter. This is the "cheerleading" gift. Exhorters make wonderful preachers and counselors. They have a knack for applying Scripture to life. Their sermons often become "how to" sermons. The exhorter frequently gives a list of things to do that will help people solve their problems. But he often expects people to follow the list precisely; he forgets that they have to do number one on the list before they can proceed to number two.

The pastor who is an exhorter gets discouraged when people do not follow his directions. Perhaps that is why his admonition is to rejoice in hope. If we say something enough times, we tend to think maybe the people will eventually get it. The exhorter must not give up on people. He must keep hoping they will get it. He must be patient and prayerful. After all, only God can change people. The exhorter may be *a* change agent, but he is not *the* Change Agent. He must be careful to exposit the Bible as the source of instruction. The pastor is not the instruction book; the Bible is.

Verse 13 relates also to verse 8, and it gives an admonition to the pastor who has the gift of giving. While all Christians are commanded to be givers, certain Christians have a special gift in this regard. They often become wealthy because God will bless abundantly when he finds a person who will be a channel of blessing to others. Luke 6:38, although only one verse in the Bible, is included for good reason. While prosperity theology may be suspect, Luke 6:38 is not. The admonition in Romans 12:8 to the pastor who has this gift is that he should practice it with liberality. In verse 13 he is warned that he must not become content with giving his money. He should also be giving his time and personal attention. This gift could also be called the gift of hospitality.

This gift is not reserved for wealthy people. Anyone can be hospitable. Luke 6:38 declares that we give to get to give. It is important how you say that. You must start and stop on *give*, never on *get*. Every pastor ought to be a giver, but some have a God-given, special gift of giving. As a pastor's income grows, so should his giving and his hospitality. The pastor who opens his home to his members will be greatly blessed. Church members will not forget his gracious and generous spirit.

Verse 14 also relates to verse 8, and it admonishes the pastor who has the gift of leading. In the King James Version, the word is translated as "ruling." It is better translated as "leading." This is the gift of organizational ability. Some pastors have this as a natural skill. But this verse is not talking about natural born leaders. It is talking about spiritually born leaders. Pastors who have this spiritual leadership gift often become pastors of large churches, but not always. Smaller churches need organizing, or else God would not have given this gift to the church.

Note the admonition in Romans 12:14: "Bless those who persecute you; bless and do not curse." Every pastor who tries to lead understands this admonition. Even Moses discovered that rebellious people can't be led into God's best. How tragic that Moses lost his temper late in life and struck the rock rather than speaking to it as God had commanded. Every pastor should pray, "Dear Lord, help me to speak to the rock and not strike it." The effective leader will have opposition, but he must never succumb to the temptation to lash out at his opponents.

The leader should expect opposition. Opponents serve two purposes in the plan of God for a pastor. First, they make him lead his people rather than drive them. Second, they make him exercise his gift with diligence and thoroughness. If the pastor is not sure about where he is going, he cannot expect the people to follow. The leader should teach his people the great passages in the Old Testament and New Testament about leadership and followership. He should remind his people that great followers make great leaders.

Preaching through the books of the Bible will help the pastor secure his leadership in the church. The book of Numbers is about leadership and what happens when congregations do not follow. Psalm 78 is about leadership and God's kindness to rebellious people. He blesses and does not curse. The book of Joshua is about leadership. Hebrews 13:7–17 is one of the strongest passages in the Bible about pastoral leadership. Preaching and teaching the Bible is the spiritual leader's greatest tool in challenging his people to follow. Even when they resist, he is to bless them and not lose his temper over their reluctance.

Verse 8 emphasizes that a pastor with the gift of mercy needs to work at being cheerful rather than sad. Verse 15 admonishes him to think of his gift as an emotional gift—ministering to the emotional needs of his congregation. The pastor with the gift of mercy needs to function with happiness, not sadness. He is first to rejoice with those who are rejoicing so he may be allowed later to weep with them when they weep. Pastors who do not have the gift of mercy should remember that Jesus said, "Blessed are the merciful, for they shall obtain mercy" (Matt. 5:7 NKJV).

The pastor who has the gift of prophecy and lashes out at sin should remember to show mercy, even if this is not his special gift. There will come a time in every pastor's life when he needs the mercy of the church. A pastor who had the gift of prophecy preached strong messages on marital fidelity and purity of life. Yet he wept with his people when they had moral failures and did not turn his back on them. He taught them to confess their failures before the congregation and to seek restoration.

Years passed, and his own son impregnated his fiancée before they were married. With tears the couple asked the church for forgiveness. The pastor offered to resign. His people said, "Pastor, you have always preached the truth, but you have always been merciful to us when we sinned. We do not want you to resign." Blessed are the merciful, for they shall obtain mercy.

Bill Gothard[1] has challenged pastors for many years to study spiritual gifts. Much of the material in this chapter was stimulated by attending his Advanced Institute and his annual conference for pastors. He illustrates the function of these gifts in an imaginary situation. Imagine that a woman is coming out of the food line with a tray of food during a Wednesday night church supper. There is a microphone cord stretched across the floor. It has been taped down, but part of the tape has come loose and the poor woman catches the toe of her shoe on it and stumbles. She almost falls, dropping her tray in the process. Seven people with the seven different spiritual gifts spring into action.

The person with the gift of prophecy says, "The person who taped down the microphone cord should have been more careful, and you should have been more careful too." The person with the gift of service says, "Let me clean it up." The person with the gift of teaching says, "The tape should have been put down more securely. If you had lifted your foot up just an inch higher this would not have happened." The person with the gift of exhorting says, "Get up. Come on. Let's try it again. I know you can do it right this time." The person with the gift of giving says, "Let me buy you another meal." The one with the gift of mercy says, "You poor thing. Are you hurt?" The person with the gift of leading says, "George, get a broom. Mack, get a mop. Steve, get her another meal. Mary, help her over to the table." It takes all seven of these gifts to make a church in the likeness of Christ.

Happy is the pastor who discovers and cultivates his own spiritual gift, then teaches his people to discover and function according to their spiritual gifts. It also helps if he will cut a little slack for those whose gifts differ from his own. If there is a fellowship problem in the church, perhaps the people need to study spiritual gifts. It is liberating when a pastor and a church realize that Christ has gifted each of His people spiritually, and each should be filling in what is lacking in others, including the pastor. How many times has a church said, "He is a good preacher but not a good pastor"? Or, "He is a good pastor but not a good preacher." That depends on what spiritual gift he has. When Christ calls a man to preach, He also gives him the exact spiritual gift He wants him to use in his ministry.

The Pastor and His Educational Preparation

The call to preach is also a call to prepare, no matter how old a man is when he answers God's call. Pastors need theological training. Pastors should publicly tell every young man who surrenders to preach to finish high school, go to college, and go to seminary. With many online educational opportunities available, pastors have no excuse for not getting an education. The ideal education for the man who is going to be a pastor consists of three different levels of learning.

First, he needs to enroll in a Bible college or a Bible institute because he needs to know the Bible. Then he needs to get a liberal arts degree because that will help him understand the world in which he lives. Finally, he needs to go to seminary where he can study not only the Bible but also the biblical languages, theology, church history, preaching, church administration, missions, evangelism, church growth, and the multitude of other specialized courses needed to prepare him for what God is calling him to do. If he attends a Bible college, he usually will enter seminary at an advanced level. Many pastors serve churches while they are continuing their education.

Many pastors in the past never had the opportunity to go to college or seminary because of where their churches were located. Many served bivocationally and could not move to a college or seminary to study. With today's distance education and online opportunities available, no pastor can be excused for not getting theological training. It is worth the sacrifice of time and money to prepare for what God has called you to do. If you do not get an education, you put a limit on your ministry that God did not intend. The call to preach is a call to prepare.

TESTIMONY:

The Pastor
and His Preaching

David Allen
Dean of the School of Theology
Southwestern Baptist Theological Seminary,
Fort Worth, Texas

The theological foundation for preaching is a deep belief that God has spoken. J. I. Packer says that Scripture is God preaching. An expository sermon should be derived from a text of Scripture. The text is not *a resource* for the sermon; it is *the source* of the sermon. Sermon preparation must begin with exegesis of the text. When sermon preparation is complete, every preacher should scrutinize the sermon and ask, "Can the text sue me for exegetical malpractice?"

Sermon preparation is a threefold development of the text. The preacher should explain, illustrate, and apply. Like a fisherman, a preacher cannot cook what he has not caught. A sermon's greatest failure is lack of biblical content. To neglect the exposition of the text is to skirmish cleverly on its outskirts and pirouette on trifles. Exposition is enhanced by clear illustrations and cogent applications. The job of sermon preparation is to take the results of exegesis, then select, arrange, and construct a sermon that is clear and interesting.

The second greatest failure in sermon preparation is dullness. Seek to write and deliver sermons that are passionate and interesting. Work at translating the meaning of the text into the language of your own time. Remember that the simpler the expression, the deeper the impression. Write the sermon with one eye on the text and one eye on the congregation. Listen for the tired voices and broken hearts desperately crying, "Give us Jesus!"

The Pastor and His Preaching

When the first man and woman had sinned and were in need of more than just clothing, God Himself came with the *protoevangelion*, the first gospel, and preached to them the coming of One who would crush the head of the serpent. When God wanted to instruct, guide, and warn His people, He sent that group of men known as prophets to preach His Word. From the miracle-working prophets like Elijah; to the fatherly Samuel; on to the erudite Isaiah; and the rough-hewn, backwoods, bucolic Amos—they all preached the Word of God.

When God wanted to announce the coming of the kingdom, it was John the Baptist who stood at river's edge and became the voice crying in the wilderness, "Prepare ye the way of the Lord" (Mark 1:3 KJV). Then Jesus began his ministry by "preaching the gospel of God" (Mark 1:14 NASB). Soon after that He entered the synagogue in Nazareth, His hometown, and began to read and preach from the scroll of Isaiah (Luke 4:18). Jesus, speaking to Simon and his companions, said, "Let us go somewhere else to the towns nearby, in order that I may preach there also; for that is what I came out for" (Mark 1:38 NASB).

When the Holy Spirit birthed the church at Pentecost, it was the heralding of the gospel preached by Peter that accompanied its birth. All through the Word of God and down through the annals of history, when God has moved it has almost always been attended by the preaching of the Word. There is no task more important, no calling any higher, and no work more noble than preaching the Word of God.

The Call to Preach

As noted in the previous chapter, the call to preach is the most singularly unique appointment in life. It is not a call to a vocation or a job, nor is it a call to a profession. It can only be described as the call of Almighty God and the touch of His hand on a person's life. A call to preach is different from a call to a church or even a call to ministry. The call to preach is more basic than that. It is a call to preach the Word of God, and that call stokes a fire within a man that, if not given outlet, becomes like "fire shut up in my bones" (Jer. 20:9 NASB).

Most everyone wants to know what the call to preach is and how you know if you have received this call. I have had people who had just lost a job come to me and tell me that God was calling them to the ministry. God may use a hurtful experience to get your attention, but having nowhere to go to work is not the same as a call to ministry. The old advice given to me is still good: "If you can do anything else but preach, then you are better off doing it."

The call is something that is an indescribable joy and an indefinable burden at the same time. There perhaps is no better way to describe it other than the words spoken to the prophet Jeremiah: "Behold, I have put My words in your mouth. See, I have appointed you this day" (Jer. 1:9–10 NASB).

If you are in the ministry and do not have a clear, unquestionable sense of God's call, even though you may not be able to explain it, then you should leave the ministry immediately. The harm you can do to people, a congregation, your family, yourself, and the kingdom is beyond description.

But if you do have that call and you know it, there will be many times when the only thing that holds your hand to the plow is your call. There have been times in my own personal life when I questioned my salvation, but there has never been a time when I questioned God's call on my life to preach.

Many who read this may be struggling with a call to ministry. You sense that God has His hand on you, but you are not sure; you feel inadequate. Paul felt that way and asked, "And who is adequate for these things?" (2 Cor. 2:16 NASB). If you do feel adequate, then you have a deeper spiritual issue.

Let's ask several questions. Do you have a consistent and growing desire to serve God? Do you love to study God's Word? Do you have any evidence that you have the gift to preach and teach? Has that been confirmed by other mature believers? If you are married, does your spouse agree? Are you busy working in the church now?

It is interesting that God in the past has called men who were busy. Moses and David were both tending sheep when God called them to shepherd His people. Gideon was threshing wheat when God called him to thrash the Midianites. Peter was fishing when Jesus called him to become a fisher of men. Paul had a trade of making camel-hair tents, a profession he used to support his itinerant ministry. He had been traveling and persecuting the church when Jesus called him to go and plant churches. God seems to call men who are already working.

If you sense God has called you, seek wise counsel from those who have been called to ministry. Solomon wrote, "Without consultation, plans are frustrated, but with many counselors they succeed" (Prov. 15:22 NASB). If Solomon—the wisest man who ever lived—needed counselors, then it is certain that we need them too. But it is critical that you turn to those who give evidence of God's call on their lives, those who walk closely with the Lord, and those who exhibit the fruit of the Spirit and godly wisdom.

Finally, allow the Holy Spirit time to work in your life. If there is one thing I am convinced of after these years of ministry, it is that hurry is almost always of the devil. God's timing is nothing like our own. Allow yourself to simmer in the Spirit of God through prayer and the study of His Word so that when the Lord speaks, you can hear clearly. When God calls, do not delay and spin off endless excuses. Isaiah 30:21 says, "And your ears will hear a word behind you, 'This is the way, walk in it,' whenever you turn to the right or to the left" (NASB).

The Content of Preaching

There is a famine in the land. It is not a famine of wheat and grain but a famine of the Word of God. On any given Sunday, what is put forth as preaching from pulpits all over our nation is little more than the stand-up routine of a Jay Leno or a David Letterman wrapped up in the cloak of contemporary piety.

When I was making the transition from First Baptist of Dallas, Texas, to First Baptist of Jacksonville, Florida, our family attended a well-known ministry for our Sunday worship time. If there was a text of Scripture used for the service, it was not expounded upon, and I am not sure the name of Jesus was ever mentioned. And this is one of the fastest-growing churches in America with one of the most dynamic ministers to be found anywhere. It was my prayer that it was an off day because I know personally that this minister wants to reach people for Jesus. It is tragic, but that has become the driving force for Sunday— "How can I reach a crowd" rather than "Thus saith the Lord."

Too often our desire to reach numbers, people, and crowds has caused us to sacrifice the Word of God on the altar of drama, theatrics, and entertainment. While there is nothing wrong with skits, great music, PowerPoint presentations, and even appropriate videos, there is something tragically wrong when we do anything other than make preaching the Word of God central in the service. You cannot separate the Word from worship.

All through Scripture you see the centrality of the Word of God being preached. Enoch, in Jude 14–15, collided with the ungodly of his generation and the Word of God. Noah, we are told in 2 Peter 2:5, preached righteousness as he built the ark. From the first moment that Jonah landed on the soil of Nineveh, he preached a hard-hitting message. Peter boldly preached to the gathered crowd at Pentecost, and three thousand people were saved. We read in Acts 2:42 that the new converts were continually devoting themselves to the teaching of the apostles.

You can move from those Old Testament and New Testament examples to the patristic fathers such as Justin Martyr, Clement of Alexandria, Theodore of Mopsuestia, and John Chrysostom. They made preaching the Word primary. When you reach the Middle Ages, also formerly known as the Dark Ages, preaching for the most part had become lost, as had the Word of God. That is perhaps why the Dark Ages were so dark. Preaching the authority of the Word of God expositionally was recovered by men such as William of Occam, John Wycliffe, John Huss, Martin Luther, Ulrich Zwingli, and John Calvin.

There are three positions that any preacher can take with the Word of God. First, he can stand *over* the Word as if he is the authority and the Word is something to be manipulated, contorted, and twisted to say what he wants it to say. This is where a lot of postmodern preaching stands. The postmodern pulpit no longer interprets; it reconstructs the text to say what people want it to say.

Second, the pastor can stand *beside* the Word of God as if he were on a par with it. This is where a great deal of nineteenth- and twentieth-century liberalism stood. To these liberals, the Bible is *a* word and not *the* Word. The sermon becomes a monologue and is used along with thoughts from the latest article in the *New Yorker* or *Time* magazine, combined with what has just aired on the Public Broadcasting Network. Scripture is just a piece of information along with all the other information people today have to sort through.

The third position is the only position to take when it comes to the Word of God—and that is to stand *under* it. The Word of God is the authority. What it says is primary. The preacher becomes the mouthpiece for the text. John Albert Bengel, speaking of the Word of God in preaching, said, "When the pulpit is in strong health, the light of Scripture shines bright; when the church is sick Scripture is corroded by neglect, and thus it happens that the outward form of Scripture and that of the church usually seem to exhibit simultaneously either health or else sickness; and as a rule the way in which Scripture is being treated is in exact correspondence with the condition of the church."[1]

The centrality of the Word of God is of utmost importance. Whenever a preacher steps into the pulpit, what he does with the text influences the health of the church. If there is any hope of winning the lost to Jesus Christ, if there is any hope of maturing the vast majority of those in the pews who are in desperate need of growing, then the preacher must preach the Word. The only thing that will relieve the famine in our land is commitment to content. Preach the Word!

The Commitment to Preach

When God calls a man to preach, He calls him to do just that—preach. There are so many aspects to the ministry to which God calls us. While pastoring Green Street Baptist Church in High Point, North Carolina, I was elected president of the North Carolina Baptist State

Convention, and I found myself in over my head. When the Lord called me to Dallas, there was a host of responsibilities that went with being pastor of that great and historic church. In Dallas I was also chancellor of Criswell College and also had the responsibility of a radio station, a homeless shelter, a pregnancy center, and an academy, to say nothing of the day-to-day operations of a budget that would rival a Fortune 100 corporation. But with all of that, the greatest sense of urgency was what I would preach.

Regardless of where you are and the responsibilities you have, the greatest priority of your ministry should be to preach the Word of God. All the other tasks of ministry have their place and are important, but nothing should ever usurp your commitment to preach the Word of God. Paul tells us, "God was well-pleased through the foolishness of the message preached to save those who believe" (1 Cor. 1:21 NASB). What an awesome responsibility and great privilege—to be part of those down through history who have stood and preached the unsearchable riches of Jesus Christ. The Lord said to Jeremiah, "Behold, I am making My words in your mouth fire and this people wood, and it will consume them" (Jer. 5:14 NASB).

Think about that for a moment. When you preach the Word of God, it is like fire that sets people aflame. No U.S. president in any state-of-the-union speech can claim that. No Hollywood writer, actor, or producer can do anything like that. No athlete in any winner's circle can make a speech that sets the audience on fire. But the man of God has the promise of God that when he speaks the Word of God, it is like fire that burns wood and like a hammer that shatters rock (see Jer. 23:29).

Construction of Biblical Preaching

There are numerous types of sermons—topical, textual, biographical, dramatic monologue, and confessional. Kenton Anderson, in his book *Choosing to Preach*, discusses the declarative sermon, the pragmatic sermon, the narrative, visionary, and integrative sermons.[2] But for our purposes we will look at just one type of preaching, and that is expository preaching. The great Baptist preacher and professor, John A. Broadus, said that the well-being of the church "is directly related to the strength of the pulpit."[3] Listen to what he said: "When the message from the pulpit has been uncertain and faltering, the church has been weak; when the pulpit has given a positive, declarative message, the church has been strong."[4]

Walter Kaiser believes there is a crisis in the pulpit that is precipitated by a lack of discipline in exegesis.[5] Expositional preaching follows in the great tradition of men such as Chrysostom, Ambrose, Augustine, and the Reformers like Martin Luther, Ulrich Zwingli, and John Calvin. "Those who have been known as the greatest preachers have been expository preachers."[6]

When you begin to work on a sermon, the most critical issue is prayer. Rather than just choosing a passage, it is far better to allow the Lord to lead you to a passage to preach. The Word of God is spiritually apprised (1 Cor. 2:14). Without the illumination of the Holy Spirit, everything you do with a text will lack the anointing of God.

Take the time to read through the text, carefully making notes as you go about what you observe in the text. For example, who are the people, the places, and the purpose that are being discussed? What kind of literature is it—dialogue, narrative, historical, epistolary, wisdom literature? This will make a great difference in how you approach the text.

From there, studies on the background of the book from which the text is taken will be helpful. What is the background of the passage, the context of the verses in question? If you are dealing with Joshua and the battle of Jericho in Joshua 6, it will make a great deal of difference if you understand what blowing the *shofarim* meant when they blew those ram's horns and the walls of Jericho fell.

Those ram's horns were blown at the beginning of the year of Jubilee. When the year of Jubilee was observed, all property that had been lost due to debt reverted back to the original owner. When the priests blew those ram's horns at the walls of Jericho, it was as if God said that this land was reverting back to the original owner—and He was the original owner. God took that land back from the pagan idolaters at Jericho and gave it to His people. That background study makes a great difference in how you approach the text.

When you begin to do the work of exegesis on the text, you need to observe the following steps.

Step One

1. Begin at the paragraph level and move to the sentence and clause level.

2. Identify the verbs, participle, infinitives, and so forth.

3. Parse the verbs and take special notice of their tenses, voice, and mood and decline the nouns.[7]

4. Identify the meaning of the words by use of a Hebrew or Greek dictionary.

5. Diagram the paragraph and the sentences. This can be done in English, but it is best if you are able to do it in the original language.

6. What is the primary thought and what are the secondary ideas or thoughts? Diagramming will help with this.

7. How do these sentences and ideas relate to one another?

Step Two

1. Identify phrases in the paragraph.

2. Determine the syntax and the structure of the paragraph.

3. Are there certain phrases that stand out? For example, in Galatians 3:1 there are two phrases that are very important: "who has bewitched you" (NASB), and "publicly portrayed" (NASB).

Step Three

1. Conduct word studies of particular words that are significant, using concordances and lexicons.

2. Take note of how many times a word is used in the Bible or if there are several different words used to describe the same thing.

Step Four

1. Consult various translations.

2. Consult good, sound commentaries. In purchasing commentaries, it is better to purchase by individual author rather than by sets. Sets often are uneven; this is why purchasing by author is a better way to acquire good, solid commentaries on each book. Be sure that your commentaries are not all devotional. In fact, you want to study out of the heavy exegetical commentaries before you move to the devotional commentaries.

Step Five

1. Determine the main idea of the text and be able to write this in a present tense sentence. If you cannot do this, you are not ready to write the message and you certainly are not ready to preach the passage.

2. Develop the points based on the main idea of the text.

3. Each point should reflect three elements: exposition, illustration, and application.

4. The introduction should capture the attention of the congregation. If you do not capture their attention in the first thirty seconds, you may lose them for the next thirty minutes. In the introduction you capture their attention and introduce your thesis, the main idea of the text. In this introduction you show them the relevancy of God's Word to their lives and their world.

5. The conclusion should be thoughtful, moving, and reflective of the sermon. When the people leave the worship center, the conclusion is what will ring in their minds and hearts. It must be as planned out as the rest of the sermon. Leave them with an encapsulating thought that conveys the entire message. When you approach the conclusion, you are preaching for a response, not just a conclusion. In these final sentences you are bringing the whole thrust of the message to a point of decision. Always preach for decision. Be sure that you use the second person personal pronoun *you* often.

6. Type the sermon out in full, complete with introduction and conclusion. When you take the time to write the sermon out, with illustrations, you help get the message into your mind. Beyond that you have a record of the message that you can refer to in the future. One of the best things to do when typing your message is to include footnotes, especially on the illustrations. Every week I receive calls and e-mails from across the country on illustrations I have used in my sermons. It is easy to respond to the requests when you have the source footnoted.

Conclusion

Paul wrote in 1 Timothy 4:13 and instructed those who are called to preach, "Until I come, give your attention to public reading, exhortation, and teaching." Paul made it clear that we are to preach and teach the Word. In order to do that we have to be immersed in the Word. When Paul said we are to "give attention to," the word he used is *proseka*. This verb is in the present tense, which calls for continuous action. The word means to give attention to and implies a previous preparation.[8] Paul was telling Timothy that he was to devote himself completely to the preaching and teaching of God's Word, and he was to do this consistently. That is God's Word to all who are called to preach.

Too often people in the pulpit as well as those in the pew think that the preacher's first responsibility is to cast a vision, to attend the latest convention, to be at every class drop-in, or to be at the hospital. But the first and most important responsibility of the pastor is to preach the Word of God.

TESTIMONY:

The Pastor and His Prayer Life

Daniel Henderson
Senior Pastor, Grace Church,
Prairie Eden, Minnesota

Shortly after I graduated from seminary, the Lord gripped my heart with the apostles' bold declaration in Acts 6:4, "We will devote ourselves to prayer and to the preaching ministry."

While I was grateful for the seven years of formal training in the ministry of the Word, I realized I knew very little about the pastoral ministry of prayer or how to lead a church in shaping a culture of prayer. My journey over the past twenty-five years has given me the privilege of leading multiple corporate prayer meetings every week of my life in the congregations I've been called to pastor.

The entire journey has resulted in transformation. My three major pastoral assignments have included two congregations shattered by the moral failure of my predecessor. In the third, I followed a beloved forty-year predecessor. None was an easy assignment. Yet the power of united prayer resulted in Christ-honoring renewal in each case.

Through almost forty three-day congregational prayer summits, mid-week prayer meetings that attracted hundreds of participants, earnest intercession during Sunday morning services, and dozens of other weekly prayer gatherings, transformation has occurred.

I have learned that the prayer level of a local church will never rise above the personal example of the senior pastor. I have also learned the power of worship-based prayer versus a request-based approach. As the senior pastor calls his people to consistent, biblical, and balanced prayer experiences, a new culture emerges in an environment of authentic, Christ-centered renewal.

CHAPTER 4
The Pastor and His Prayer Life

One of the most neglected disciplines among pastors is prayer. Most pastors do not have a regular prayer life. About twenty years ago, a layman approached a major evangelical seminary with the offer to endow a chair of prayer. When his offer was brought before the faculty, the first question was, "Who would teach it?" As it turned out, there were only two faculty members who knew enough about personal prayer to teach it. When the chair was finally approved, it was broadened to a chair of spiritual formations. How can we neglect the study and practice of prayer when it is so central in the Bible?

Jesus taught and modeled prayer in the Sermon on the Mount (Matt. 6:5–15; 7:7–11). He spent the last hours on the night He was arrested in prayer in the Garden of Gethsemane (Matt. 26:36–46). The first and last words He spoke from the cross were prayers (Luke 23:34,46). The church was born in a ten-day prayer meeting (Acts 1:13–14). Deacons were first selected in order to relieve the apostles of pastoral ministry duties so they might give themselves "to prayer and to the preaching ministry" (Acts 6:4).

The last words Stephen spoke before he became the first Christian martyr were words of a prayer (Acts 7:59–60). It was in prayer that Ananias was told to find Saul of Tarsus and lay hands on him in prayer. When that command was given, God added about Saul, "He [Saul] is praying" (Acts 9:11). While he was in prayer, Cornelius was advised to send people to Joppa to find Simon Peter, a person who could tell him about Christ. And it was in prayer that God told Simon Peter not to reject that request, even though it had come from a Gentile (Acts 10).

It was prayer that oiled the hinges of the prison gates in Jerusalem as they opened miraculously to let Simon Peter out of prison (Acts 12:5–10). It was in prayer that Christian missions began (Acts 12:2–3). Hardly a page in the book of Acts can be found that does not contain a prayer. Most of the letters of Paul place heavy emphasis on prayer, as do the general letters. The book of Revelation is replete with angels and men bowing before God in worship and prayer. The Bible is full of prayer. Prayer is a wonderful way to do the work of God! You can do a lot of things for God after you pray, but you can't really do anything for Him until you pray.

The Pastor and His Personal Prayer Life

When this author (Bryant) was a young preacher, he worked as an assistant to Paul R. VanGorder, a wonderful pastor in Atlanta, Georgia, for fourteen months between college and seminary. When the young man asked about his pastor's prayer life, he was told that every morning, when he had his devotions, he prayed over an open Bible. When the young preacher went to seminary in Texas, he served for four years under W. Fred Swank, another wonderful pastor of a large church. When he asked about this pastor's prayer life, he told him he prayed in his car while driving to and from the hospitals to visit his people. That was the only time he was alone. (This was BCP, "before cell phones.")

Some years later, this young preacher had the privilege to work under W. A. Criswell at the First Baptist Church of Dallas, Texas. When he asked Dr. Criswell about his prayer life, he shared how he prayed in his study every morning, as he poured over the Scriptures in preparing his Sunday messages. (He had a Bible with tear stains on the pages.)

Based on what those three pastors had taught him, this young preacher prayed when he had his devotionals, he prayed as he studied the Scriptures in preparation for preaching, and he prayed on the way to the hospitals. After five years on the staff of the First Baptist Church of Dallas, he was called as pastor of Hoffmantown Baptist Church in Albuquerque, New Mexico. After preaching for Dr. Criswell that last Sunday evening, as he told the people good-bye, Dr. George Davis, then a professor at Criswell Bible Institute (now Criswell College), placed in the young pastor's hands as a going-away gift E. M. Bounds's book, *Power Through Prayer*.[1]

The author took this little book on a family vacation in Colorado between churches. He and his family stayed in a friend's cabin beside the Little Arkansas River in Poncha Springs, Colorado. Each morning his wife sat by the fire to have her devotions. His sons climbed up the mountain to have their time with the Lord, and he walked through an apple orchard beside the river and read Bounds's little book. He read these words that struck deeply into his heart: "What the Church needs today is not more machinery or better, not new organizations or more and novel methods, but men whom the Holy Ghost can use—men of prayer, men mighty in prayer. The Holy Ghost does not flow through methods, but through men. He does not come on machinery, but on men. He does not anoint plans, but men—men of prayer."[2]

In his book Bounds advised pastors not to do their praying during their devotionals, while doing their sermon preparation, or even while driving to the hospitals, but to give full attention to God. As this young pastor read those words, he walked, and read, and wept, and determined to begin—for the first time, really—a life of prayer.

When he arrived in Albuquerque, he told the church he would have his study at home and would not come to the church office until afternoon, giving his mornings to God, prayer, and the study of the Scriptures. He determined to get up an hour before the rest of the family each day, to spend that hour on his knees in prayer before God. The first day he prayed for every need he knew and for every person he could think of, then looked at his watch. Only ten minutes had passed. What would he do for the rest of the hour? He had been given a Rolodex file with the names and addresses of all members of the church. He began to pray through the membership list. After a few weeks of this approach to prayer, a strange and wonderful thing happened.

As he prayed through the church roll, he knew personally only a few of the people. Then as he met them at church, he would say, "I prayed for you and your family last week." The effect of this was tremendous. Word got around about what he was doing. People began to call and say, "I have heard you are praying through the church roll, but my name is way down in the alphabet and I have a need now. Would you move me and my family up on the list and pray for us?"

It was a great way to get to know the church members. People who were not members of the church heard that the pastor was praying for individuals. In time, lost people began to call and ask for prayer. Backslidden Christians called and asked for prayer. Much of the visitation and soul winning occurred as a result of the pastor praying. Prayer is a wonderful way to do the work of God!

The Pastor and His Family Prayer Life

G. Campbell Morgan pointed out that Jesus outlined two basic responsibilities for prayer—the practice of prayer personally and the practice of prayer collectively.[3] The practice of personal prayer is based on Matthew 6:5–8 where Jesus tells us to go into our closets to pray. This is not an injunction against public prayer, but simply Jesus' advice about private prayer. Jesus adds that when we pray secretly, the Father will reward us openly. People can tell a difference in a pastor who prays.

The pastor should establish his own family altar of devotions and prayer and then teach his people to do the same thing. When the children are young, the family altar must be brief and put on a child's level. As they grow older, they can absorb more. As teenagers, they can sometimes be led to take the lead in devotionals. After they are grown and gone, they will still call on Mom and Dad to pray for them. The family altar is not a time for preaching or deep Bible study. Bible study can be done privately with each child. This author remembers taking his older son, at ten years of age, through the book of Proverbs, rearranging the individual proverbs by topic. It was enriching for both father and son. But a family altar is different. It is for praying. In our home we prayed daily, not only for our own needs but also for our denomination's missionaries by name on their birthdays.

The practice of prayer collectively is based on Matthew 18:19–20 where Jesus says that if two of us agree on earth concerning anything that they ask, the Father in heaven will do it for them. This passage primarily is about church discipline, but Jesus widened it beyond that when He said, "concerning anything" (NKJV). There is a power, I think unmatched, when a man and his wife pray together. The pastor and his wife should pray together regularly. As long as children are at home, the pastor should teach his children to pray the same way Jesus taught His disciples to pray—by praying with them. Of all the things that a pastor can teach his children, none will be more valuable as they grow up and go out on their own than to pray. This is true for laymen as well.

In one of the churches pastored by this author, a young man came to see the pastor and asked for help with his finances. What he really needed was to be discipled. For weeks he and the pastor met weekly for an hour and the pastor discipled the young man. The first financial question the pastor asked was if the young man was tithing. He showed him Haggai 1:9, which teaches that if we withhold the tithe that belongs to God from Him, we will not prosper. It's like putting our money in a bag with holes in it.

The young man said he could not afford to tithe. When asked why he did not budget the tithe in his monthly budget, he said he did not have a budget. The pastor asked him to bring all of his bills the next week and he would teach him how to make a budget. When the pastor looked at the bills, he discovered the young man was telling the truth. He could not afford to tithe. In fact, he could not afford to eat! His credit card bills exceeded what both he and his wife were earning.

The pastor taught the young man to get his family together and to cut up their credit cards. He explained they would have to have cash to buy anything from then on. Then he told him to call the credit card companies and explain that he would send something monthly but not the full amount. Almost any credit card company will work with a person like that. About that time their oven quit working. The wife said she would cook on top of the stove. Their Sunday school class found out about this problem and took up an offering to buy them a new oven. It was humbling, but they could see that God was providing for their needs through prayer.

This couple's ten-year-old son had a broken bicycle. They did not have the seven dollars needed to fix the bike. The little boy said, "Then let's pray about it when we have our family prayer time tonight." When they prayed, the little boy asked God for a new bike. What they didn't know was that his grandparents had already bought him a new bike for his birthday the next month. They didn't know that his bike was broken, but they decided to give him the bike ahead of time. That little boy learned that God answers prayer. Family prayers are powerful.

The Pastor and His Church's Prayer Life

One of the sad commentaries on American Christianity is that prayer meeting is no longer prayer meeting. If a midweek service is held at all, it is primarily a Bible study and not a prayer meeting. The little bit of praying done in the average church prayer meeting today is prayer for people who are sick. Seldom does the church pray for the lost to be saved. We seem to spend more time praying to keep Christians out of heaven than we do praying to keep lost people out of hell!

One of the greatest churches in modern history was Charles Haddon Spurgeon's Metropolitan Tabernacle in London, England. Because he was the "Prince of Preachers" in England, it is easy to suppose that the church was built on Spurgeon's preaching. My guess is that Spurgeon would say that it was built on prayer. Over three hundred men and women were on their knees in prayer in the basement every time their pastor was preaching in the pulpit upstairs. His church at that time seated approximately six thousand people. He filled it with a different crowd up to five times every Sunday.

Spurgeon did have a midweek Bible study, but he gave a separate evening each week to prayer. Thousands of his members came, and they came to pray. He spoke briefly, but the evening was given to prayer. He described those services in his little book, *Only a Prayer Meeting*,[4] in the second chapter: "Prayer Meetings as They Were and as They Should Be." He listed several characteristics of prayer meetings as they were and suggested these were the reasons so many prayer meetings died.

First, prayer meetings died because the prayers were too long. He suggested the pastor admonish the long-winded pray-er and if that did no good, to "jog his elbow when the people are getting weary."[5] His other characterizations of the old prayer meetings that failed included using well-worn catch phrases, monotonous repetition, and "mistaking preaching for prayer."[6] I knew a preacher who would make announcements in his closing prayer. "God bless our deacons who are going to meet in my office immediately after this service."

Spurgeon then gave six suggestions for promoting and sustaining a regular prayer meeting in the church.

1. Let the minister himself set a very high value on this means of grace.
2. Let the brethren labor after brevity.
3. Persuade all the brethren to pray aloud.
4. Encourage the attendants to send in special [written] requests for prayer.
5. Suffer neither hymn, nor chapter, nor address to supplant prayer.
6. It is not amiss at all to let two or even three brethren succeed each other without a pause, but this must be done judiciously; and if one of the three become prolix [long-winded], let the pause come as soon as he has finished. Sing only one verse or at the most two between prayers, and let those be such as would not distract the mind from the subject, being alien to the spirit of the meeting.[7]

God has raised up a young pastor today with both a burden for corporate prayer and an understanding of it. His excellent little book is a must for every pastor's library and can be life-changing and church-changing. *Fresh Encounters* is the book.[8] Daniel Henderson, whom this author has known since he was fourteen years old and was his pastor when God called Daniel to preach, considers him a contemporary Andrew Murray. Daniel has pastored two great churches—Arcade Baptist Church in Sacramento, California, and Grace Church in Eden Prairie, Minnesota. God gave him a vision for building a church with a "worship-based" prayer ministry rather than a "request-based" prayer ministry.

During his eleven years at Sacramento, Daniel led the church in more than thirty prayer summits. These were three-day prayer retreats. He and his staff had daily prayer meetings. Each week there were thirteen different prayer meetings in his church. More than one hundred people served as the pastor's prayer partners. Every Thursday evening a "Fresh Encounter" prayer service was held with four hundred to five hundred in attendance. The church began an annual prayer conference that attracted more than five hundred attendees from fourteen different states. He organized a world prayer center where many people came to pray individually for worldwide revival and evangelization an hour each week.

Andrew Murray once said, "The man who mobilizes the Christian Church to prayer will make the greatest contribution to world-evangelization in history." When Daniel Henderson made prayer a priority in his church, he said, "It was the closest to genuine revival I have ever experienced."[9] Prayer is a wonderful way to do the work of God!

Jesus quoted God the Father when He said, "My house will be called a house of prayer . . . but you have made it a den of thieves" (Mark 11:17; see Isa. 56:7; Jer. 7:11). One of the chief responsibilities of a pastor is to lead his church to become a house of prayer. Churches today are known as houses of praise, houses of preaching, and even houses of great fellowship. But are they known as houses of prayer? It is the pastor's responsibility to develop a life of prayer personally, with his family, and with his church. Spurgeon is quoted as having said, "I would rather teach one man to pray than ten men to preach."[10]

A pastor who fails to make prayer a priority in his ministry robs himself of the Holy Spirit's anointed power, robs the church of personal contact with God, robs the lost of an opportunity to hear the gospel in a powerful setting, and robs the world of an awakening. The first prerequisite of a God-sent awakening is God's people humbling themselves and praying (2 Chron. 7:14). Pastor, give yourself to a ministry of prayer.

TESTIMONY:
The Pastor and His Family

H. B. London Jr.
Vice President of Church, Clergy, and Medical Outreach
Focus on the Family

The most important sheep in a pastor's flock are his family. They must love one another and demonstrate that love verbally through appropriate embrace and in the proper scheduling of time. I doubt you can say "I love you" too often. We must honor and respect one another. We must not take one another for granted. Dad should be affirmed for his ministry, Mom for her multitasking, and each child for his or her achievements.

There also needs to be an attitude of shared ministry. We must recognize the unique nature of the clergy home. We must recognize that the call from God makes a pastor's family different from other families. That may not be fair, but it is true.

Every clergy home should be characterized by compassion and forgiveness. Each member of the family must realize that the role is to be a part of the solution rather than the problem. The sun should never go down on our anger.

The words "As for me and my family, we will worship the LORD" (Josh. 24:15) must become more than just a beautiful slogan. It can and should reflect a way of life, not perfect, but constantly exploring new ways to validate love for one another and determination to glorify God by the lives that are lived. Are these things easy to accomplish? Not at all. Are they necessary and achievable? Yes, but only as all family members accept their God-given assignments.

CHAPTER 5 The Pastor and His Family

This is one of the most important chapters in this book. The pastor's family can be his credibility or it can be his liability. It certainly will be his vulnerability. Some years ago a leading pastor of a large church in the southeast was on an airplane traveling to a speaking assignment. The man next to him did not order any kind of beverage, nor did he accept the traditional peanuts. There was a meal served on that particular flight. The man did not accept the meal. The pastor asked him if he were ill. The man explained that he was fasting. The pastor asked the man's denomination, assuming he was a Christian.

As it turned out, the man was a Satanist. He explained that his church of Satan had called for a fast every Monday and Thursday to support prayers to Satan that the families of leading Christian pastors would be destroyed. Even the devil knows that if he can destroy a pastor's family, he can destroy his ministry.

Perhaps the greatest pressure on a pastor comes at the point of his family. The importance of a successful family to a pastor's ministry is made clear in the qualifications given in the New Testament for a pastor. In 1 Timothy 3, at the head of the list of qualifications are these words: "An overseer [or bishop, another word for pastor], therefore, must be above reproach, the husband of one wife" (1 Tim. 3:2). Two verses later Paul adds, "one who manages his own household competently, having his children under control with all dignity" (1 Tim. 3:4). In Titus, Paul puts at the head of the list of qualifications for an elder [another word for pastor], "blameless, the husband of one wife, having faithful children not accused of wildness or rebellion" (Titus 1:6). God ordained the family long before He ordained the church.

A Matter of Priority

If a pastor does not make a distinction between his personal relationship to God and his job in the church, he can never order his priorities according to God's will. He often tells his church members to put God first, their families second, and their jobs last. But if he does not separate God from his job as a pastor, his family will always come in third place. The effect on his family and the poor example for the church will be devastating.

An evangelist tells of another evangelist who was virtually never home. He preached between forty and fifty meetings a year. In the middle of a meeting his wife called him to come home. Their sixteen-year-old son had been seriously injured in an automobile accident. He had been drinking. His father did not even know his son drank. As he paced the waiting room outside the intensive care unit, waiting for his son to die, he quoted Song of Solomon 1:6 over and over, "They made me a keeper of the vineyards. I have not kept my own vineyard."

Of course, there are times when you have to "rob Peter to pay Paul," as the saying goes. Priorities sometimes do conflict with one another. But if a pastor regularly neglects his family, he, his family, and his ministry will pay for it dearly.

The wise pastor will set aside a day each week to be with his wife. If not a day, then certainly an evening should be set aside for her. If a pastor lives near his or his wife's parents, grandparents love to keep grandchildren. If grandparents are miles away, people in the church will gladly take care of the children while their pastor takes his wife out on a date. When this author was a young minister, making very little money, going to seminary, working at a church, I could not afford a babysitter. An old couple in the church where I served as an assistant to the pastor became surrogate grandparents for our children. Most of our sons' friends had only two sets of grandparents. Our children had three. One set was in Georgia, another set lived in Illinois (later they moved to Florida), and the third set was in Texas where we lived.

The wise pastor will also set aside a day for his children. When our children were little, that day was Saturday. As seminary students, we would take our sons to a local lake most Saturdays in the summer. Sometimes we would cook breakfast, lunch, and dinner by the lake.

As they grew up, we would do this on Mondays, my day off each week. When we moved to New Mexico, we went to the mountains by a stream where the boys could fish and swim. In a daytime camping area, we were often the only ones around. It was a great time in our lives.

The pastor and his entire family should eat at least one meal a day together, preferably two. On Saturdays and Sundays it may be all three. All of us have heard the old saying, "Families that pray together stay together." That is true. I would like to add, "Families that eat together stay together." In my years of counseling couples with marital problems, one of the first questions I asked was if they were eating their meals together. Almost always they were not. The husband would be late coming home from work. The wife and whatever children were at home at dinnertime would sit down and eat. The husband would come in later and eat his meal standing at the kitchen counter. Families that eat together stay together. How can a pastor have regular family devotions if his family does not eat together?

Speaking of family devotions, the family altar needs to be geared to the age of the children, both in content and in time. Kenneth Taylor's *The Living Bible* began as an attempt to put his family devotions in language his five young children could understand. The family altar is not a place for preaching but a place for family worship and praying.

Pastor, when your family is at home, remember that just because you live together under one roof does not mean you have a successful family. Going your separate ways, watching multiple television sets, working on separate computers, talking on different cell phones, pursuing separate hobbies—these things do not add up to a family. You need to interact verbally, intellectually, emotionally, spiritually, and spatially.

Speaking of television and computers, a wise pastor will limit the amount of television his children watch each day as well as monitor what they watch. There should be no television until all homework from school is finished and inspected. Most television cable networks have software to lock out adult-content shows. The same is true of computers. The pastor should limit and monitor the time his children spend online each day. Whatever happened to reading? Table games? Conversation? Pastor, lead your family to be successful and to interact with one another.

When children get into sports, their father should be at their games. A college student told me recently that his father, a pastor, never missed one of his football games when he was a high school football player. No wonder this son and father are close as adults.

It is also true that families that play together stay together. Vacations are important. The wise pastor will budget for vacations with his family each year. When we were poor seminary students, the only vacation we could afford was going to see our parents. When we did not have money to stop in a motel, we would start out about 10:00 p.m. on a fourteen-hour trip. The boys would sleep through the night. We packed a cooler with food to eat along the way. As our income improved, we would stop at a motel on the way to see grandparents. Both sons learned to swim in motel swimming pools on vacation. As our income improved, vacations improved. When they were teenagers we took them on ski trips over Christmas. Our sons, now in their forties, still talk about those winter vacations. Pastor, give priority to your family.

Family Failures

In a 2004 survey of pastors who left the pastorate without another church to go to, seven motivations for leaving the pastorate were discovered. Some had found another ministry outside the church. Some had taken ministry positions with their denomination. Some had conflict in the local congregation. Some had become discouraged and burned out. The other three reasons related to the family. Some left the pastorate to care for their children or families. Some left due to sexual misconduct. Some left due to divorce or marital problems.[1] The most devastating failure a pastor can go through is the failure of his family.

In researching the sources on pastoral theology, we discovered that almost no books exist on the topic of the pastor and his family. There are a lot of books on the Christian man and his family, but few on the pastor and his family. Some books, like this one, have a chapter on this subject, but few are devoted totally to the pastor and his family. One of the few exceptions is Andy Stanley's book, *Choosing to Cheat.*[2]

Some children raised in a pastor's home turn away from God and the church as older teenagers and young adults. Why? Perhaps they are victims of living in a fish bowl. Every pastor understands this analogy. His family seems to be under closer scrutiny than the families of lay-men in the church. Sometimes pastors are responsible for this mental-ity. They force their children to participate in every church event and go to church all the time, even when they are not feeling well, just because they are the pastor's kids.

A good suggestion for a pastor is to set the parameters of partici-pation by his children to include attendance on Sunday morning, Sunday evening, and Wednesday night. Beyond that, let participation be a matter of choice. This author's boys chose to participate in youth choir, youth camps, and mission tours, but they were not required to do so. Consequently, they never felt like church was being "pushed down their throats." The pastor should try to make his children's lives as normal as possible.

The Pastor and Divorce

There are two questions that loom large for a pastor in the matter of divorce. One has to do with biblical justification for any divorce in the church. What does the Bible say about divorce? This will be dealt with in chapter 13. The other question has to do with what happens when a pastor divorces. The answers to these questions are varied. The issues are complex.

Ordination and Divorce

This brings up the question of whether to ordain as deacons or ministers those who have been divorced. The question is what is the meaning of "the husband of one wife" in 1 Timothy 3:2,12 and Titus 1:6? Some say it means "one at a time." In other words, the issue was polygamy, which was rampant in the first-century world. If this is what the qualification means, any divorced man could be considered for ordination as a deacon or minister.

The problem with this interpretation is twofold. First, in 1 Timothy 5:9 the same grammatical construction is used in speaking of the quali-fications of a true widow who is to be supported by the church. Among those qualifications is that she must have been "the wife of one hus-band." That cannot mean one at a time, because she is not married to anyone. She is a widow. If "the wife of one husband" must mean that she had only one husband, then how can "the husband of one wife" mean "one at a time"?

The second problem with interpreting "the husband of one wife" as "one at a time" is that such an interpretation leaves part of the New Testament with little application today in a nation where polygamy is forbidden. Polygamy was considered normal and was widespread in the first-century Roman world. As the church expanded beyond Judaism, it must have been faced with the question of what to do with the Gentile polygamists who were converted to Christ. Were they to be baptized and added to the church or were they to be rejected? Must a man kick out of his home all but his first wife and her children before he could join the church? If the gospel is intended for the whole world, what about these polygamists?

The decision was made, in the providence of God, to reject polygamy but to accept polygamists into the church but not allow them to become leaders. The church would illustrate God's glorious ideal of one man and one woman for life in the church's ordained leadership—its deacons and her pastors. In three hundred years polygamy virtually disappeared from the ancient Roman world. If a church today ordains men who have been divorced, how can it teach God's glorious ideal of one man and one woman for life? If a church ordains deacons or pastors who have been divorced, how can they teach God's glorious ideal?

If a Pastor Divorces

Denominations deal with the question, "What if a pastor divorces?" in different ways. Some apply the same test to a pastor's divorce that would be applied to any divorce in the church. If the spouse was unfaithful, then the divorce is allowed. Some churches have retained pastors after they were divorced as long as they did not initiate the divorce and as long as they had not been unfaithful to their wives. They usually refer to John Wesley, whose wife left him, yet he continued to preach. In most churches, if the pastor divorces he will be asked to resign, no matter how loved he may be. If a successful vote is taken for him to stay, many of the members who voted against it will leave in protest. So what should a pastor do if he gets divorced?

First, a distinction must be made between preaching and pastoring a church. The call to preach is irrevocable. Paul said, "God's gracious gifts and calling are irrevocable" (Rom. 11:29). A divorce does not disqualify a man from preaching, but it does disqualify him from being the senior pastor of a church. He no longer meets the qualifications of a pastor as stated in 1 Timothy 3:2, 4 and Titus 1:6. Out of loyalty to the Bible and concern for the testimony of the church, a pastor who goes through a divorce should step down as pastor. He can be an evangelist. He can be a lay preacher while he earns his income at a secular job. He can develop a writing ministry. He may even develop a seminar ministry. But he should not continue to be a pastor. This is difficult to say but hard to avoid if you want to follow the Bible. He cannot keep the vineyards of others if he has not kept his own vineyard.

A Biblical Example

Noah was a preacher. Second Peter 2:5 calls him a "preacher of righteousness." As you read about him in Genesis 6:9, Noah met all of the qualifications for a pastor that would be given later by Paul. He is said by God to have been "blameless." No subsequent preacher preached as many years as Noah. He preached over one hundred years. One might think Noah was a failure. In over one hundred years he had only seven converts. Everyone else ignored what he preached. In Matthew 24:37–39 Jesus said, "As the days of Noah were, so also will the coming of the Son of Man be. For as in the days before the flood, they were eating and drinking, marrying and giving in marriage, until the day that Noah entered the ark, and did not know until the flood came and took them all away, so also will the coming of the Son of Man be" (NKJV).

Why did they not know? Certainly Noah had told them in his preaching, but they ignored him. Noah did not save many people, but he saved his entire family—and through that the entire human race from extinction. Pastor, save your family! This may be your greatest contribution to the kingdom of God.

TESTIMONY:
The Pastor and His First Church

Wade Rials
Associate Pastor, Salem Baptist Church
McDonough, Georgia

A pastor's first church plays a pivotal role in forming the shape and focus of his entire ministry. My first church, Laton Hill Baptist Church in southwestern Alabama, accomplished this in my life. The most important life lesson I learned from Laton Hill is the importance of pastoral love. As I entered this first pastorate, I anticipated that my training, theological expertise, and exegetical preaching would be the keys to growing and building this church. The wonderful people of this church in Chatom, Alabama, taught me about love.

Pastoral ministry is grounded in a deep-seated love for people. The greatest opportunities for ministry are not always found on Sundays in the pulpit. I found that true ministry occurred while sitting on an elderly couple's back porch drinking sweet tea, eating homemade peach pie, and listening to stories about the past. The best discipleship occurred on fishing and hunting excursions. Numerous young people were reached when I volunteered to help coach the local high school football team. Pastoral ministry is earned while sitting with families in hospitals, holding an elderly woman's hand as she leaves this world and goes to be with Jesus, bear-hugging an elderly man whose wife just departed this world, and sitting with two dear parents whose son had just died tragically in a car accident. Laton Hill Baptist Church called me to be their preacher; they allowed me to earn the privilege of being their pastor.

CHAPTER 6 The Pastor and His First Church

There are very few books written about a pastor's first church. Most books on pastoral ministry are written for pastors who are already established in their ministry. Pastoring one's first church is like having one's first child. You don't have any experience at the task. If a pastor is in a denomination with a bishop, he is given the assignment following completion of his education and ordination. If, like the authors of this book, he is in a Baptist church, the process is quite different.

A student arrived at a Southern Baptist seminary in 1959, hundreds of miles from his home. He went to the placement office and asked if they could help him find a church. After all, the seminary catalog stated that more than 50 percent of the students were pastors. (The percentage is much lower now.) He wanted to get a church. He had been ordained by his home church and had served as assistant pastor for fourteen months between college and seminary. How does one go about getting his first church?

The placement officer gave him some excellent advice. After learning that the student did not know any pastors in the town where the seminary was located, he suggested that the student join a church and become an active volunteer in it. If a church were to consider him and find that he had no local church membership, that consideration would probably end. A couple of Sundays later, the young minister and his wife joined a large church in the city. Shortly afterward the pastor asked him to work part-time visiting newcomers in the community. When their first child arrived, the young minister was given a salaried job that allowed him to continue in seminary on a reduced class schedule. When he completed his Master of Divinity degree and began work on the Doctor of Theology degree, his pastor recommended him to a small church across town to become their pastor.

The pulpit committee came to hear him preach in the church where he had served as assistant pastor for four years. They met with him, talked about the parsonage they provided and the salary, and asked him to preach in view of a call on a given Sunday. After he preached, the pulpit committee recommended to the church they call him as pastor. About 95 percent of them voted positively. (In a Baptist church there are seldom unanimous votes on calling a pastor.) He, his wife, and his two small sons moved across town to begin what would be a five-year pastorate, his very first one.

Considering One's First Church

Considering one's first church is rather simple. The pastor tends to follow Jesus' words in Revelation 3:8, first spoken to the church at Philadelphia but included in the Bible to speak to us today: "I know your works. See, I have set before you an open door" (NKJV). With a pastor's first church, he simply walks through the open door, assuming that Jesus has opened the door. It is important for the new pastor to become convinced on his knees that Jesus has opened the door. If he and his family have been praying about it, the first open door is usually God's answer to that prayer.

The pastor may want to ask the history of the church. Did it begin as a mission? Is it a newly planted church? Is it committed to his denomination? How many pastors have they had? Why did they leave? Is the church basically united? Do they want to reach people for Christ and do they want to grow? Do they have a constitution and bylaws? Do they have a personnel policies and procedures manual? Do they have a financial policies and procedures manual? What do they say about the duties and responsibilities of the pastor? Are there other employees of the church? Will they be answerable to the pastor? How do the deacons view their role in the church?

The pastor will want to see the latest financial statement. Is the church solvent? Has it been able to live within its means? He will also want to visit the church facilities. Do they plan to build further buildings? When and how will they be financed? He will want to visit the parsonage. Does the church pay for the utilities or does the pastor? Will the church make repairs as needed? Perhaps the house needs new carpet or needs to be painted. Are they willing to do that? If there is no parsonage, is an adequate housing allowance available to rent or buy a home? If he is still in school, will they allow him to continue his education?

Lyle Schaller, an expert on church growth, suggests in his book, *The Pastor and the People*, that there are four types of questions a prospective pastor should ask the pulpit committee.[1]

First are the *what* questions. Ask the committee members: What is the reason you belong to this particular church? What does your church do best? What would you change about your church if you could? What was the period of your church's greatest strength? Then ask the *why* questions. Why has your church grown or declined or stayed the same? Why do you have the staff members you have now? Why has the number of staff increased or decreased? Why did you or did you not relocate? Why has your budget increased or decreased? Then ask the *what's the type* questions. What type of church are you? What is the type of your community? What is the type of your people? Finally, ask the *what are your expectations* questions. What are your priorities?

The young candidate for pastor should not talk about salary and benefits until he is reasonably sure it is God's will for him to consider the church further. If he asks for a financial statement, the pastor's salary may be itemized on it. As a final consideration, he should ask if the itemized salary is the salary that he would be paid. Does the church pay one-half of the Social Security, or is their pastor considered self-employed? What are the benefits? Does the church pay for the pastor and family's health insurance? Does the church participate in the denominational retirement program? What is the church's policy on vacations? Will the pastor be allowed to attend denominational meetings? Will the church pay for it? Will he be allowed to hold revivals at other churches? Most churches allow a pastor up to two weeks a year to preach revivals in other churches, with his salary continuing. Is there a book allowance or an automobile allowance? Will the church pay for all moving expenses?

All of these things should be spelled out in writing before the pastor preaches in view of a call. The pulpit committee should be unanimous in their recommendation of him to the church. If they are not, the pastor should not proceed. He should also ask if the church has a minimum percentage requirement for the church vote to call a pastor. The vote should be at least 90 percent in favor of the call. If that is not required and the actual vote is less than 90 percent, the pastor should pray long before proceeding. How close to 90 percent was it? If it was barely over 50 percent or 60 percent, the church is divided. That would be a hard first church to pastor.

The pastor should be willing to have a credit check run on him by the church. It would be wise to get a credit report himself, available free online. If it is incorrect, he should correct the report before giving permission to the pastor search committee to request such a report. He should also be prepared if the church asks for a criminal background check to be conducted. In this day and time, he should not be offended by such a request.

Preaching in View of a Call

When the weekend arrives, the pastor and his family should be present for Sunday morning and possibly Sunday night services if asked. If the church is in a different city than the one where he lives, the church should pay transportation for the pastor and his family to travel to their church. They should also provide housing and food while they are visiting the church field. The prospective pastor and his family should arrive on Thursday or Friday before the Sunday of preaching. They will be housed either in a home or in a motel. If they did not drive from their home, it would be nice to have a car provided for the long weekend. The pastor can suggest this. A car could be borrowed from one of the members or it could be rented, with the church paying for the rental.

If the church is a small country church, usually a dinner will be held for the pastor and his family to enable them to meet the church members. If not, perhaps a fellowship could be held after the Sunday evening service. The pastor needs to see the members in an informal as well as a formal setting.

When the vote is taken, the pastor and his family should leave the worship center. Some churches vote the same day the candidate is heard. Others vote at a later service. If the vote is taken while the pastor is still in the building, he may be asked to respond to the vote.

It would be wise for the young pastor to thank them for the call, tell them that he and his family will pray about it, and that he will let them know his decision within a week. If the call is strong, the pastor may feel led to accept on the spot. If the call is weak, he should go home and pray about it.

How to Begin

If a pastor in his first church has never been ordained, this needs to be done. If he is in a denomination that ordains, his bishop or district superintendent can be asked to proceed with ordination. If he is in a Baptist church and has not yet been ordained to the gospel ministry, the church calling him as pastor should vote to ask their new pastor's home church to ordain him to the gospel ministry. If that is not feasible, the church can ask the local Baptist association to guide them in proceeding with ordination of their new pastor. Then he is ready to begin. Where does he start?

Andrew Blackwood, in his classic book *Pastoral Work*,[2] has a chapter entitled "The First Days in a New Field." He lists four principles that will get a pastor off to a good start with his new congregation.

Getting to Know the People

First, Blackwood advises that the new pastor get to know the people in their homes. This is especially true in one's first church. It is usually small enough for the pastor to schedule several home visits a week and get into everyone's home within a few months. His wife should go with him on these visits. If she cannot, he should take a deacon with him. In a larger church, families can be asked to come by the pastor's office for a visit.

W. A. Criswell, pastor of the First Baptist Church of Dallas, Texas, for nearly fifty years, was very effective at this. When children made professions of faith, he asked the entire family to come by his office with the child for a talk. This is a wonderful evangelistic opportunity. Zig Ziglar, the great sales motivator, was led to Christ while listening to Dr. Criswell talk to Zig's young son after he made a profession of faith in Christ. They were baptized together.

Bill Bennett, while pastor of the First Baptist Church of Fort Smith, Arkansas, had tea and coffee in his office for downtown businessmen at four o'clock most afternoons. He would mix church members and prospects in those meetings.

Learning and Remembering Names

Second, Blackwood says that the pastor should win the hearts of his people. The initial step toward this goal is to learn and remember the church members' names. One pastor who was especially good at this was asked how he remembered so many persons' names. He told about the turtle that climbed a tree. Of course, turtles cannot climb trees, but this one had an alligator after him! The need to know church members' names is an alligator. The wise pastor will learn and remember the names of his people, especially in his first church.

Blackwood quotes William M. Anderson Sr., a pastor from Dallas, Texas, in the 1940s. Anderson advised, "Be sure to get the name. Spell it distinctively. Write it down; say it aloud, more than once. Associate it with something fixed, facially. Visualize for the other person with a 'camera eye.' Talk over at night every new name or face. Take time. Use all your senses. Will to know. Determine by God's grace to excel in this art."[3] Jesus said, "I am the good shepherd. I know My own sheep, and they know Me" (John 10:14). He added, "My sheep hear My voice, I know them, and they follow Me" (John 10:27).

If a pastor wants his people to follow him, let him learn and remember their names. Nothing more negative could be said about a pastor by one of his members than "he doesn't know who I am." In a larger church, the new pastor can ask from the pulpit that his members repeat their names to him for the first few times they speak with him, but this only goes so far. After a few Sundays people expect a pastor to remember their names.

Learning About Your New Church

Third, Blackwood suggests that the pastor ought to learn the facts about his new church. This may take time, but as he visits with the church members, the new pastor will learn where the skeletons are buried and not dig there.

Finally, the new minister should gladly accept the church's customs. A vice president of a large electric company shared with his new pastor a leadership secret. When he was a line foreman and was assigned to a new crew, he would watch how they picked up a telephone pole. If they picked up the light end first, he did not correct them. But the next time he would say, "Hey fellows, let's try something different. Try picking up the pole by the heavy end first. It's a lot easier."

Many a well-meaning pastor has rushed into his new church and started changing everything immediately and then wondered why he was meeting resistance. People do not like change. They will change if the pastor explains why the change is necessary and brings his congregation along with him. Effective pastors should follow the advice of George W. Truett, a pastor in the first half of the twentieth century. He said this about preaching a sermon: "Start low, go slow, rise higher, catch fire." This is also good advice to the new pastor when implementing changes.

How to Stay at a Church

Very few pastors stay at their first church throughout their entire pastoral career. When they do, they are greatly beloved and many times able to see their churches grow to become either very large or very elite. One notable example is George W. Truett, who served only one church throughout his entire ministry—the First Baptist Church of Dallas, Texas, where he stayed for forty-seven years. Rick Warren is another notable example. Saddleback Community Church, a Southern Baptist church, is the only church he has pastored. He is the only pastor that congregation has ever had. Both Truett and Warren show the value of staying at a church for a long time.

A large number of churches have had only one pastor for their first twenty-five or thirty years, but it was not their pastor's first church. If a pastor grows and his church grows, there is no reason why he should leave unless God clearly directs him to leave.

Many young pastors make mistakes in their first church that would be fatal if the church were not small, loving, and forgiving. Many small churches in a seminary town have a ministry of giving young, new pastors their start. Hopefully, a young seminary student should be able to stay at his first church until he finishes his education. How can he do that?

In almost any relationship, there are periods of adjustment that need to be made every eighteen months or so. This is true in a marriage. It is also true in a church. The pastor who stays at a church must be willing to make adjustments about every year or two. If this doesn't happen, conflict may drive him away or the church may decline or even split.

It is never wise for a pastor to split a church. The spiritual and emotional effects on him, his wife, his children, the church, and even the community are usually devastating. How many pastors' wives have become bitter toward the ministry because of a church split? How many pastors' children have left Christ and the church because of a church split? Neither of the authors of this book would allow a church to split over them.

Jesus prayed in His high priestly prayer, "While I was with them, I was protecting them by Your name that You have given Me. I guarded them and not one of them is lost, except the son of destruction, so that the Scripture may be fulfilled" (John 17:12). If a church member stops attending or even joins another church, the pastor should call on him and find out why. Sometimes this is a painful thing to do. Washing another person's feet is not pleasant, but Jesus did it. He admonished us to serve others with basin and towel.

Sometimes people stop coming to church because of fellowship problems with others in the congregation. Sometimes the pastor has failed them in some way. The pastor may not be able to get other members to apologize to the offended member, but he can and should apologize for his own failures. All pastors are frail. No pastor always does what is right. If he is humble enough to admit his frailty and failures, usually he can stay at a church as long as he wants. People appreciate honesty and humility.

If a pastor wants to stay at a church, he should learn to practice servant leadership rather than raw pastoral authority, in spite of what many church growth publications suggest. The pastor who leads as a servant will gradually be given pastoral authority and is likely to stay a long time as pastor. The longer he stays, the more authority he will have. The pastor who insists on pastoral authority may never be granted it by his people. Peter advised elders (another word for pastors), "Shepherd [Pastor] God's flock among you, not overseeing [or bishoping, another word for pastoring] out of compulsion but freely, according to God's will; not for the money but eagerly; not lording it over those entrusted to you, but being examples to the flock" (1 Pet. 5:2–3).

One challenge that sometimes comes up in small churches that begin to grow is that a group of laypeople, who have been able to control the small church, begin to resist the pastor's leadership. They cannot control the new members, and they feel they are losing control. New members tend to follow the pastor. The wise pastor, even though young and inexperienced, will find a way to challenge the people who have been in the church for many years to open their hearts and their circle of fellowship and service to the new members who join.

The Great Commission involves discipleship, not just evangelism. You cannot disciple people until you win them to Christ, but you do not fulfill the Great Commission just by winning souls. In fact, the command of Christ is not to win souls but to make disciples. As the pastor wins the hearts of his people and disciples them from the pulpit and in small groups, enlisting the members to help him in this discipleship process, they will automatically widen the circle of fellowship and leadership to include new members.

Jesus taught that the church's credibility and even His credibility in the world is in the church's unity: "I pray not only for these, but also for those who believe in Me through their message. May they all be one, as You, Father, are in Me, and I am in You. May they also be one in Us, so the world may believe You sent Me" (John 17:20–21). Church unity is essential for church growth, and it is vital if a pastor is to stay at a church.

A pastor should never insist on his own way at all costs. He should never threaten to resign if the church doesn't go along with his ideas. Nobody gets his own way all the time. It is better to back off and approach the matter at a later time in a different manner.

A teenager had an accident because he saw that the traffic light was about to turn green, and he assumed the other driver would stop. The other driver was trying to beat the light. He hit the teen broadside. The boy was furious that the other driver had not stopped. His father quoted him an epitaph from a tombstone:

> Here lies the body of Mike O'Day
> Who died maintaining his right of way.
> His right was clear. His will was strong.
> But he's just as dead as if he'd been wrong.

Solomon said, "A live dog is better than a dead lion" (Eccles. 9:4). I wonder, are there pastors like Mike O'Day?

When a pastor does leave his first church, it should be a heartbreaking decision on his part. Hopefully, his leaving should be for a good reason, such as going to another church or furthering his theological education. It should not be because he is forced to leave. (We will deal with that problem in another chapter.) Stay with it. Wait for the words of Jesus, "Well done, good and faithful slave! You were faithful over a few things; I will put you in charge of many things. Share your master's joy!" (Matt. 25:23).

Some pastors grow so unhappy in their first assignment that they think they are going to die. It is not wrong to feel this way. You just need to remember that Paul said he experienced that; he died daily (1 Cor. 15:31). Many commentators think Paul was talking about dying to self, not physical threat. God has used many difficult churches in the lives of pastors to teach them how to be crucified with Christ and to stay on the cross like Jesus did. With the possible exception of the church at Philippi, all of Paul's churches were difficult assignments. Jesus said, "Be faithful until death, and I will give you the crown of life" (Rev. 2:10). The promise of a crown gives richness to any pastor who suffers for Jesus. Galatians 2:20 is in the Bible for good reason. The default attitude for the pastor is to stay, not to leave.

TESTIMONY:

The Pastor and His Leadership

Zig Ziglar
Motivational Speaker
Dallas, Texas

People do not care how much you know until they know how much you care. For that reason a pastor with a flair for leadership makes it a point to let his people know that he cares for them, whether they be staff, volunteers, visitors to the church, consistent members, or people who are lost and in need of love. He knows they are all created in the image of God and loved by God. Leadership is love in action. That's what the pastor must radiate as he relates to and communicates with God's people. His time is their time, but he uses his time wisely.

The pastor should follow the biblical mandate to be no respecter of persons. He has time for all of God's little ones, and he ministers to them in a loving way. By the same token, when he interacts with deacons and other church leaders, he is also careful to follow biblical admonitions, understanding that he is the shepherd to whom they look for guidance and leadership. When there is lack of harmony in the body of the church, the pastor with leadership qualities takes the necessary action to bring his congregation together through prayer, counseling, and loving them into following the path our Lord wants them to take. The pastor is to display leadership at home, at the church, with the members and leaders of his congregation, and throughout his community. Lead, pastor, lead!

CHAPTER 7
The Pastor and His Leadership

A church can call you to be a pastor because *Pastor* is a title. The call does not make you a leader. *Leader* is not a title but a role. You only become a leader by functioning as one.[1]

The world today is suffering from a leadership crisis, and the church is no exception. James Means, in his excellent book *Leadership in Christian Ministry*,[2] gives five convincing reasons the church is experiencing such a crisis in leadership:

1. The absence of meaningful growth in the churches.
2. The amount of discord and disharmony among congregations.
3. The number of brief pastorates and ministerial burnouts.
4. The rise of a spectator religion that caters to the fallout from churches with leadership problems.
5. The high percentage of nonministering churches.

What is happening to the leadership in our nation, our denominations, our homes, and our churches? If you walk through a bookstore, the number of books on leadership will overwhelm you. There are seminars everywhere on leadership. Yet with all that is being written and taught, we are living in a vacuum where it seems as if leadership does not exist.

In America on the eve of the American Revolution, the population of the colonies was about 2.1 million people.[3] The population of our country at this writing is more than 300 million. Yet look at the leadership difference. In 1770, in a pool of just over two million people, the leadership of that day consisted of the likes of George Washington, Benjamin Franklin, James Madison, John Adams, and Thomas Jefferson. And these were just a few of the great leaders who founded this country. Today we have a pool to draw from that they could not have imagined, but we are in a leadership crisis.

This is also true of the church. We look back to men such as John Wycliffe, Martin Luther, and John Calvin. We can move beyond them in history to men such as Joseph Parker, Charles Spurgeon, and Alexander Maclaren. Where are leaders like John Broadus, E. Y. Mullins, George W. Truett, R. G. Lee, and W. A. Criswell? We have such a vast pool of people to draw from today, but where are the great leaders whom we desperately need?

Is it possible that in our day of ecclesiastical drift, denominational demise, and megachurch melt-downs, we have confused leadership with lordship and substituted success for servanthood? We have looked to a business model for leadership for kingdom work. While we can learn from the business world, the church is not a business; it is a bride. Even the secular world is beginning to recognize that leadership as outlined in Scripture—servant leadership—is more effective. Myron Rush, in his book *The New Leader*, states, "Servant leaders are more effective leaders than traditional leaders."[4]

Jim Collins, author of the best-selling book *Good to Great*, says, "Social sector organizations increasingly look to business for leadership models and talent, yet I suppose we will find more true leadership in the social sectors than in the business sector."[5] Listen carefully to what he says: "How can I say that? Because, as George MacGregor Burns taught in his classic 1978 text, *Leadership*, the practice of leadership is not the same as the exercise of power. If I put a loaded gun to your head, I can get you to do things you might not otherwise do, but I've not practiced leadership; I've exercised power. True leadership only exists if people follow when they have the freedom not to."[6]

While people in the church are busying themselves looking to the business sector for leadership techniques, those in the business sector are discovering that raw power is not leadership. What Scripture teaches about leadership is now capturing the minds of the business world. There is a book out by two women, Linda Thaler and Robin Koval, who opened an ad agency in 1977 with only one customer. Today they have some of the largest accounts in the world with billings in excess of a billion dollars. The book is entitled *The Power of Nice*. What is interesting is the subtitle, *How to Conquer the*

Business World with Kindness. That is amazing, since kindness is one of the fruits of the Spirit!

The Mandate for Biblical Leadership

You cannot get around the fact that throughout God's Word there is a mandate for godly leadership. We understand that every football team has a quarterback who calls the plays inside the huddle. We also know that there is a coach standing on the sidelines who is ultimately sending in the plays. Every team has a captain, and every church is supposed to have a pastor who receives his word from the Lord and then leads the congregation.

God has always had leaders. Moses was a unique but chosen leader of God's people. Joshua followed in his footsteps and became the leader of God's people. We can look back to the Old Testament and see great leaders such as David, Solomon, and Hezekiah. In the New Testament Jesus led the disciples for three years. He chose Peter to be the one who would lead the apostolic band after He had been crucified, resurrected, and ascended back to the right hand of the Father.

In the church in Jerusalem in the book of Acts, James was head of the church as well as the Jerusalem Council. When Barnabas and Saul set out on their first missionary journey, Barnabas was clearly the leader, but this changed when Saul of Tarsus became Paul the apostle, the leader of the first Christian missionary trips. Paul made it clear that things were not right in the church without proper leadership: "For this reason I left you in Crete, that you might set in order what remains, and appoint elders in every city as I directed you" (Titus 1:5 NASB).

Leadership is not born nor is it manufactured. It is given. In the church, leadership is God-called. God calls a man, and He does not call a man who is already equipped. God gives him the gift of leadership. This is not to say that the man does not already have some abilities, but leadership according to Romans 12 is a gift given by the sovereign discretion of God.

Leadership is not something we should fear or shy away from. If God calls us, He will equip us to do what He has planned. George W. Truett was convinced he was not to be a preacher, but everyone else was convinced that he was. On a Saturday afternoon in the Baptist church in Whitewright, Texas, packed out for its Saturday conference, Truett arrived surprised at the crowd. At the close of the meeting a deacon stood and said there was still one piece of business to take care of; it was to call for an ordination council to ordain the young George W. Truett.

The young man had no idea this was going to take place. The vote was about to be taken when he pleaded with the members of the church to wait six months. But the church responded that it would not wait six more hours. The next day Truett answered the call of God and gave in to the vote of the church.[7] There was a fear and an apprehension on Truett's part that went beyond his desire to be a lawyer. God took that fearful, timid young man and made a mountain out of him for His glory. Truett led the great church in Dallas, the Southern Baptist Convention, and even the nation. Little did he know what God would do with him as He called and gifted him for leadership.

The Motive for Biblical Leadership

Paul stated, "Our exhortation didn't come from error or impurity or an intent to deceive. Instead, just as we have been approved by God to be entrusted with the gospel, so we speak, not to please men, but rather God, who examines our hearts" (1 Thess. 2:3–4). Note carefully what Paul says here:

- not pleasing men
- not with flattering speech
- nor with a pretext for greed
- nor with a desire for glory
- nor did we assert our authority

Paul told us what did not motivate him. His desire was not to please men but to please God. So often in the ministry we are tempted to become "men-pleasers." O. S. Hawkins, in his excellent manual *The Pastor's Primer*, talks about two leadership styles. There is the style of the pastor who leads by public consensus. This person does not take a stand until he can get a "read" on what the people are thinking. This is exactly what Paul is talking about—those who will do nothing unless they know it makes everyone happy.

The other style is that of the pastor who leads by personal conviction. "Those who lead by personal conviction have convictions deep in the fiber of their being about what is right or wrong and they lead that way, come what may. Those who lead by public consensus lead people to do whatever the people *want* to do. Those who lead by personal conviction lead people to do what the people *need* to do."[8]

Paul stated that he did not come to the people of his time with flattering speech. The idea behind this was the wearing of a mask in an effort to conceal real motives and intentions. The motive behind that was greed. There were people in Paul's day who traveled among the churches solely for self-aggrandizement. From the early days of the church until now, some people have wanted to profit from the people of God. Paul said that they were motivated by greed.

The great apostle also stated that he was not seeking glory. This is more of an issue than greed. It is a desire for personal reputation. This has overtaken more men in the ministry than we want to admit. How many ministries have failed because some pastor was more interested in reputation among the brethren than winning the smile of God?

Finally, Paul stated that he did not demand the honor that was due him because he was an apostle of Christ. He did not come throwing his authority around. This is closely tied to the idea that precedes this statement, which was seeking glory from men. Paul did not come seeking the applause of men and desiring to be honored because of his position.

What is the motivation behind your actions? That is always an appropriate question to ask yourself. Before you cast a vision, before you lead a new program, before you make a staff adjustment, even before you preach a sermon, ask, What is my motivation in doing this? You can be sure that others in your church will be asking this question—if not publicly, then privately in their own hearts.

The Method of Biblical Leadership

We do not have to wonder what biblical leadership looks like. There are so many good examples for us throughout the Word of God. Let's look at one Old Testament example and one New Testament example.

The Shepherding Method: Psalm 78:70–72

Psalm 78 is a picture of Israel from the time the nation was in Egyptian slavery until the days of the Davidic kingdom. In this psalm there is a warning not to repeat the sins of the previous generations. Also it is a psalm that shows the constant grace and miraculous power of God intervening on behalf of His people. It is a narrative that looks back over the waywardness of Israel in contrast to the love and faithfulness of God. He chose David from out of the sheepfolds. "From the care of the ewes with suckling lambs He brought him, to shepherd Jacob His people, and Israel His inheritance" (Ps. 78:71 NASB). Then the psalmist concludes with these words: "So he shepherded them according to the integrity of his heart and guided them with his skillful hands" (Ps. 78:72 NASB).

It is obvious that God chose someone who was tender and gentle and a reflection of Himself. Paul sounds a lot like David when he says, "We proved to be gentle among you, as a nursing mother tenderly cares for her own children" (1 Thess. 2:7 NASB). There is no doubt that God calls those in leadership of His people to be tender, compassionate, and gentle. In fact, this is the picture of Jesus when He looked out on the multitude: "He felt compassion for them, because they were distressed and downcast like sheep without a shepherd" (Matt. 9:36 NASB).

The method of biblical leadership is one of tenderness, gentleness, and compassion. We are never more like Christ than when we are shepherding God's people. If you doubt this, consider what Paul said to the Ephesian elders: "Be on guard for yourselves and for all the flock, among which the Holy Spirit has made you overseers (*episcopoi*), to shepherd the church of God which He purchased with His own blood" (Acts 20:28 NASB).

Did you notice why the Holy Spirit has made you an overseer? It is so you can shepherd the flock of God, the very ones Christ purchased with His blood. This is an incredible thought—that God has placed under our care as pastors a portion of His sheep. It is also an awesome responsibility—that we are to shepherd His people, knowing that they were purchased by the blood of Christ. We did not redeem them; we did not buy them. He bought them!

This means that our responsibility as pastors is not just to preach and teach or just to cast a vision and lead; it also requires that we care for God's people. This does not mean that we care only for those people whom we are naturally drawn to but also for those who are hard to get along with and difficult to love. Jesus shepherded His twelve disciples even when He knew that one was a devil, one would deny Him, and all would desert Him.

God's people are referred to again and again in the Bible as a flock of sheep. "Like a shepherd He will tend His flock, in His arm He will gather the lambs, and carry them in His bosom; He will gently lead the nursing ewes" (Isa. 40:11 NASB).

When Isaiah described the coming Messiah, it was in terms of a shepherd. Peter called Jesus the chief Shepherd in 1 Peter 5:4. Isaiah spoke of the flock in a collective sense; then he referred to lambs and some that had to be carried. Finally he spoke of the nursing ewes. He described the various needs within a flock. Some are little lambs that are injured or frightened, and they need to be carried close to the shepherd. Others are in the process of gestation or have delivered, and they have special needs. As a pastor of God's people, everyone will not be at the same place spiritually, emotionally, mentally, or physically. Some will require a little more attention than others. Still others will not need you except in emergencies.

One act of shepherding that I have followed through the years is standing at the front of the worship center after Sunday night and Wednesday night services to let people talk to me. Debbie and I are usually some of the last people out of church on those evenings because we can "shepherd" a great number of people by allowing them to come up and share their hearts, speak, get close enough to shake hands, or get a hug if they are hurting.

Many times people will come up and say, "I need to talk to you." I can tell them to call my office for an appointment so I can see them there, but I sometimes respond, "Why don't you tell me now what's going on so I can be praying about it?" They will usually share with me their needs, hurts, or desires on the spot. Many times they just need someone to listen, and an appointment for more extensive conversation is not necessary.

In every church you will encounter "needy" people. These are folks who simply have a need to get close because they have no close relationships with anyone else, or they have some emotional problems, or they are people who feel "left out." To get close to the pastor, to shake his hand, to say a word, and to hear a kind word spoken by him in return—this is what they need. At First Baptist of Dallas and at First Baptist of Jacksonville, I have had a great number of people who repeatedly come down after the service to reach out and touch my hand and wait for me to say a word to them. I am never representing Christ more than when I take a few minutes with these people. This is shepherding, and this is leadership.

The Serving Method: John 13:1–17

Perhaps no picture of Christ is more moving than the one we find in John 13. Here we see our Lord with a towel wrapped around His waist, on His knees, washing the feet of His disciples. This was a job for the most menial of servants. In fact, a Jewish slave could not be commanded to do this; therefore, it was left for Gentile slaves to do.

When Jesus finished this task He explained what He had done: "I gave you an example that you also should do as I did to you" (John 13:15 NASB). Then He told His disciples that they were blessed if they served others in this way (John 13:17). It is one thing to know what to do; it is quite another thing to do it. Jesus washed His disciples' feet, leaving them and us an example to follow. This is servant leadership.

Ken Blanchard is a businessman, consultant, speaker, trainer, and author on management and leadership. He wrote the popular *One Minute Manager*[9] that has sold over seven million copies and has been translated into twenty languages. In his unique book *Lead Like Jesus*, he opens with these words, "The world is in desperate need of a different leadership role model."[10] He goes on to tell us what leadership style the world needs: "There is a way to lead that honors God and restores health and effectiveness to organizations and relationships. It is the way Jesus calls us to follow as leaders: to serve rather than to be served."[11] It is amazing that the business world seems to understand this better than those who are called to shepherd the flock of God.

After I arrived at First Baptist of Jacksonville, the ladies of the church were hosting a women's conference on a Saturday. Deb needed to be there and I decided I would go along, get there early, and help serve the women breakfast. That is exactly what Deb and I did, and you cannot imagine the response. We simply walked around from table to table with coffee pots and refilled the coffee cups of these women. It gave us an opportunity to meet and serve these people who spend so much of their time serving others. I still get letters and e-mails about that one simple act of servanthood.

Servant leadership is more caught than taught. What your people see you do, they will eventually copy. What they see you emphasize, they will begin to emphasize. When they learn your heart—if it is one of servanthood—that will become their heart. That is leadership.

The Manner of Biblical Leadership

The "how" of leadership is critical. How do we lead the people of God? What manner, shape, and fashion does our leadership take? The Word of God gives clear instruction about the manner of leadership.

We Lead Most Effectively When We Lead from Humility (Acts 20:18–19)

When Paul said farewell to the elders of the church at Ephesus, he began with these words: "You yourselves know, from the first day that I set foot in Asia, how I was with you the whole time, serving the Lord with all humility" (Acts 20:18–19 NASB). Humility is a lost virtue even among God's people. Humility is not self-effacing; it is self-awareness. I know who I am and that I am nothing apart from God's grace. Those who lead most effectively lead with humility.

We Lead Most Effectively When We Lead from Gentleness (1 Thess. 2:7, 11)

Paul told the church at Thessalonica that he was as gentle as a nursing mother to them. At the same time, in 1 Thessalonians 2:11, he stated that he exhorted, encouraged, and implored them as if they were his children. Being humble and gentle does not mean that you cannot be direct when the occasion calls for it. But it does describe the manner of your directness.

We Lead Best When We Lead without Partiality (1 Tim. 5:21)

Paul charged Timothy to maintain the principles he had laid out and to do it "without bias, doing nothing in a spirit of partiality" (NASB). Paul used two words in this passage. *Bias* means to judge beforehand. This means you have your mind settled in a certain direction before you even know the facts. The second word is *partiality*. The Greek prefix *pros* means "toward" or "to lean in the direction of something." When a pastor shows partiality, favoritism, or bias, the rest of the church picks up on it and resents it. Too often a pastor will bond with men in the church whom he is most like. If the pastor likes to play golf or hunt or is interested in certain sports, he will be tempted to gravitate toward those people who share these interests.

The opposite of that is also true. The people who are interested in things that do not interest the pastor will tend to feel alienated. They will think that the pastor is aloof, distant, and uncaring. As you carry out your preaching assignments and your pastoral duties, your leadership must be without bias and partiality.

We Lead Most Effectively When We Lead with Decisiveness (2 Cor. 1:17)

Paul in this passage discussed the radical change in his travel schedule. This upset the Corinthians. Paul explained that he intended to come to Corinth but did not. Some of the Corinthian Christians accused him of vacillating, but Paul stated the church knew that he did not make erratic decisions. He was not wishy-washy when it came to making decisions. Nor did he, like so many people, make decisions "according to the flesh" (NASB). That is, the decisions he made were not based on his own selfish desires or his need for personal gratification. People do not have confidence in a leader who consistently makes decisions based on his personal preferences or who is constantly changing direction.

Of course, there are times when a pastor needs to change a decision. In fact, if you are unable to change decisions that need to be changed, people will lose confidence in you just as they will if you are constantly changing directions. A good leader will take the time to seek counsel, think, pray, and carefully make decisions that will not have to be changed. Yet, when a decision needs to be changed, he should have the courage to do so. The people should understand that he is not vacillating but has their best interest at heart.

We Lead Most Effectively When We Understand Timing (Eccles. 3:1, 3)

In this familiar passage, Solomon talks about time and seasons. Timing is critical in everything that a pastor does. One of the great ploys of Satan is to rush us and bring the pressure of a quick decision into play. Over the years I have come to the conclusion that noise and haste are usually of the devil. As pastors we tend to think that everything has to be done immediately. This can lead to tragedy, confusion, and misunderstanding. Besides that, so much of what is done in haste lacks the excellence that should characterize church work.

Many young pastors, when they enter a new field of work, a new church, or a new ministry, feel as if they must have a plan ready for implementation. One of the smartest things you can do when entering a new work is not to be pressed into a plan. People will want to know, "What is your vision?" Staff will constantly ask, "What is your plan?" It is best not to go into a new work with a plan but with a process.

Take your time at the beginning to establish a list of critical issues and top priorities and begin to focus on them. As you do, leaning on the Lord, He will direct your steps in His timing. "The steps of a good man are ordered by the LORD" (Ps. 37:23 NKJV). Over and over throughout Scripture we are told to wait on the Lord. "Let integrity and uprightness preserve me, for I wait for Thee" (Ps. 25:21 NASB). "Rest in the LORD and wait patiently for Him" (Ps. 37:7 NASB). "Wait for the LORD; be strong, and let your heart take courage; yes, wait for the LORD" (Ps. 27:14 NASB).

In fact, you rarely read where God tells His people to hurry unless it is in connection with salvation. God's Word to us over and over is to wait on the Lord. That, for Americans, is perhaps the hardest directive we could have. Timing is something that has to be God-directed. We need to spend time in prayer. This is not wasted time. I do not know of a better way to determine God's timing than to be still and quiet and to wait on Him.

We Lead Most Effectively When We Keep Our Heads (2 Tim. 4:5)

Paul was awaiting execution when he counseled believers to be sober in all things. We could translate this, "Keep your head in every situation." I will never forget memorizing as a young teen the famous poem "If" by Rudyard Kipling. The opening line goes, "If you can keep your head when all about you are losing theirs and blaming it on you." There will be times in a crisis when everyone around you is literally "losing their heads." Someone had better stay calm and collected— that someone should be the pastor!

There was an occasion, soon after I arrived at Green Street Baptist Church, when the deacon body was split over sending the former pastor a financial gift. He had been fired, and some deacons felt that the church had always taken up a love offering for pastors when they left. Even though he had left under adverse circumstances, some wanted to extend to him a financial gift. As a young pastor, I sat and watched as the deacons wrangled over this issue.

The senior adult pastor was in the meeting. After a while he simply said to the deacons, "Do not be overcome by evil, but overcome evil with good" (Rom. 12:21 NASB). I just sat and stared at him and thought, *Why didn't I think of that?* It was a word aptly spoken, and it settled everyone down. Counsel like that comes with age and godly wisdom.

We Lead Most Effectively When We Are Trustworthy (1 Cor. 4:2)

Paul stated, "In this case, moreover, it is required of stewards that one be found trustworthy" (NASB). Paul had just stated that we are stewards of the mysteries of God. A steward, an *oikonomos*, was a chief household slave—a person who answered directly to and gave an account to his master.[12] God's desire is that we be faithful. He does not call His servants to be eloquent or successful but to be faithful.

You as a pastor should be faithful to your assigned tasks. When you handle the Word of God, you are to be faithful. When it comes to your family, you are to be faithful. When it comes to finances, you are to be faithful. When it comes to handling critically sensitive issues concerning the membership of the church, you are to be faithful.

Being trustworthy means you set your feelings aside to do what is right. You should determine ahead of time that you will do the right thing—not the easy thing, the popular thing, or the feel-good thing. You will do the godly thing. Leadership is an inside job. It involves character, integrity, the right attitude, and knowing how to submit yourself to authority. My dad always told me, "Heaven help the people who get a leader who does not know how to submit to authority." Lead yourself because that is where leadership begins.

TESTIMONY:

The Pastor and His Staff

Bill Taylor
Executive Pastor for Education
First Baptist Church, Jacksonville, Florida

*The best executive is the one who has sense enough to pick good men
to do what he wants done, and self-restraint enough
to keep from meddling with them while they do it.*
—Theodore Roosevelt

One of the wisest investments a pastor can make is the time and energy that he invests in the men and women who make up his staff. One cannot place too high a premium on this strategic step in practical ministry.

Examine the great leaders in history. George Washington only had to ride his horse through the ranks of ill-equipped troops to stir up their fervor, which ultimately won independence for America. A kind word from Robert E. Lee brought about victory after victory for the Confederacy. It was said of Napoleon, the great military genius, "Napoleon lived with his men, ate and drank with them, trained them, praised and chastised them, listened to them and when the going got tough, led them personally."

A marker in London has the following quote from Stafford Gripps, Britain's chancellor of the exchequer: "If a man neglects the things of the Spirit and puts aside the full armour of God, he will seal the doom of future generations." A pastor who does not neglect his staff will be honored by them. A pastor who loves and builds relationships with these godly servants will also be honored by God.

CHAPTER 8 The Pastor and His Staff

The plurality of elders taught in the New Testament has great implications for the pastor and his staff. We are using the word *elder* as synonymous with the word *pastor*. We recognize that not every denomination uses the two words synonymously. There are four different words used in the Greek New Testament to speak of the leaders of a church.

Episcopos means literally "overseer." It is usually translated as "bishop." *Presbuteros* means literally "elder," and it is usually translated that way. *Poimen* means literally "shepherd." It is usually translated as "shepherd," which usually refers to the pastor. *Pastor* is of Latin derivation and is usually used today to speak of the preaching head of the church. *Diakonos* means literally "servant," and this word is usually translated into English as "deacon."

Baptists usually equate the first three terms as referring to the same office, the office of pastor. Because of that equation Baptists usually maintain that there are only two ordained offices in the church—pastor and deacon. Because of Acts 6,[1] Baptist churches traditionally have recognized the pastor's responsibilities to include preaching, teaching, and praying. Business affairs were left up to the deacons. But the business outlined in Acts 6 was visiting and serving the needs of the widows in the church.

In Baptist history, particularly in the southern United States, there were not enough pastors to provide a full-time pastor for every church. Two churches, sometimes four churches, had the same pastor. He would spend a week at each of his quarter-time churches. These pastors were sometimes called circuit riders. I can remember visiting my grandmother when I was a child. Her church, Benton Baptist Church in Benton, Alabama, was a quarter-time church. (It is a full-time church today.)

Three Sundays out of the month they would have only Sunday school at the Benton church. They had coordinated their preaching schedule with three other churches of different denominations. On those three Sundays they would announce during Sunday school the locations in the community where preaching would be held that day. On the fourth Sunday preaching would be at their church, Benton Baptist Church.

Who was in charge three out of the four weeks each month? Not the pastor. He was traveling his circuit. The deacons were in charge. All the pastor did was preach and visit one Sunday out of the month. If a funeral was necessary, he would come back for the funeral, but weddings were always scheduled during the pastor's week at the church.

After World War II, when the urban movement brought Baptists from the country to the city in large numbers, churches that had been quarter-time churches soon grew to full-time churches. Now they had a pastor on the church field all the time. Tensions often arose over who was in charge—the pastor or the deacons. That tension still exists in many churches today.

As mentioned in a previous chapter, when Adrian Rogers became pastor of Bellevue Baptist Church in Memphis, Tennessee, the deacons were accustomed to running the church. R. G. Lee, the famed pastor of that church for many decades, wanted it that way. He was frequently gone during the week, preaching in other churches. When Lee died, Ramsey Pollard became pastor. He was unable to wrest control of the church away from the deacons.

When Adrian Rogers became pastor of this church, he had a deep conviction that deacons of today should function as deacons did in Acts 6. They should assist the pastor in the pastoral ministry of the church. He met with the deacons one Sunday afternoon a month. He took the first forty-five minutes of the one-hour meeting and taught them what the Bible says about deacons. He left fifteen minutes for them to spend on business. Some of them did not like this approach, so they left the church. But most stayed. Bellevue was transformed from a deacon-led church to a pastor-and-staff-led church in just a few years.

The Development of the Church Staff

Prior to the twentieth century, most churches had only one paid staff member—the pastor. But these churches still had leadership in the areas beside preaching and pastoring. Volunteer laymen functioned as staff members. A layman led the music. Laymen were in charge of the education program, as the Sunday school superintendent, and the Church Training director. A layman was in charge of the youth program and so on.

This was not a bad pattern, getting staff members from the congregation. In fact, the first pastors mentioned in the book of Acts did not come from seminaries because there were no institutions of this type. They came out of the congregation. "So when they [Paul and Barnabas] had appointed elders [another word for pastors] in every church" (Acts 14:23 NKJV). The point I am making is that laymen make wonderful ministers in the church.

If you as pastor are the only paid staff member in the church, you can still have a staff. See appendix 6 for a staff organization chart for churches with only one paid staff member—the pastor. But even larger churches can expand their staff by using volunteer laymen. The First Baptist Church of Dallas, Texas, reorganized their staff in 2005 to include a large number of volunteers as departmental secretaries, hospital visitors, Stephen Ministry[2] care leaders, and even skilled maintenance workers. Most of these were recently retired persons and did not work full-time. This is the day of volunteers.

As the Staff Grows

As the staff grows, care must be taken to see that staff members work under authority. There is a principle in the Bible about authority. There is a God-given pattern of authority in the home. The husband is to be the head of his family. There is a God-given pattern of authority in the government. We are told, "Let every soul be subject to the governing authorities. For there is no authority except from God, and the authorities that exist are appointed by God" (Rom. 13:1 NKJV). There is a God-given pattern of authority in the church. "Remember those who rule over you, who have spoken the word of God to you"

(Heb. 13:7 NKJV). Even stronger is this admonition, "Obey those who rule over you" (Heb. 13:17 NKJV).

Ample warning is given to every pastor about how he exercises his God-given authority in the church. The New Testament concept, and the example of Jesus, is clearly what is known as servant leadership, not pastoral authority. This does not mean that the pastor is not in charge, but it does mean that being in charge involves serving as the chief servant, not the CEO. While God's business is big business, the church must be run differently from a business. This does not mean that sound business principles should not be followed in a church, but it does mean that exemplary service is the underlying principle of leadership. The pastor is not to be a commanding general barking out orders. He should be like the file leader of the paratroopers who says, "Come on, men; stand up, hook up, and follow me."

As the staff grows, it must be organized. Job descriptions should be written, signed, and accepted by an incoming staff member. (I always added one final duty to every job description: "And any other assignment made by the pastor.") The personnel committee should be led by the pastor to write and have the church approve a personnel policies and procedures manual. Regular staff meetings should be conducted where the church calendar is reviewed together, programs are evaluated and planned, and decisions are made by the pastor, who should preside over the meeting, unless he has an executive pastor to whom he has assigned this responsibility.

Even in that situation, the pastor should attend every staff meeting so that he knows what is going on and can guide the decisions being made. A printed agenda should be prepared for each staff meeting. Each meeting should begin with a time of prayer.

Church Polity

The denomination or church's view of church governance will affect how the staff is organized and led. Out of those words used in the New Testament for leaders come three different types of church governance.

From the word *episcopos* comes the episcopal form of church government. An *episcopos* is a bishop. So the episcopal form of church government has a hierarchy presided over by a bishop. Roman Catholics, Episcopalians, Anglicans, and Methodists all have bishops. The bishop owns the church property and appoints the pastors. The pastors are accountable to the bishop, not to the congregation.

From the word *presbuteros* comes the presbyterian form of church government. A *presbuteros* is an elder. Presbyterian churches have what is known as elder rule. The pastor is only one of the elders, and he is responsible to the other elders of the church.

The word *poimen* or "pastor" is the word used by free churches that are congregationally governed. The congregation calls the pastor. It owns its own buildings and has the final say in all decision making. This is known as congregational polity. This type of church government is often cumbersome, and many pastors feel frustrated by it. A church that has congregational government can be led to put in its bylaws what decisions must be referred to the congregation and what decisions can be made by the pastor and staff. If the pastor has good leadership skills, a congregation can usually be led to follow him, although congregational meetings must allow discussion and even opposition, with the congregation settling the issue at hand.

Periodically in Baptist life, some churches have turned from pure congregationalism to elder rule. Anytime Calvinism experiences a resurgence among Baptists, there is a tendency to adopt Calvin's elder rule. If a Baptist church adopts elder rule and wants to remain Baptist, the elders should be elected by the church and not be a self-perpetuating body. Also, ultimate decisions such as calling or dismissing a pastor, buying or selling property, and building facilities should be taken by the elders to the congregation for approval.

Periodically among Baptists there is a discussion of church polity. A recent book entitled *Perspectives on Church Government*[3] surveys five different views of church polity (how a church should be run or governed). This book contains a chapter on "The Single-Elder-Led Church" that recognizes the principle of a plurality of elders in the book of Acts, but it views them as the staff and not as equals to the pastor. Other chapters include "The Presbytery-Led Church," "The Congregation-Led Church," "The Bishop-Led Church," and "The Plural-Elder-Led Church." We believe the single-elder-led church best meets New Testament teaching from a historic Baptist perspective.

When I (Bryant) was a pastor, I considered my ordained staff my fellow elders. I involved them in decision making, but they were still under my supervision and authority. When I was called as pastor of Hoffmantown Baptist Church in Albuquerque, New Mexico, this church had been historically a deacon-and-committee-led church. Before I would accept the call, I asked them to change the bylaws to put the staff and program under the pastor. The revised bylaws specified that the pastor would select the ministerial staff, with the advice and consent of the personnel committee and with the affirmation of the church. The pastor, with the advice and consent of the personnel committee, could dismiss ministerial staff without a congregational vote. They also specified that the pastor had full responsibility for the nonprofessional staff. This placed the staff clearly under the pastor.

That church had also used a church council to plan the calendar and program of the church. Then the church had to approve the calendar and any subsequent changes. I asked them to change the bylaws to specify that the pastor and staff would plan the calendar and program of the church. It worked like a charm. The church was released from the previous bureaucracy to follow its pastoral leadership and to grow. The staff functioned as elders, yet there was only one pastor, and they were under his supervision. The church followed the pastor and staff. The limitations on church growth were removed, and the church was enabled to follow leadership and to grow at a brisk pace.

Where Do You Find Staff?

At all of the churches I pastored, we had wonderful staff members. Other pastors used to ask me, "Where do you get your staff?" Even pastors of megachurches have asked me that question. I looked for staff people before I needed them. In my travels to preach at other churches and to denominational meetings, I would meet and mingle with staff members as well as other pastors. If they were potential staff members, I would correspond with them and keep up with them. In short, I would love them and show interest in them and their families. Then when a vacancy occurred on my staff, I already had a friendship with the person whom I knew could fill that vacancy.

If you want to attract good staff members, love the staff you have, support them, pay them well, enable them, empower them, encourage them, and brag on them. They will talk to their friends about what a good pastor you are to work with. Your reputation as a pastor who loves and takes care of his staff will attract the best of the best future staff members. If you hire highly qualified staff members, when they leave your church they will always go to bigger and better churches. That makes you and your church look good. Continue to keep up with them after they leave. I have former staff members who still call me for counseling and advice. Your staff should be among your best friends.

Have a Good Time

Fellowshipping with your staff should be fun for you as well as them. In my churches I always asked that part of my salary be designated for entertainment. I used this account mostly to take staff members and their wives to dinner in nice restaurants. When my staff members would go to professional conferences where they would see their peers in the same field, I would have a basket of fruit waiting for them at the hotel with a card that said, "To the World's Best (Minister of Music, Educational Director, Youth Director, or Administrator)." I always took my staff on an annual planning retreat, usually in January. We would plan the calendar for the next eighteen months during the first part of the week and then spend a day skiing before we returned home. Church work should be fun for you, your staff, and your people.

Pay Your Staff Appropriately

Appendix 8 tells you how to find the appropriate format for presenting to the personnel committee the pastor and staff salary and benefits. In many large churches there is a big gap between the salary and benefits of the senior pastor and the ministers one level below him. This is unwise. Denominations have salary schedules that can guide you in paying those under you appropriately. Obviously, these people should not earn more than you do. I have known several pastors who asked their churches to freeze their salaries when their children were grown and gone because they did not need the money anymore. In every case, the staff under them suffered because they stopped getting raises they needed to keep up with the cost of living.

A pastor should make sure that the staff has the same basic benefits the church extends to him. For instance, if the pastor has retirement benefits, so should the staff. If the pastor has health insurance, so should the staff. If the pastor has allowances to travel to denominational meetings or personal development conferences, so should the staff. Vacations can be scheduled according to tenure.

Be a Pastor to Your Staff

Of all the people you should pastor, next to your own family, you should do so for your staff. You may not be able to meet the pastoral needs of the entire congregation, but you had better meet the pastoral needs of your staff. They need spiritual help just like anyone else. More than one former staff member has said to me, "I am in a different church now, but you are still my pastor." They will love and follow their present pastor, but they will never forget you. That is as it should be if you love your staff.

TESTIMONY:

The Pastor and Worship

Scott W. Bryant
Associate Pastor of Worship Ministries
Lamar Baptist Church, Arlington, Texas

A number of years ago the phrase "worship wars" was coined to describe controversy over worship style. If your church is involved in a worship war, I pray that our church's journey will be of encouragement to you.

Anything of eternal consequence related to the ministry of worship in our church is strictly by God's grace and to His glory. As our individual church members have grown in their daily walk with the Lord, musical style has become less of an issue. Compliments and complaints about music have given way to reflections of touched hearts and changed lives. Criticism faded as we allowed God to become the center of attention in our services.

I've been blessed to work with a number of pastors who were not only bosses and supervisors but friends as well. These gifted men varied in leadership style and worship preference. God placed undershepherds in churches as spiritual leaders. As such, I submitted to their authority and led others to do the same. God blessed this obedience, trust was built, love was fostered, and freedom was given. What a perfect atmosphere in which true worship can blossom! I love seeing senior adults worshiping God with a praise song. I get a kick out of seeing youth connecting to the Lord with a hymn. This would not be happening without our pastor, staff, and church members living out Mark 12:30–31.

CHAPTER 9 The Pastor and Worship

The notion that America has a major problem in the area of worship is an inescapable conclusion. Perhaps the most striking feature of the research is the revelation that our problem is not an inability to craft services or experiences that are culturally relevant . . . . The problem is that American Christians do not have a heart that is thirsting for an experience with God, eager to express gratitude and praise to Him, and open to His response to their efforts to convey humility, appreciation, acknowledgment of His love and character, and joy in knowing and serving Him.[1]

When you say the word *worship* today, the image that comes to most pastors and staff is not style, approach, or manner, but it is a feud like that of the legendary Hatfields and McCoys.

Over the past thirty years or so the church has experienced what has been termed "worship wars." Churches have fought, split, ranted, and ruined their witness in the community over the issue of music style. You can preach heresy and get by with it, but do not change the tempo of the hymns or the style of the music. The ecclesiastical landscape is littered with the ministries of pastors who introduced a new piece of music with a different beat.

Our task is not to debate the issues of contemporary worship versus traditional worship styles. Every pastor needs to be as wise as a serpent and as harmless as a dove when it comes to changing, rearranging, and reordering the worship style of a congregation. Changes should be made prayerfully and carefully and with great sensitivity.

Years ago, the church where I currently serve as senior pastor was very high church and formal in its style. This was when

Homer Lindsay Sr. was pastor. The church at that time reflected the worship style across our denomination. When Homer Lindsay Jr. became pastor, he introduced drums, instruments, and gospel music. It was not the easiest transition, but very carefully, slowly, and with sensitivity he changed the style of worship at First Baptist of Jacksonville. Applause also became an issue under Homer Lindsay Jr. Once again with humor and sensitivity, he slowly moved the congregation through what could have been a divisive issue.

We have already looked at timing in the chapter on leadership, but timing and time are two of the pastor's best assets if he uses them wisely.

Old Testament Worship

From the gates of Eden, with the killing of animals so their skins could clothe Adam and Eve, sacrifice became a part of worship. Something had to die so Adam and Eve's nakedness could be covered. Blood was spilled, life was taken, and sin was covered. In Genesis 4, Abel came to worship God with an animal sacrifice. Then Cain, having seen this, brought to God a sacrifice from the ground. Some interpreters speculate about whether an animal was required and Cain sinned by not bringing something from the flock. Others claim that it was something quite different; perhaps Cain was not worshiping God in spirit and in truth. This may be the first indication to us in Scripture that worship is more a matter of the heart than anything we do externally. Worship became tied to sacrifice.

From there we come to Moses and the fire and smoke and the dread and fear of Mount Sinai in the book of Exodus. Worship at that point became connected to the tabernacle and later to the temple where sacrifices were made. In the Old Testament, God had a temple for His people. God gave Moses the law along with instructions about how He was to be worshiped.

In Leviticus 10 we see the judgment that falls on those who do not approach God in the prescribed way. Nadab and Abihu took their firepans and put incense in them and offered what is termed "strange fire" (NASB) to the Lord. Some think that they went too far into the Holy Place and went behind the veil into the Holy of Holies. Others think they did not put the prescribed incense (Exod. 30:9) on the coals in the firepan. Still others believe that Leviticus 10:8 indicates they had been drinking.

But the text is clear that the fire they offered was "strange" fire. Most likely they did not use coals from the high altar where, in the previous chapter, God had ignited the fire on the altar (see Lev. 9:23–24). The text does not say where the coals came from. Anything we say is speculation, but it seems certain the coals were not the type prescribed by the Lord. This made it "strange" or, as the word means literally, "foreign" fire.

Following that, the chapter begins with these words: "The LORD spoke to Moses after the death of two of Aaron's sons when they approached the presence of the LORD and died" (Lev. 16:1).

Then the Lord again gave specific instructions on how the high priest was to approach God. Following that incident, God reinforced how He is to be approached because He is holy and is to be treated as holy. That lays the foundation of Old Testament worship with fear, fire, thunder, and trembling. That is worship under the shadow of Mount Sinai.

New Testament Worship

With the coming of Jesus Christ, there was the dawning of a new covenant or New Testament. No longer did man have to go to Mount Sinai, but now he could go to Mount Calvary. There is no more earthly high priest because Jesus Christ alone is now the great High Priest (Heb. 9:11–14). There is no more need for sacrifice because the sacrifice of Jesus Christ is all that is needed for the atonement of sin (Heb. 10:10). We have a new covenant (Heb. 8:6). We have access now to the Father through Jesus (Heb. 10:19–22). Simply put, there is no more sacrifice, priesthood, or temple because all of that has been fulfilled in Jesus Christ.

There are no longer any special days of worship because now every day is a day of worship. We no longer have to go to the temple to worship; we can now worship anywhere and everywhere. We no longer need to bring a sacrifice because our lives are to be presented as a living sacrifice to God (Rom. 12:1). With that background in mind, let's look at some elements to remember when it comes to worship.

The Why of Worship

Perhaps the greatest answer to the "why" of worship lies in the Reformed Catechism. I realize that this sounds strange coming from a Baptist. But when I started dating the young lady who would one day become my wife, I went to church with her on certain Sundays. She was an Associate Reformed Presbyterian and had gone through their catechism at age twelve. In sharing our testimonies, she shared with me on one occasion that the chief end of man was to glorify God and enjoy Him forever. (That is part of the Westminster Shorter Catechism.) Never having heard an explanation of why man exists, I had no good Baptist response.

She explained 1 Peter 4:11: "So that in everything God may be glorified through Jesus Christ. To Him belong the glory and the power forever and ever. Amen." The chief end of man is to glorify God and enjoy Him forever; that is the "why" of worship.

When God created man, He breathed into him the breath of life. God exhaled His breath, the spark of life, into man's nostrils; and man became a living soul. Man was created to worship. In the words of Augustine, "Our hearts are restless until they find rest in Thee." Adam and Eve experienced unbroken, pure worship with God as they walked with Him in the garden in the cool of the day. Every aspect of their lives in the garden was unadulterated worship. That ended when they chose to listen to the voice of Satan rather than the voice of God. But the Fall did not negate man's deep need to worship or his longing for a relationship with his Creator.

Man was not only created for worship, but he was also redeemed to worship. Jesus said that the Son of Man came into the world to seek and to save that which was lost (Luke 19:10). In John 4:23 we see one of the primary reasons Jesus came to redeem mankind: "The Father wants such people to worship Him."

D. A. Carson, in his excellent book *Worship by the Book*, says, "We should not begin by asking ourselves whether or not we enjoy worship, but by asking, 'What does God expect of us?'"[2] We often sing this chorus in worship: "Let's forget about ourselves, and magnify the Lord, and worship Him." But the truth is we do not forget about ourselves, we rarely magnify the Lord, and we are not worshiping Him because we are more interested in what we are getting out of the worship experience. In that context, true worship cannot take place.

Listen to the wisdom of Warren Wiersbe: "If we look upon worship only as a means of getting something from God, rather than giving something to God, then we make God our servant instead of our Lord, and the elements of worship become a cheap formula for selfish gratification."[3]

Why do we worship? Because only in worshiping the true and living God are we doing what we were created to do and what we have been redeemed to do. Some people will respond that worship completes us, it gets us through the week, and it enables us to handle life. These may be some of the benefits of worship, but they are not the "why" of worship. If that is your primary reason for worship, you have made worship a me-centered event instead of a God-centered event. In the words of the current culture, "It's not about you."

As pastors we have failed our people if we do not teach them the "why" of worship. One of the major ways to do this is to spend time on the doctrine of God and the doctrine of man.

The Who of Worship

In Jesus' encounter in the wilderness of temptation, Satan suggested that Jesus bow down and worship him. Jesus answered the "who" of worship when He quoted Deuteronomy 6:13: "Worship the LORD your God and serve Him only" (Luke 4:8 NASB). When Jesus encountered the woman at the well, three times He mentioned worshiping the Father (see John 4).

When you come to the book of the Revelation, the fulcrum around which the worship of heaven and the ages takes place is the throne of God. In Revelation 4 God is worshiped as Creator. The entire chapter sets the scene for worship. God is the object of worship by the twenty-four elders who will fall down before Him and worship. There are the four great beasts who do not cease to say, "Holy, holy, holy, Lord God, the Almighty, who was, who is, and who is coming" (Rev. 4:8). They worship the Lord because we are told in Revelation 4:11, "Because You have created all things, and because of Your will they exist and were created."

Here are creatures that recognize God as the Creator. All through the New Testament there is an emphasis on God as Creator. When the New Testament speaks of the incarnation, it begins at the beginning: "In the beginning was the Word, and the Word was with God, and the Word was God. . . . All things were created through Him, and apart from Him not one thing was created that has been created" (John 1:1, 3).

When the resurrected Jesus wanted to explain to the men on the road to Emmaus what had happened in the crucifixion and the resurrection, He began with Moses and the prophets. He went back to the books of Moses, which include Genesis. Paul opened the book of Romans with the statement that man the creature has rejected the Creator. When Paul was speaking of order in the church and home, he turned to creation (1 Cor. 11:8–9). His epistle to the Colossians opens with these words, "All things have been created through Him and for Him" (Col. 1:16).

The writer of Hebrews opened his great epistle by speaking of Christ who is the exact representation of God and is heir of all things. He is also the Creator of all things (Heb. 1:2). The apostle John began His first epistle with a reference to the beginning (1 John 1:1). Over and over throughout the New Testament, the Holy Spirit draws our attention to the fact that God is Creator. That is the "who" of worship.

When you turn to Revelation 5, you see God worshiped as Redeemer. In this chapter that evokes awe and wonder, we see Jesus Christ as the Lamb of God. He is worshiped because He is worthy. The old Anglo-Saxon word *weorthscipe* gives us our English word *worship*, which is related to the idea of worth, value, and worthiness. Worship is ascribing to God His worth and supreme value.

Jesus is also worshiped because He was slain. The Greek word *sfadzo* means "slaughtered," but it can also mean "stretched out," which indicates crucifixion.

Jesus is also worshiped because He purchased for God people from every tribe, tongue, people, and nation; because He purchased us with His own blood; because He made us to be a kingdom of priests and ensured that we will reign eternally with Him.

When we worship the Lamb of God, we are essentially proclaiming the gospel of Jesus Christ. Worship of the Lamb becomes an act of witness to the Good News. The "who" of worship is none other than the triune God who is both Creator and Redeemer.

The What of Worship

With all that goes on in churches today in the name of worship, is it possible that we have come to the place where we worship *worship* rather than worship God? The mechanics of worship have become the goal, and the means has become the end. Worship must keep one thing in focus—God Almighty! With that in mind, let's look at the critical elements for worship.

The Planning of the Worship Service Is Critical

The worship of God's people is far too important to be left to spontaneity or chance. The planning of the service should be done early in the week so the pastor and the minister of music are not rushed. It is good to go over the previous week's service in staff meeting and to focus the collective mind of all the ministers on the flow of the service. While the pastor is the primary worship leader, he needs to incorporate elements of worship suggested by other staff team members. This keeps the services fresh and new and corrects problems that might be overlooked by a one-person planning approach.

When planning the service, do not leave anything up for grabs. Plan the entire service from the prelude to the postlude. If bulletins with the order of service are not used by the congregation, the staff at least should have an order of service in mind so they know what is going to happen next.

A service when there is confusion about who is up next or what is next in the order of service will cheapen the service, make it seem as if it is not really that important, and create a distraction that will be nearly impossible to overcome when it is time to preach.

In baseball the team at bat always has a person in the batter's box. In football specialty teams are ready at a moment's notice to rush to their places. What takes place in a worship service is far more important than what happens on a baseball diamond or on a football field. Every person involved in the leadership of worship should know exactly where the service is going and what is supposed to happen next, and should be ready to move into place at the right time.

Some people will claim that the Holy Spirit cannot break into such a regulated and scheduled worship service. The Holy Spirit will have no trouble moving on sensitive hearts that are attuned to Him. When a service has been prepared, planned, and prayed over, the Holy Spirit has been at work all week in the lives, hearts, and thoughts of His worship leaders. In a sense the Holy Spirit has already shown up. Nothing can substitute for planning the worship of God's people.

The Priority of the Word Must Be Clear

In the Church of Scotland during the days of the Reformation, there was a tradition that the congregation was seated, the doors were opened, and the Word of God was carried into the service high over the minister's head. As the Bible passed, the people stood in reverence for the Word of God. At the end of the service the Bible was closed and lifted up again over the heads of the clergy. As the Bible passed, once again the people stood in reverence as the Word of God led the procession out of the church. From beginning to end the service was Word-centered. God said, "Take to heart all these words I am giving as a warning to you today, so that you may command your children to carefully follow all the words of this law. For they are not meaningless words to you but they are your life" (Deut. 32:46–47).

These words emphasize the way God saw His Word and the priority it should have among His people. In Nehemiah 8 it was the people who requested that the Word of God be read. They also had constructed a podium which they had made for this purpose (Neh. 8:4). In our Baptist churches, the pulpit should have the place of prominence. There is no divided chancery. The Word and the preaching should not be separated.[4]

When Ezra took the Word and opened it in the presence of the people, they all stood out of reverence for God's Word. Personally I think it is good to have the congregation stand when the Word of God is read in the worship service. There should be a place for the reading of the Word. At First Baptist of Dallas, the people would stand and read a passage of Scripture in unison. It was a passage that reflected the planned theme of the service.

Nothing should take the place of the Word of God preached in a service. Of course, some services may be dedicated to music, prayer, drama, or times of information. But this should be the exception rather than the rule. What the pastor gives priority to in worship is what the priority of the people becomes. If the Word is regularly, systematically, and consistently preached, the people develop a hunger for the Word of God.

Pastor, you will be surprised how much pastoring you can do through a sermon. You will also be surprised how much counseling you can accomplish through an expositional sermon. You will grow the people through the Word of God. They will pick up on how to handle the issues that arise in their lives in a biblical way. Nothing should take precedence over the Word of God in worship.

The Passion of Prayer Should Be Felt

All of us realize that prayer should not be dispassionate. As you read through the prayers of Scripture, notice the passion and intensity with which the person praying talked to God. In Psalm 51, a penitential psalm, David prayed with gut-wrenching passion. When Mary prayed the Magnificat after learning of God's choice of her to bear the Messiah, she prayed with great intensity. When Hannah prayed for a son, it was with such passion that Eli, the old priest, thought she was drunk. Then consider our Lord in the garden as He prayed fervently, "My Father! . . . not as I will, but as You will" (Matt. 26:39). Scripture is full of passionate praying.

Perhaps you are thinking, *That is not my personality.* To take prayer seriously is not a personality issue; it is a heart issue. I am not referring to being demonstrative but to intensiveness, earnestness, and seriousness with which we approach prayer.

Prayer should be strategically planned into the worship service. One of the things that W. A. Criswell did years ago was to have kneelers installed in the First Baptist Church of Dallas. At every service we would kneel and pray as a congregation. What an incredible blessing and a sense of unity this brought to the services. I miss having kneelers; I want to install them some day in the great First Baptist Church of Jacksonville.

It is important to give people the opportunity to come and kneel at the altar to pray. From time to time, in the traditional/blended services, and almost every week in the contemporary service in Dallas, I would call people to the altar during the pastoral prayer. I began to train some of the laypeople and staff members to come at invitation time and pray with those who came and knelt for prayer. Hurting people are uplifted and encouraged when someone kneels beside them to lift them up in prayer.

At times I have asked parents to pray for their children or I have given spouses the opportunity to pray for their mates. I have called my children, my wife, and my family at various times to come to the altar and let me pray for them. You cannot begin to know the impact it has when a father prays aloud over his children or his wife. To hear my wife pray for me moves me deeply, creating a desire in me to be a better husband.

There are so many ways in which we can lead our people to pray. But it takes time in prayer and a leading of the Lord to know the right timing and the right manner in which to lead in these ways I have mentioned. But it is always the right time to pray.

Being a Baptist, I have always shied away from reading prayers in a worship service. But in my personal devotional time, I have benefited greatly from reading the prayers of the great saints of God. Just as so many of those old hymns have great theology, so also do some of the prayers of God's great servants. The depth of your prayers will reflect your time spent in prayer. As you spend more time with God in prayer, your prayer life will take on a dimension that you cannot learn from a book. Over the years my conversations with my wife have matured, developed, and deepened. There are times when we can say a lot to each other in very few words. We don't have to verbalize our thoughts. We are content just to sit next to each other. Sometimes I find myself getting on my knees or just "sitting" next to God. His presence is more than enough. That is passionate praying!

Giving Should Be an Integral Part of Worship

When Melchizedek came out to bless Abraham, Abraham gave him a tenth of what he had (Gen. 14:18–20). Jacob promised the Lord a tenth (Gen. 28:22). When Araunah the Jebusite offered a threshing floor to David and oxen and implements of plowing for free, David said, "No, I insist on buying it from you for a price, for I will not offer to the LORD my God burnt offerings that cost me nothing" (2 Sam. 24:24).

Giving was established in Genesis 4 when Cain and Abel brought offerings to the Lord. In fact, by the time of the Mosaic Law, it was already a part of the life of God's people. In the law it was ratified and codified. By New Testament times, it had been so ingrained that there was no question about the tithe in Israel.

Giving is an important part of worship. The time of giving should be a celebration time in the service. We have not just failed to teach our people about giving, tithing, offerings, and gifts, but we have reduced it to drudgery. Several things about giving should be emphasized.

- Giving is an act of worship.
- A church should have a systematic plan for giving.
- Set aside a time each year to emphasize stewardship. I cannot begin to tell you how this has blessed my life as well as the church and countless believers.
- Stewardship involves more than your finances. It includes time, energy, talent, abilities, family, gifts, marriage, children, and work.
- Teach your teachers to teach stewardship.
- Use tithing testimonies. People grow when other laypeople share their stories of how they learned to trust God in the area of their finances.
- Easy-to-use envelopes are helpful to those who want to give. This also helps the church keep accurate records of gifts given. Some companies will mail these to the homes of church members.
- Online giving, automatic withdrawal, and other banking options will appeal to some people in the congregation. Some

ministers believe these methods are unbiblical, and they prefer to have people bring their offerings to the church. But a number of people in the churches I have served wanted these electronic options. The important issue is that we teach our people to tithe, that it is biblical, and that it is a part of worship.

The Praise God Is Due Must Be Given to Him

We read in Revelation 19:5, "A voice came from the throne, saying: Praise our God, all you His servants, you who fear Him, both small and great!"

Music is an important part of worship. Music warms the heart and helps focus attention on the Lord. Music should complement the message and the truth of God's Word. Opening the service with a hymn or song sets the stage for the rest of the service. Kent Hughes states that music is to be the servant of preaching.[5] Regardless of the style of music, it must be biblical and it should teach theological truth.

During the past year, I have worked with a worship team to help design the worship service at First Baptist of Jacksonville so that every element will point to the biblical truth to be preached. When the music supports the message, it drives home the spiritual truth. This means that the pastor has to plan his preaching in advance. He knows the direction he is going with his sermons, and the worship team helps build the service, the choir specials, and solos around the theme. This takes creativity, time, planning, and prayer. Music is an incredible force in worship, and it should be well planned and well executed.

The Public Invitation

I have always given an invitation at the end of the Sunday morning and Sunday evening worship services. On those few times when I have not done so, someone has said to me, "I was coming tonight to make a decision or to join the church." I had occasionally given an invitation on Wednesday nights, but since I have been at First Baptist of Jacksonville, I have given an invitation every Wednesday night. It has always been my custom to give a gospel presentation at the end of children's programs, musicals, various other events, and then issue an invitation. I have seen many people who didn't usually attend church come to Christ at these special events. In every sermon, present the gospel; then give people an opportunity to respond.

There are more ways to respond to the gospel than walking down the aisle. On one Sunday night in Jacksonville, two young men in their teens came to Jesus Christ after the service. I took them to a side pew and shared with them the plan of salvation. Then I prayed with them, and they prayed to receive Christ.

It is important for the pastor and staff to be available at the front of the worship center after the service so people can come to talk about their spiritual needs and decisions that need to be made. This is a perfect time to "pastor" people and to lead people to repentance and to Christ.

Invitations should not be prolonged unless there is clear indication that the Holy Spirit is moving. Do not give a high-pressure invitation or extend it too long. People will begin to resent it and will think of the invitation as a time of human manipulation rather than the spiritual work of the Holy Spirit. For guidance about the content of a public invitation, see appendix 13.

When the Service Is Over

People can tell a lot about the health of a church by what happens when the service is over. If fellowship is strained, there will be a great sucking sound as people rush from the church to their cars. If the fellowship is sweet, they will stay and visit with one another. In Brazil it is customary at the end of a worship service for the congregation to sit down and wait. They are waiting on God, not wanting to rush out of His presence. The people are also waiting on the pastor to come down from the pulpit and walk down the aisle to the back door to greet them as they leave.

Much of what happens when the service is over depends on the pastor. If he rushes out of the worship center, the people will rush out too. If he stays and visits with the people, the congregation will likely follow his example. It is my conviction that the larger the church, the more determined the pastor must be to stay after the service to speak with the people. W. A. Criswell, pastor of the First Baptist Church of Dallas, Texas, stayed as long as necessary to allow everyone who waited to speak with him personally. He gave them his full attention. He did not reach out to any other person while talking to an individual. Visitors were amazed that a pastor as prominent and as busy as he would take time to talk with them. Members felt as if they really knew him and that he cared for them.

Sometimes people wait to speak with the pastor because God has touched them during the sermon. What a wonderful opportunity to make an appointment, to give a word of encouragement, and to pronounce a blessing on people. It could be that success in pastoral leadership rises or falls with how the pastor treats people when the church service is over.

If you are in a small church, explain to the janitor or the deacon responsible for locking up the building that he should not turn off any lights or stand at the door hurrying people outside. God told Aaron, "Fire must be kept burning on the altar continually; it must not go out" (Lev. 6:13). We should not dash into God's presence. Nor should we dash out.

TESTIMONY:
The Pastor and Technology

Sal Saberna
Lead Pastor, Metropolitan Baptist Church,
Houston, Texas

Most children and teenagers reside on the Internet. What is important to them will be most crucial to your congregation in a few years, if not already. George Barna in *Boiling Point*[1] says that 10 to 20 percent of the population will rely on the Internet for their spiritual input by the year 2010. If a church doesn't have a presence on the Web, then that church does not exist for most people. More and more people visit a church's Web site before they physically visit the church. When people go online to find truth about God, life, and today's issues, who is answering their questions?

No matter what the size of a church, there are several ways a pastor can use technology to stay connected with people and clarify the message of the church.

- E-mail is a quick, effective way to respond to questions and issues or to announce important events within the church.
- Many pastors are using "blogs" (online journals) as a sounding board to clarify their thoughts and the direction of their churches or simply to share insights into current events.
- Displaying graphics through a data projection system, online streaming video, or through iPods are other ways to clarify visually the message each week during worship services.

Technology is a tool. It cannot replace a pastor's heart, passion, or calling. But it can enhance what a pastor does, and it allows him to reach more people in more ways.

CHAPTER 10 The Pastor and Technology

It was Christmas Eve, 1906. Wireless operators sitting off the coast of New England wondered what was happening. While they were listening to the dots and dashes of Morse Code, suddenly through their headsets came a voice reading the Christmas story from the Gospel of Luke and a violin in the background playing "Silent Night." The voice then wished them a merry Christmas, and the dots and dashes started again.[2]

It was the voice of Reginald Fessenden (1866–1932), an inventor and engineer who had been working on producing voice radio. Fessenden was a leading pioneer in voice radio transmissions, and Christians were leading the way in this new technology. In fact, the first person to theorize the existence of radio waves was the Christian physicist James Clerk Maxwell. One writer pointed out that "his studies of light led him to the electromagnetic theory and in 1865, he proved mathematically that radio waves are possible."[3]

The first church service to be broadcast was the worship service from Pittsburgh's Calvary Episcopal Church on January 2, 1921. A Westinghouse engineer happened to be a member there, and he made the arrangements. It was the first remote broadcast. The assistant pastor, Lewis B. Whittemore, preached that morning because the senior pastor was "leery of the new medium."[4]

All of this seems so humorous and antiquated in a day of streaming Internet and pod-casts. Christians have been on the front end of technology and at the same time Christians have resisted technology vigorously. In our seminaries we are teaching Greek, Hebrew, German, French, and Latin, but the language of the twenty-first century is "technese."[5]

One evening I walked into the den to find my wife typing on her laptop, my son Wills on his laptop and a cell phone, my other son Trey on his laptop, and his wife Rachel on her laptop computer. They were all hooked up to the Internet, wirelessly, and the television was on. I thought to myself as a pastor, *I am going to have to learn to communicate in a new language if I want to reach the next generation for Christ.* The message does not change, but the language I communicate with will have to change.

Far too many of our churches that use technology today are doing so reluctantly. They are being dragged kicking and screaming, "We don't want to go." Many people today will not even listen to you if you are not perceived to be technologically savvy. We stand to lose a great many people simply because we are not willing to learn and utilize technology. Technology is neither spiritual nor unspiritual; it is simply a tool to reach the next generation for Christ.

If you think only a small number of people are using technology to access information about religion, then you have no idea what is happening. In 2004, 64 percent of the 128 million Internet users in the United States used it for religious and spiritual matters. That is over 82 million Americans, and the number is growing exponentially.[6]

While it is impossible to cover every area of technology in this chapter, there are several things that the church needs to know about and be involved in. If you are making no effort in the area of technology, you will lose members. On the other hand, some ministers only want to add the latest toy to the church media room. There is a sensible solution to all of this.

Technology in Ministry

The use of technology in the church is not only beneficial in its day-to-day operations but it can also enhance the worship experience as well. All over the world *The Jesus Film* has been used to win hundreds of thousands of people to Jesus Christ. There is a place for technology in ministry. Here are some helpful guidelines on how to use technology in your work as a pastor.

Do your homework. The pastor needs to spend some time learning the basics about the technology that will be used in the church office and the worship services.

Have a strategy. You would not dare get up and preach without a planned and prayed-over message, and the same should be true of technology. A strategy will help to determine what you want to accomplish, which in turn will lead you to the technology you need. Too often we have "things" lying around the church that we acquired but never used because we had no strategy for what we wanted to accomplish.

Don't attempt to do everything by yourself. I have discovered that there are many people in the church who have technological abilities and training. Some of them are just waiting to be asked if they can help in these areas. A "tech team" provides an excellent opportunity to use these people, to learn about the technology, and to support the work once it is started.

Beyond those people available in your church, a host of ministries specialize in helping pastors and churches with today's technology. Many of them are willing to give direction, information, and advice without an initial charge or at a nominal fee because they see this as a ministry.

While pastoring larger churches I have always put my staff at the disposal of smaller churches with lesser resources that needed help. Often our media and technology staff spends hours helping other churches and ministers because we have a sense of stewardship about what God has given us. Don't hesitate to call other churches and talk to them about helping, giving advice, and making suggestions about the technological areas where you are in need.

Don't overwhelm your congregation with the latest gadgetry. Too much technology all at one time can be difficult for some church members to handle. The way you introduce the technology will make a difference in its acceptance. If you want to use video clips, do so very carefully. Be sure that there is nothing offensive in the clip or that it does not promote a movie or anything else that would be offensive. Often people will see the use of a clip as an endorsement of a movie or program. News clips are much safer and usually not offensive. Some online companies have excellent video clips for use in churches.

Don't use technology to impress people. The use of any technology should have a purpose. We are not trying to impress people with our technology; we should be trying to preach Jesus Christ. Technology is just a tool for enhancing the gospel message.

Some churches use video clips, drama, and special lighting effects every service. This is probably overkill. Occasionally I will use a video clip, a personal testimony, or some other means of communicating the gospel. It is far more meaningful if it is not overdone.

Technology gives you the opportunity to minister to people you would never meet or reach any other way. Almost any size church today can pod-cast its services or stream them live on the Internet. Many churches of various sizes put their services on the net at a very nominal cost. There may be people in your church who have this on their heart as a ministry and will supplement the cost just to get the gospel out. It does not require large budgets, the latest in television equipment, or multiple staff personnel to get the church service to people. The ever-changing world of technology and equipment as well as lower prices make ministry to people more feasible than ever before.

Technology in the Worship Service

Good audio in the worship service is a must. If people can't hear you, nothing else matters. Use digital audio boards. Allow for a small console to have several different inputs and, with the use of a computer interface, have many inputs into the board. Properly sized audio for the size of the room is a must.

One of the mistakes churches often make is not having adequate power in their sound systems. The more powerful the system, the more control and the better quality your church will get from its sound system. The myth that you only need a powerful system for concerts has cost congregations a lot of intelligibility during worship. Inadequate sound systems tend to muddle the sound and cause the congregation not to be able to hear lyrics and even the spoken word clearly.

Be sure to check the sound system before every service. Nothing is more disruptive than a blast of feedback or having the system not turned on when you get up to start the service or when a person begins to sing. It is difficult to refocus the people's attention after a sound mishap.

Good lighting is not a luxury. Adequate stage lighting is a must. People not only need to hear; if you're to hold their attention for several minutes, they need to be able to see the speaker. Many church pulpits are dimly lit, and this means people have to work hard to pay attention. If they can't see you because you are in a dark spot, they will check out mentally.

Theatrical lighting is a great help. One of the most important usages of theatrical lighting is to create environments by simply changing the lighting in a room. A powerful worship song can be enhanced by the proper use of lighting fixtures with color gels or gobos (metal or glass fixtures that allow for different shapes to be projected on screens, walls, or any surface). Moveable lights are not that expensive, and they can change the look of the pulpit area. Lighting can change for a solo, a testimony, or preaching. This is an effective way to hold the attention of the congregation and set the right atmosphere for the elements of the service.

Some pastors want the lighting to be darkened over the congregation while they preach. But I want all the light I can get when I preach. I want the lights bright over the pulpit as well as the congregation so the people can follow in their Bibles and take notes on the sermon.

Projection systems are important. In a sight and sound world, projection screens, LCDs, or active matrix projection systems are no longer luxuries for megachurches. We live with screens in everything we do. From the GPS system standard in most new cars, to television on cell phones, or movies on iPods, the screen is part of our lives and it's not going away anytime soon. Creating compelling videos to enhance the preaching or to illustrate a point is a great way to use these tools beyond the words for worship songs that most churches already project.

Projection systems usually require separate projectors and separate screens. They come with front-projection or rear-projection options. The more ambient light you have in your worship center or auditorium, the more powerful a projector you will need. The new breed of digital projectors is high-definition-ready. They can project brilliant images that capture people's attention. The larger the screen, the more effective it will be in helping the congregation see and become immersed in the worship experience.

The worship center at First Baptist of Jacksonville is very large. From many angles people cannot see the pulpit area very well. With the new large screen that we added, people feel a part of what is taking place. But a caution goes along with this. With big screens and especially if you have high-definition cameras, people will see every hair that is out of place and every pore on your nose! But what you can accomplish with a big screen is worth the cost and the extra effort.

LCD and plasma screens are often thin, and they have incredibly strong power (measured in lumens). They can be seen in broad daylight. They don't require a projector since the video input comes directly into the screen. Some LCD screens are quite large and can cost over a million dollars. Willow Creek Community Church in Chicago has two large screens on a track that can be moved anywhere on stage, even coming together to form one large screen fifty feet wide by twelve feet tall. At the time of this writing, the cost of flat screens is dropping rapidly. They take up much less space than rear-projection and front-projection systems.

Church Growth and Your Online Strategy

Chances are your church Web site was initially launched by a volunteer with good intentions and that it has "grown" on its own—much like the proverbial ugly stepchild that no one wants to acknowledge. Some churches have begun to tap into the great potential the Internet offers churches and nonprofits. Political campaigns, for example, raise millions of dollars from online donors. Nationwide Christian ministries have seen their call center costs reduced drastically by establishing an online community with their partners. Fast-growing churches are using the Internet for outreach, education, and even assimilation of new members. So what separates the successful sites from the rest?

Resources

A good Web site will cost you—in both time and money. From hosting fees, to bandwidth fees to design and specialty software, a great Web site is not cheap. It takes a commitment of both energy and finances to launch and maintain a great site.

Strategy

The first question you ask should be, What do we want to accomplish online? Today's Web-savvy ministries have a wide variety of options online. You should look at several aspects of your ministry and think how the Web could be beneficial. Here are some major areas to focus on.

- Outreach: making a first impression before people get to your church. Let them know what to expect before they arrive. Some churches feature their current message series online as well.
- Inreach: how can we communicate with our own people more effectively?
- What about our music and arts department?
- What about assimilation of new members? Community Bible Church in San Antonio, Texas, has more than three hundred small groups posted online. You can search for groups by affinity, days of the week, age group, location, and so forth. Their entire small group structure is also managed online, saving them a lot of time. Group leaders input their information from home, work, or anywhere in the world that has a Web connection. Once the information is in the system, the church's online software does the rest. It even prints out a paper directory for distribution during recruitment time.
- Stewardship: how can we make it easy for people to give to the church other than during a weekend service or by mailing a check at a later time? Online donations are becoming popular. People would rather go online at their convenience and give instead of having to deal with checkbooks during the worship services. "I don't think our people will use this feature," said one pastor, not long before his own people were giving more than $100,000 online every month. Oh, you of little faith!

Streaming audio and video is a great way to "show" people who you are instead of telling them. They also help in making announcements to your congregation about important things. Some churches are using "v-mail" on a weekly basis to communicate with their congregation. Instead of getting an e-mail from your church, you get a video e-mail with the latest news and images of what's going on.

Innovative churches usually market their sermon series to the community through various forms of media, such as newspapers, direct mail, billboards, and TV and radio spots. But they are also directing people to a Web site that gives further information and captures their attention. Second Baptist Church of Houston had billboards all over town that said "MyBadMarriage.com." The site was part of Pastor Ed Young's sermon series on marriage, and it received hundreds of thousands of hits from curious people who wanted to know more (and whose bad marriages needed help).

Getting Started

Find professional help that you can trust. Make sure the person or firm you are considering has the experience and the know-how to do the job right. One of the great mistakes people make is assuming that a Web designer knows how to program the code that will make the site function. A great Web site must have all these elements in order to create a successful experience: good architecture, streamlined design, and strong backend support. What people *don't* see—how well it functions—is as important as what they *do* see. The challenge in using a single person to oversee your Web site is finding that rare individual who has strengths in the areas of design, programming, and multimedia all rolled into one.

Make your online strategy a vital part of your ministry focus. The Web is not a "fad" that will be replaced by the next "big thing." It's a great, cost-effective, multidimensional tool every growing church should take advantage of. It should be one of the pillars of your communication strategy, for outreach as well as inreach.

TESTIMONY:
The Pastor, Missions, and Evangelism

Johnny Hunt
Senior Pastor, First Baptist Church,
Woodstock, Georgia

We are on a mission to share the gospel of Jesus Christ. Our churches need to have His heartbeat for the world. We are to be busy locally and globally, sharing the story of Christ. I have the deep conviction that it is possible to take the gospel to the whole world in our lifetime. It is my prayer that God will do something deep in your heart that will cause you to go with Christ to the nations beyond and to your own neighborhood, sharing the good news of Jesus.

The Bible says that the Lord Jesus came to seek and to save that which was lost. Nothing brings greater joy to the heart of our Savior than to know that we, His servants, are busy about what concerned Him when He was here on earth. Through His Holy Spirit He continues to be with us as we take His story to those who have never heard the gospel.

There are approximately 1.6 billion people in the world today who have never heard the name of Jesus. If we are committed to the task of missions and evangelism, God will use us to reach these people. As we go with the gospel, Jesus has promised, "Remember, I am with you always" (Matt. 28:20). Go today into your world with His presence.

CHAPTER 11 The Pastor, Missions, and Evangelism

It was a Wednesday evening Bible study around the tables at Green Street Baptist Church in High Point, North Carolina. I was teaching through the book of 1 Corinthians. At the end of each lesson I asked, "Are there any questions?" Members of the class usually asked several questions about the passage we were studying that evening.

A young woman who was visiting asked a question. I do not remember specifically what it was, but I do remember that it was a "seeking" type of question. She was searching and it was obvious. I answered her question and followed it up with a question that related to her personal relationship with Jesus Christ.

It seemed as if everyone else in the room faded away, and it was just the two of us carrying on this conversation. I asked her if she had come to the place in her life where she had personally asked Christ to forgive her of her sins and had received His free gift of forgiveness and salvation. She replied that she had not. I began to share with her passages from the Bible about the plan of salvation. Then I asked her if she wanted to ask Jesus to forgive her and to receive Him as her Lord and Savior. She replied that she did. I told her to pray with me, and I led her through the sinner's prayer. After the prayer I explained to her what she had just done and some things she needed to do.

There in front of about eight hundred people on a Wednesday night, I led this young wife and mother to Jesus Christ. Then I used this event to challenge all those who were there to do what I had just done. It was a transformational moment for many people to see their pastor lead a person to Jesus Christ.

Pastoring the First Baptist Church of Jacksonville comes with a great heritage of personal evangelism. This great church in the River City knows how to evangelize. The privilege of my ministry has been to follow great soul winners. Homer Lindsey Jr. was a great personal soul winner. Jerry Vines, my immediate predecessor, is a great personal soul winner. W. A. Criswell was a great personal soul winner. You catch Dr. Criswell's heart for evangelism in this line from his pastor's manual: "There is a reason for the growth of great churches. That reason is evangelism—evangelism in the pulpit, in the Sunday school, in the city, in the country. Evangelism, the soul and spirit of every organization and endeavor of the church."[1]

The Lord's purpose, plan, and desire is the salvation of mankind. Saving the lost was the purpose for which Christ came into this world. When Jesus called the disciples, He called them to follow Him and to become "fishers of men." In Matthew 28:18–20, Jesus commissioned the disciples to evangelize the world, which they began to do as soon as they had received power from the Holy Spirit (Acts 1:8; 2:1–4). Evangelism and missions are the tasks of the church and of every believer.

We need to remember that nowhere in Scripture is the unbeliever told to come and get the gospel, but the church is commanded to go and take the gospel to the lost. Roy Fish and J. E. Conant, in their excellent book *Every Member Evangelism*, state that "the responsibility of every Christian is not to bring the lost to the Gospel but to take the Gospel to the lost."[2]

Personal Imperative

Paul told the young preacher Timothy that he was to do the work of an evangelist (2 Tim. 4:5). That was a personal imperative to Timothy, and it is a personal imperative to everyone who is called to ministry. God has called us to be evangelists in the sense that we are to share with others the gospel of Jesus Christ. As pastors, we must do this every time we preach. Every pastor, in every message, should include the gospel. We are to preach the love of God, the cross of Christ, that Jesus died for man's sins, that He was buried, that He rose from the dead, that He is Lord of all. Then we must call on people to believe on Him, to repent of their sins, and to receive His free gift of salvation.

How many opportunities do we miss to make an impact for Christ every Sunday because we fail to preach the gospel? Someone may be asking, "Should every sermon be an evangelistic sermon?" Not necessarily, but every sermon should contain the gospel. Too many pastors try to preach an accommodating message—a sermon that will accommodate any sin, a sermon that is designed not to confront out of fear that it will come across as judgmental and offend someone. While no sermon should purposefully set out to be offensive, the gospel itself will offend many people.

In a clear messianic passage, the prophet Isaiah wrote that the Messiah would become a stone of stumbling and a rock of offense (Isa. 8:14). First Peter 2:8 quotes this same verse. We are also told that many of the disciples turned away from following Jesus because His sayings were too hard for them to accept (John 6:60–66). The gospel does not have to be preached in an offensive way. We should always seek to be appealing rather than appalling.

The pastor should be involved in personal evangelism. In 1 Timothy 4:12 and Titus 2:7, pastors are told that we are to be examples in personal evangelism. This involves one person leading another person to Christ. You see this in Andrew, who found his brother, Simon Peter, and told him about Jesus (John 1:40–42). This is what you see when Jesus spoke to the woman at the well (John 4:7–15). Pastors are to set the example in evangelism by their own personal lifestyle. Nothing will promote, enhance, and encourage the church toward evangelism like the pastor's preaching the gospel and being personally involved in sharing Jesus Christ with others.

Practical Implication

While the pastor is to do the work of an evangelist, the pastor is not to do the work of the entire congregation. Paul is very clear in Ephesians 4:11–12 that pastors are given "for the training of the saints in the work of ministry." God gives to the church pastors and staff to equip the body to carry out the work of ministry.

The methods for outreach are as numerous as the recipes in a Baptist women's cookbook. In fact, the subject of methodology is an issue that we seem to love to debate. We spend too much time arguing about which method we should use, and evangelism never takes place. If Satan cannot convince us not to be evangelistic, he will be satisfied by getting us to debate evangelism to the point that we never tell anyone about Jesus.

Every church should have a systematic evangelism and missions plan. This covers everything from the moment guests set foot on the property of the church and how we reach out to them, to the person who walks the aisle at invitation time and wants to make a decision for Christ.

Evangelistic Training

A formal program of training believers for evangelistic encounters is needed in every church. There are so many good programs to choose from that it would be impossible to list them all. The main thing is to select one and begin to equip the people for evangelism. Pastor, nothing will make this succeed like your presence and participation.

Evangelistic Visitation

Even before you start an equipping program, you need a strategy. I am convinced that evangelism works best when we work it through the Sunday school. Part of recruiting teachers for Sunday school is an understanding that they will make evangelistic visits and will encourage their class to visit as well.

Through the Sunday school you can funnel the list of prospects, guests, and names that are given for visits. The organization is already in place. People will respond to people their own age, and this makes the Sunday school perfect for evangelism. Young people will visit their own age group; middle adults will do the same. If you know that a prospect has a teenager at home, it is good to take a teen along on the visit.

Part of the strategy needs to be a consistent time for visitation. At First Baptist of Jacksonville, we have daytime visitation on certain days as well as every Tuesday night. That is part of our strategy. Not everyone can go visiting at the same time. We make our approach flexible so more people can go out and visit.

Also, when the Sunday school takes the name of a prospect, an appropriate class member can follow up with that person over the course of several weeks. People want to know that they are more than numbers and that they matter. Once they discover that they count, they are open to the gospel. This takes time to develop, so the Sunday school is the best unit to follow up with prospects.

The Sunday school will also provide accountability. Everyone needs to be accountable, especially when it comes to dealing with prospects. The teacher or outreach leader can regularly follow up with visits made and track who is being contacted and who is doing the contacting.

At First Baptist of Jacksonville, each Sunday school class is built around a zip code. Classes will reach, minister, and visit those people who come to the church from their zip codes. This way members of a class are close by, and they do not need to come to the church and then go back out on the night of visitation. We have multiple classes in zip codes so the area can be further broken down and covered more efficiently. All of this comes from a well-thought-out and prayed-over strategy.

Evangelistic Events

An evangelistic event can be anything from a church picnic to a concert, a play, or a church fair. The issue is not the event but the fact that it is geared toward evangelism. Does your church have a strategy in place to share the gospel, gather names, get information, and present Jesus to those people who attend your services?

On a Father's Day Sunday night we moved our worship services to the Jacksonville Suns' baseball stadium. We had the choir perform the national anthem and "Take Me Out to the Ball Game." Then some children put on a skit, followed by some comedy. At that point I went to the pitcher's mound and proceeded to give the plan of salvation. We saw fifteen people come to Jesus Christ that night, and we attracted people who would have never attended a church service. This service was not expensive. It was short—no more than fifty minutes—and it gave families an opportunity to spend the afternoon together. Any event can be an evangelistic opportunity if you plan ahead.

Evangelistic Home Socials

As spread out as church members are and as busy as people are today, it is more convenient to do an evangelistic social in a home. It can be an evening where you invite people for dinner, for dessert, or for a Bible study, or even for games. At some point in the evening the host can share the gospel by giving his personal testimony. Today there are great DVDs that present the gospel very effectively.

A Sunday school class in our church had a dinner at the teacher's home. They each invited their mate and an additional couple. The class that normally has about twenty-five in attendance had sixty-eight people present. The next Sunday they were up to almost forty in the class, and one woman accepted Jesus Christ as Lord and Savior. Evangelism must be intentional.

Evangelistic Revivals

In many churches today, revivals are a thing of the past. But revivals are still an effective evangelistic tool. Revival is actually for the church. But God still uses these meetings for the winning of the lost. In my opinion, a revival's "success"—if we can use that term in a sanctified manner—is determined by the amount of prayer that precedes it.

Purposeful Intentions

It is worth noting that no one in the New Testament ever came to Jesus Christ apart from human agency. Consider the story of the Ethiopian (Acts 8:26–38). This government official had been to Jerusalem to worship. He had probably heard of the Jewish religion that majored on worshiping one God. He apparently knew about the acts of this God and was drawn to the Lord. He was reading from a scroll of Isaiah. He was puzzled by Isaiah 53:7.

Philip asked him if he understood what he was reading. His reply was honest and sincere: "How could I, unless someone guides me?" (Acts 8:31 NASB). This Ethiopian official invited Philip to sit with him in his chariot and to explain the passage. Note his question,

"Please tell me, of whom does the prophet say this? Of himself, or of someone else?" (Acts 8:34 NASB). Philip began with that Scripture and preached Jesus to this man.

One of the amazing things about this account in Acts is how Philip knew where to meet this Ethiopian. An angel of the Lord had spoken to Philip and told him what to do and had given him precise directions about where to go (Acts 8:26). Why didn't the angel just speak directly to the Ethiopian?

Consider also the story of Cornelius. Peter was summoned to the house of this Gentile Roman centurion. You know the story—how Peter went and shared with Cornelius and all those gathered there that day (Acts 10). An angel had appeared to Cornelius and told him that his prayers would be answered. The angel gave him instruction to send messengers to Joppa and to invite Simon Peter to come to his house (Acts 10:30–33). If the angel could tell Cornelius all of that, why didn't he just tell this centurion directly about Jesus Christ? Why was a person sent? Can God not get the job done apart from human agency?

The obvious answer is that He can. God is not dependent on man. But in His sovereignty and in His perfect plan, God has chosen people to communicate the gospel to other people. This is why when it comes to evangelism and missions, there must be purposeful intention.

Edward Kimball sold shoes. But on Sunday he taught Sunday school. He was one of those meek and mild-mannered men who had a heart for sharing the gospel. One day Edward shared the gospel with a young salesman by the name of D. L. Moody, and the rest of that story is history. Edward, the shoe salesman, led to Christ a young man who became one of history's greatest evangelists.

Under the preaching of D. L. Moody, a young preacher by the name of Frederick Meyer was in the congregation. God moved on his heart to start a nationwide preaching ministry. One evening while Meyer was preaching a young man by the name of Wilbur Chapman prayed to receive Christ as his Lord and Savior.

Eventually Chapman felt called to evangelism. While he was out preaching he came to the conclusion he needed help. He knew a young man by the name of Billy Sunday who was looking for a job. Chapman hired Billy and asked him if he would preach for him from time to time. You know how that story turned out. Sunday became a great revivalist and evangelist.

Billy Sunday was preaching in Charlotte, North Carolina, and God was moving in an unusual way. Many people were saved. Many were convicted and convinced that they needed to have another gospel meeting, so they called on a preacher by the name of Mordecai Ham. One night in that meeting a young man named Billy Graham came to faith in Jesus Christ.[3]

All of that began not with a preacher, not with an evangelist, but with a shoe salesman who taught Sunday school—with a man who had a passion for sharing Jesus Christ. There must be a purposeful intention to our evangelism.

The Missions Mandate

When Jesus issued what we call the Great Commission, He was entrusting to His followers the greatest message of all time. In fact, it was the most important message that any person can hear. Just before His ascension Jesus told that crowd of five hundred that they were to be His witnesses "in Jerusalem, in all Judea and Samaria, and to the ends of the earth" (Acts 1:8). This message was not left with professional speakers, trained theologians, or confident ambassadors. He gave that message to people who were still wondering if the kingdom was about to be restored to Israel!

If we are saved, we have a missions mandate: "Go, therefore, and make disciples of all nations" (Matt. 28:19). Our Lord has entrusted us with the most important message of all time. In fact, this commission goes beyond the New Testament. The idea of being witnesses emerges from the pages of the Old Testament. In Isaiah we read, "All the nations are gathered together, and the peoples are assembled . . . You are My witnesses" (Isa. 43:9–10).

The message is "repent and be saved," and this is to be preached to the ends of the earth. The church that neglects the mission mandate misses the last command of our Lord and does so to its spiritual detriment.

Mission Possible

Mission strategy is undergoing a revolution in our day. Yet the tragic truth is there are very few churches that are involved in missions. It has been my experience that people are hungry to be involved in missions. Many people who are unwilling to make a commitment or to give of their resources will surprise you when it comes to hands-on missions. Suddenly they become very passionate, committed, and willing to give. The problem is that they have lacked vision and direction.

If your church is to be involved in missions, you as the pastor must be involved in missions. Missions today begins as soon as you leave the church parking lot! The world has literally come to us. When I was pastoring in downtown Dallas, there were some 104 different languages spoken downtown. While we are in worship on Sunday morning at First Baptist of Jacksonville, we have Japanese, Chinese, Vietnamese, Spanish, and Ukrainians worshiping at the same time in their languages on the church campus.

In every city, town, and hamlet in America, you will find a population of non-English-speaking people who desperately need to hear the gospel of Jesus Christ. You don't have to venture overseas to do missions anymore. Beyond that, you don't have to go to those who are not native-born Americans. The unchurched population in America doubled from 1991 to 2004. There is a mission field right here in our own country.

We have a sweet older couple at First Baptist of Jacksonville who use a strategy and a plan to reach the inner-city children of our city. They have a trailer they pull behind their truck that opens out into a small stage. Three days a week they go to three different public housing projects and put on "Funday School." They do all kinds of activities with the children. In the midst of it they share the gospel, teach them the Bible, and disciple those kids who otherwise would never come to our church. If that is not missions, then I don't know what missions is.

While there is plenty of ministry around us, we are also called to go to the most remote part of the earth. Nothing in my ministry has been as life-changing as taking Christians on a mission trip. There on the streets of Kiev, Ukraine; or Saint Petersburg, Russia; or Buenos Aries, Argentina, I have seen Christians who have wanted to share the gospel but had never done it in the United States. When they began to share the gospel abroad, they were transformed into witnessing machines when they returned home.

The doors are so open, the possibilities are so limitless, and almost any place on this earth is so accessible that every church needs a strategy to go somewhere locally, nationally, and internationally to be a part of God's kingdom work. Pastor, you should repeatedly challenge your church to reach the world for Jesus. A global vision is as necessary as a local vision. Every church should be a global church. We need both a local and a global strategy that involves our people. Some will not want to go overseas. That is fine. There are plenty of opportunities right in your church's neighborhood. Then there are others who will not be involved locally but are challenged by the opportunities overseas.

How do you go about starting a "mission possible" program? Here are several ways that your church can get involved in missions around the world.

- Familiarize yourself with missions and mission projects by contacting the International Mission Board, if you are Southern Baptist, or your own denominational mission board, or a fellow pastor who is already involved in missions.
- Take a select few people to a missions fair offered at another church to introduce them to what is possible for a church in the area of overseas missions.
- Pray. Nothing in the church should ever be done, especially in missions, until it is bathed in prayer. Recruit some laypeople to pray with you.
- Preach a series of sermons on the Great Commission, missions, or the missionary trips of Paul as outlined in Acts.
- Ask the congregation to pray, and give them some direction for their praying. Everyone can pray if they cannot go and even if they cannot give. Everyone has the opportunity to be a part of missions.
- Look for a mentoring church and a mentoring pastor. Many churches and pastors are involved in overseas trips, and they

are willing to help other churches launch a missions ministry. If they have a heart for lost people, they will have a heart to help mobilize others to reach lost people. I cannot remember a single trip that I have taken that I did not take with me laypeople and other pastors from churches who wanted to be involved in missions.

- Adopt a mission opportunity that will be strategic and intentional. You want opportunities where you can help plant reproducing churches.

- Do not bite off more than you can chew and yet at the same time do not have too small a vision. Pace yourself and the church. Once you become involved, the tendency is to jump in and take on too much. This will often scare some leadership in your church. Satan will look for every opportunity to discourage you and the church. Be balanced in what you do.

- Set a missions goal for the year. Do not set it too low or too high. Stretch your people with a goal and step out on faith. You will discover that as you give to missions, God will bless the rest of the church budget. In Dallas, the year we began a thirty-eight-million-dollar building project, we also gave more than one million dollars to the Southern Baptist Lottie Moon Christmas Offering for International Missions. Do not buy into the lie that if we do something for missions, it means we will have less to spend at home on ministry. That is not true. When we set God's priorities as our own priorities and when we seek first the kingdom of God, the church will experience God's blessings.

- Once you have completed a mission project, look for a pastor and another church to mentor and do for them what was done for you.

The International Mission Board's Church Services Office of Mobilization is a great asset for Southern Baptists in planning a mission. Personnel there are available to come and speak, mentor, and share with you and your church.

People who need Jesus and are dying and headed for a real devil's hell are all around us. Most of these people have tried to be good, they have tried to be religious, and some have even joined a church. But the fact remains that they have no personal relationship with Jesus Christ. We see people who have become experts at masking the fact that they are needy. Therefore we pass them by, thinking, *These people do not need what I have.*

Cindy Crawford, the beautiful model, was once on a flight from California to New York City. She stated that halfway through the flight the plane ran into some turbulent weather. As the plane bumped its way through the storm, she looked over and saw a person whom she knew. She thought to herself, *This plane will never go down with him on board.* With that she comforted herself for the rest of the flight. That someone whom she saw was John F. Kennedy Jr., "John-John," who later died tragically when the plane he was piloting went down over Martha's Vineyard, taking his life, the life of his wife, and the life of his sister-in-law.

The Word of God is clear, and the message that the world needs to know is, "There is no other name under heaven given to people by which we must be saved" (Acts 4:12).

TESTIMONY:
The Pastor and the Ordinances

Paige Patterson
President, Southwestern Baptist Theological Seminary
Fort Worth, Texas

Unforgettable! That is the only adequate word to describe my reaction the first time I watched W. A. Criswell lead the congregation at the First Baptist Church of Dallas in the observance of the Lord's Supper. Not only was the pastor's handling of the Lord's Supper unique, but it was also an act of beauty.

Criswell had similar contributions to make when he stepped into the baptismal waters. He often said to younger pastors, "When you see a family lay their loved one to rest at a funeral, they do so with great gentleness. Likewise, the waters of baptism should hardly ripple as the candidate is gently laid away and then lifted up to walk in newness of life with Christ."

All of this leads me to the conclusion that we as Baptists have a marvelous story to tell through the ordinances of baptism and the Lord's Supper. The ordinances of the early church were not focused on ritual but on redemption. The two ordinances ordained by Christ—baptism and the Lord's Supper—together paint a beautiful picture of redemption. Jesus' body was broken and His blood was shed for our sins. The Lord's Supper pictures that Jesus died. He was buried, and then He was raised again. Baptism pictures that. The church is commanded to practice these two ordinances because they focus on the central facts of the gospel.

CHAPTER 12 The Pastor and the Ordinances

Every Christian denomination observes at least two ordinances: baptism and the Lord's Supper. Roman Catholics and some other denominations are sacramental in their approach to what Protestants call "ordinances." The difference between a sacrament and an ordinance is that the former is believed to carry with it, almost automatically, some measure of grace, while the latter is more symbolic.

Typically, denominations that believe in sacraments view baptism as imparting grace. Augustine, whom Roman Catholics follow closely, believed that the sacrament of baptism washed away what he called "original sin."[1] Thus, Roman Catholics baptize infants to cleanse them of original sin. A baptized infant is considered to be justified, saved, and rightly related to God. The Lord's Supper is also considered to impart grace to those who receive it after confirmation at age twelve. The sacrament of the eucharist, as Catholics call it, keeps the communicant in a right relationship with God.

When the Protestant Reformation took place in the early 1500s, a difference in belief occurred that was a primary element in the separation of Protestants from Catholics. Since 1215, Roman Catholics had believed in what came to be called "transubstantiation." This is the belief that the physical elements in the eucharist, the bread and the wine, are transubstantiated into the physical flesh and blood of Christ. There is not a change in the form of the elements; they still look like, feel like, and taste like bread and wine. But in substance they become the literal, physical body and blood of Christ.

Martin Luther, the first reformer in Germany, at first maintained that there were only three sacraments (in contrast to the Catholic seven): baptism, the eucharist, and penance. He later dropped penance and kept only the first two. He continued to baptize infants, saying that he intended to keep all Catholic practices not specifically forbidden in the Bible. Since idolatry and images were prohibited in the Bible, he tore down all of the statues and images of Mary and the saints. But he kept infant baptism.

Luther retained the Augustinian view of baptism, that it washed away original sin. In his view of the eucharist, Luther adopted a view called "consubstantiation." He rejected Catholic transubstantiation. He believed that the elements of bread and wine did not change in either substance or form, but when the words "this is My body" and "this is My blood" are spoken over the elements and the communicant takes them in faith, the literal, physical body and blood of Christ come into the believer "with" (*con* in Latin) those elements. Both Catholics and Lutherans believe in what is called the "real presence of Christ" in the eucharist.

John Calvin, who appeared later in Geneva, Switzerland, taught the real spiritual presence of Christ in the eucharist, but not the real physical presence. He, like Luther, retained infant baptism, believing in replacement theology: the belief that the church had permanently replaced Israel in the plan of God. He saw baptism as the New Testament parallel to Old Testament circumcision. He also believed that infants born to believing Christian parents were automatically in God's covenant and, thus, should be granted baptism.

Contemporary with Luther was a reformer in Zurich, Switzerland, named Ulrich Zwingli. He rejected both the Catholic and Lutheran views of the Lord's Supper and proposed what is called the symbolic view, or "memorialism." Neither the bread nor the wine change in form or substance, nor does the physical presence of Christ come with the elements. They are symbolic of the broken body and shed blood of Christ. Most evangelicals today, in what is known as the free church tradition, hold to this symbolic view of the Lord's Supper. Zwingli looked upon both baptism and the Lord's Supper as symbolic. The Anabaptists,[2] perhaps the earliest Baptists, followed Zwingli and called baptism and the Lord's Supper "ordinances," or simply practices ordained by Christ. They saw them as symbolic.

Believer's Baptism

These early Anabaptists recovered the New Testament teaching of "believer's baptism." This came from their reading the book of Acts in the first printed Greek New Testament, published by Erasmus in 1516. They noted that the only people baptized in the Greek New Testament were believers who were old enough to confess Christ publicly. There are no instances of infant baptism in the New Testament.[3]

Since both authors of this book are Baptists, we will assume that there are only two New Testament ordinances—baptism and the Lord's Supper—and that they are symbolic in nature. Baptism symbolizes the death, burial, and resurrection of Christ, according to Romans 6:4–5. The word "likeness" in verse 5 indicates the symbolism. Baptists maintain that the symbolic view of baptism is in fact New Testament baptism. And it is for believers only, not for infants.

The author visited an Anabaptist church in Zurich, Switzerland, once and discovered that the baptistry was in the foyer of the church, not in the back of the choir loft, as it is in most Baptist churches. The baptistry was in the shape of a casket. The person being baptized sat down in the lower part of the casket. The pastor stood on the outside and then lowered the person backward into the water, saying, "Buried in the likeness of His death; raised in the likeness of His resurrection; to walk in newness of life."

Those baptized in that church will never forget that New Testament baptism symbolizes the death, burial, and resurrection of Christ. Every Baptist pastor should speak the words spoken by that Anabaptist pastor as he baptizes his converts to Christ. By repeating these words from Romans 6:5, the meaning of New Testament baptism is taught and guarded. It is symbolic of the death, burial, and resurrection of Christ.

Another word that should be spoken at every baptism comes from Jesus' command to the church to baptize its converts. Every pastor should ask the candidate for baptism, "Are you following Jesus in baptism because you know that you have accepted Him as your own personal Lord and Savior?" After the candidate has publicly confessed Christ in that way, the pastor should add, "I baptize you, my brother (sister) in Christ, in the name of the Father, and of the Son, and of the Holy Spirit" (see Matt. 28:19–20). By repeating these words before each baptism, the doctrine of the Trinity is taught and guarded.

A new pastor should practice baptizing, using one of the members of his family or one of his deacons. The easiest way to baptize a person is to have the candidate fold his arms across his chest. With one hand behind the candidate's neck, and the other hand holding on to the candidate's folded arm, lower the person backward under the water, saying, "Buried in the likeness of His death." Then pull the person back up to a standing position, saying, "Raised in the likeness of His resurrection." Then as the person turns to walk out of the baptistry, say, "To walk in newness of life."

Some pastors have the candidate hold his nose with one hand. The pastor can hold the arm connected to that hand when lowering and raising the person from the water. I always found it helpful to have a tall or heavy candidate place one foot slightly behind the other and bend his legs and go almost straight down under the water. Then he will have his foot underneath him to help push himself back up to a standing position. However the pastor feels most comfortable, he should practice enough to make baptism smooth and graceful.

Under no circumstances should a pastor baptize a person without first talking with him to make sure he has been truly saved. This conversation should include going over the plan of salvation once again to make sure the person understands and has assurance of salvation. It is also an opportunity to guard the ordinance of baptism by explaining that baptism does not save a person. It does not wash away sin. Nothing spiritual, magical, or mystical happens under the water. But baptism is something Jesus asks of a person who comes to believe in Him at the beginning of his walk with Christ.

Jesus was baptized. It certainly did not wash away His sin. He had no sin. Jesus was baptized to set an example for us to follow as we begin to follow Christ. He was baptized by John the Baptist in the Jordan River at the beginning of His three-and-one-half-year ministry. Jesus dramatized in water at the beginning of His ministry what He would do for us at the end of His ministry. He would die, be buried, and rise again. When we are baptized, our baptism has the same timing (at the beginning of our walk with Christ), and the same meaning (to show forth His death, burial, and resurrection), as His baptism. And it is done in the same way. Since Jesus' baptism was public, our baptism should be public. In New Testament times, the profession of faith was made by coming to be baptized. What a wonderful privilege to obey Christ and follow Him!

The Memorial Supper

While baptism occurs only once (after receiving Jesus as Lord and Savior), the Lord's Supper is to occur with some measure of frequency. The churches of some denominations observe the Lord's Supper every time they gather to worship. According to Acts 2:42, the early church celebrated the Lord's Supper regularly and frequently. Some churches observe the Lord's Supper monthly, some quarterly, some only twice a year. There is a tendency to add this observance to the end of a regular service.

The author suggests celebrating the Lord's Supper quarterly and devoting the entire service to this observance. Celebrating the Lord's Supper should be a special event. It should not be "tacked on" to the end of a regular service. The sermon should be about some aspect of the Lord's Supper. What a wonderful time to preach the gospel and demonstrate it symbolically! There is a threefold emphasis in the Lord's Supper as instituted by Jesus according to Paul in 1 Corinthians 11:23–26. The bread symbolizes His broken body. The cup symbolizes His shed blood. At the end of the Lord's Supper we should recognize publicly that we will keep on doing this "until He comes."

Every pastor, especially a new pastor, should have the deacons meet and practice where they should sit, when they should stand or be seated, how they should come to the table to get the trays, how they should pass them to the congregation, and when to come back to the front of the worship center to be seated. The Lord's Supper should be one of the most beautiful events in the church.

The table should be prepared ahead of time with a cloth over the trays. The pastor and deacon chairman should have chairs behind the Lord's Supper table. They should practice removing and folding the cloth. The pastor should then read 1 Corinthians 11:17–34 and explain the various parts of that passage. The church at Corinth was a troubled church. People were bringing their own food and wine to the church. That is why the churches simplified the supper to just bread and wine. Some were even getting drunk at the supper. That is why most evangelicals serve unfermented grape juice rather than fermented wine.

From this passage, the pastor can explain the meaning of the Lord's Supper and that it is symbolic, reminding us of the broken body, the shed blood, and the promised return of Christ. Jesus said to His disciples when He first instituted the Lord's Supper, "I will not drink of this fruit of the vine until that day when I drink it in a new way in My Father's kingdom with you" (Matt. 26:29). Thus the Lord's Supper has a backward look to the broken body and shed blood of Jesus and a forward look to His return. The early Christians often said good-bye to one another at the end of the supper by saying "until He comes." What a wonderful way to teach and guard the doctrine of the second coming of Christ!

This passage also teaches how Christians are to prepare themselves spiritually to take the Lord's Supper. This is a good place to address the question of who can take the Lord's Supper. Without getting into the issue of open or closed communion,[4] let it be said that historically, most Baptists have allowed only baptized believers to take communion. This follows the same idea of believer's baptism and takes it one step further.

All Christian denominations agree that only Christians should take the Lord's Supper. Baptists add that those Christians, according to 1 Corinthians 11, should be walking in obedience to the Lord. Since Jesus commanded baptism in Matthew 28:19–20, a Christian cannot be obedient without being baptized. Children particularly want to know when they can take the Lord's Supper. I found that by addressing the children, adults who were not members of the church understood whether or not they were to join in the Lord's Supper.

To the children present I said something like this, "Many children ask, 'When can I take the Lord's Supper?' The answer is simple: after you have been saved and after you have been baptized. Until both of these things happen to you, just pass the tray on without taking the elements." That gave parents help in supervising their children as well. Then I added, "This is not my table. This is not the church's table. It is the Lord's table. The Bible says that each of us should examine himself before eating and not partake of the supper in an unworthy manner. So let us now take time to do just that. First Corinthians 11:28 says, 'So a man should examine himself; in this way he should eat of the bread and drink of the cup.'"

After the pastor leads a prayer of spiritual examination, he then takes a piece of bread and says, "Jesus took bread, He broke it, and He blessed it." Then he should call on the deacon chairman to say the blessing, thanking God for the bread and what it symbolizes. When he says, "Amen," that is the deacons' signal to stand. Then they can either come to the table and receive the trays to pass, or the pastor and deacon chairman can take the trays to them as they stand where they have been seated on the front row. After the deacon chairman and pastor return to their places behind the table, they sit down. This is the signal to the deacons to begin passing the elements.

While the bread is being passed, the pastor, while sitting behind the table, can read Isaiah 52:13–53:6 or some other passage of Scripture aloud. Some pastors have the organist play softly while the elements are being passed. After the deacons have finished passing the bread, the deacon chairman stands. This is the signal for the deacons to come back to the front row. When the deacons return the trays, the pastor and deacon chairman place them back on the table and then serve the deacons, who are standing in their places at the front row. Then the pastor and deacon chairman serve each other. The deacon chairman then sits down. When the deacon chairman sits down, the rest of the deacons also sit down while the pastor remains standing. If the organ has been playing, at this point it should stop.

With an open Bible in one hand and a piece of bread in the other, holding it above the open Bible, the pastor should say, "Jesus said, 'This is my body which is broken for you.'" Then the pastor leads the people in eating the bread. First Corinthians 11:33 says to wait and eat the bread together.

After allowing sufficient time for the people to chew and swallow the bread, the pastor can quote 1 Corinthians 11:25, "In the same way He also took the cup, after supper, and said, 'This cup is the new covenant in My blood. Do this, as often as you drink it, in remembrance of Me.'" Then he or the deacon chairman can pray, thanking

God for the cup and what it symbolizes. When he says, "Amen," this is the signal for the deacons to stand again. Then they receive the trays from the pastor and deacon chairman. When they return to their places and sit down behind the table, that is the signal for the deacons to begin passing the trays with the cups of juice. While the trays are being passed, the pastor can read aloud Isaiah 53:7–11 or the organist can play softly.

After the chairman of deacons sees that the trays have been passed and the deacons are ready to come back to the front, he and the pastor stand. This is the signal for the deacons to come back down to the front and remain standing as the pastor and deacon chairman retrieve the trays. As they retrieve them, they can serve the deacons. Then the pastor and deacon chairman return to the table and serve each other. When the deacon chairman sits down, this is the signal for the deacons to be seated. The organist should stop playing at this point.

While the pastor remains standing, he holds an open Bible in one hand and the cup of juice in the other, and says, "Jesus said, 'Drink you all of it.'" Then he leads the congregation in taking the cup at the same time. I usually ask the people to hold their empty cups in their hands for a moment and think about Christ before placing them in the cup holders in the back of the pews.[5]

The pastor can remind the congregation of the forward look to being with Christ at the marriage supper of the Lamb in heaven and taking the Lord's Supper with Him in heaven, according to 1 Corinthians 11:26. Then he can remind them that after Jesus instituted the Lord's Supper, it is written, "And when they had sung a hymn, they went out" (Matt. 26:30 NKJV). At this point a familiar hymn such as "There Is a Fountain Filled with Blood" should be sung. Just the first stanza is enough. Often I ask the people to be silent until they get outside the auditorium in order to preserve the holiness of the moment. I encourage them to say to one another outside, "Until He comes!"

W. A. Criswell, pastor of the First Baptist Church of Dallas, taught the deacons to hold the trays with both hands rather than just one. This makes the Lord's Supper more formal, more uniform, and it helps ward off the possibility of any deacon dropping a tray.

Morning or Evening?

Should the Lord's Supper be served in the morning or only in the evening? Some say that it is a supper and therefore should be served only in the evening. It is good to serve the supper occasionally in the morning because many older people cannot come out at night. Also, deacons can take the Lord's Supper to shut-ins or those in nursing homes. There are kits available at most church bookstores to use in transporting the elements.

The question also arises about serving the Lord's Supper at a wedding. Most Baptists do not do this unless the entire congregation is served. Private baptisms and private communion services are usually not a part of congregationalism, since both ordinances are church ordinances and not private matters belonging to the individual.

Baptism is not the door to heaven, but it is the door to the church. The way a person becomes a member of a church is to be baptized. Churches can then decide whether or not to accept baptism from just their own denomination or from other denominations. Very few churches practice open membership, allowing people who have not been baptized at any time or in any church to join. This issue will be addressed in the chapter on "The Pastor and His Denomination."

TESTIMONY:
The Pastor, Weddings, and Funerals

Jim Henry
Pastor Emeritus, First Baptist Church, Orlando, Florida

In my first years of pastoring, I invited one of my heroes, Dr. R. G. Lee, to preach at our little church, He had just retired as pastor of Bellevue Baptist Church in Memphis, Tennessee. I asked for any advice he could give to help me as a young pastor. I'll never forget his reply, "Stay on your knees, in the Book, and close to your people." One of the best ways to stay close to your people is to participate in two of their most important family events—weddings and funerals. People will forget most of our sermons, but they rarely forget our ministry in those monumental events of their lives.

The church I served in Orlando grew into a megachurch. Although I could not officiate at every wedding and funeral, I did so as often as possible. It kept me close to my people, and this helped my preaching. It was an opportunity for witness as well as ministry. Many people who attend weddings and funerals are not believers or they have drifted from the faith, and their hearts are receptive to eternal things. I always shared the gospel at each wedding and funeral and through the years saw many people saved. There were moments of humor, joy, deep sorrow, and worship that enriched my own faith. Jesus showed up at both weddings and funerals. If they were important for our Lord, they should be important to us as pastors.

The Pastor, Weddings, and Funerals

A man may be called as pastor of a church, but the title is not equal to the reality. An appointment, a congregational vote, or a vote by the elders of the church (all depending on the form of church government in his denomination) makes him the pastor officially and/or legally. After he has the position, it takes years for him to become the pastor in reality. The word *pastor* comes from a Latin word meaning "shepherd." The Greek word translated "pastor" in the New Testament is *poimen*. That is one of three Greek words used in the New Testament to speak of the office of pastor.

Episcopos is the Greek word translated as "bishop" or "overseer." That role has to do with the pastor's oversight of the congregation. Some denominations consider "bishop" to refer to an office above the office of pastor, but denominations such as the Baptists, who follow a congregational polity, consider the terms synonymous. Those denominations that have bishops above local church pastors operate under an episcopal form of church government, with a hierarchy of ascending leadership. In such denominations the hierarchy is often thought of as the church.

Presbuteros is the Greek word used most frequently in the New Testament to refer to the office of pastor. It is translated literally as "elder." This role speaks of the pastor's leadership and place of respect in the congregation. Some denominations consider the office of elder to be separate from that of deacons and pastors. Those denominations have a presbyterian form of church government, practicing what is known as "elder rule." In such denominations the elders are usually the final authority in the church.

The Greek word *poimen*, translated as "pastor," is the term used in most churches that are "free churches," those that practice congregational government. The traditional Baptist ecclesiology or church government recognizes only two ordained offices in the church—pastors and deacons. Throughout Baptist history some Baptist churches have ordained elders in addition to pastors and deacons, but the elders are not the final authority in the church; the congregation is. Nor are elders in a Baptist setting self-perpetuating; they are elected by the congregation.

Since pastors are referred to frequently in the New Testament as "elders," there is a current debate going on among Southern Baptists over a "single-elder church" (having only one pastor, though perhaps multiple assistants) and a "plural-elder church" (having a board of elders in addition to the pastor and deacons). Several books debating this issue have been published.[1] The authors of this book lean toward a single-elder rule, with ordained staff functioning as a plurality of elders ministerially but not authoritatively. It is clear in the New Testament that most if not all churches had more than one elder, but a single elder seemed to be in charge, even in the Jerusalem church in Acts 15.[2]

Of the three words used for the main church leader, the term *pastor* seems to be the most endearing in churches today. Pastors are far more than preachers. Large churches may have teaching or preaching pastors (the equivalent of a senior pastor), but they may also have other pastors to carry on what has come to be known as pastoral ministry. This includes duties such as ministering to families who have serious illness, domestic problems, deaths, and other needs.

The wise pastor will not relegate all of these duties to his staff. If all he does is preach on Sundays, he may be the preacher, but he will not become the pastor of the flock. The shepherd lives with the sheep. This is what Jesus did. This is known as an "incarnational" ministry. If you do not have a desire to live with your people, perhaps you have mistaken your call. Maybe you have been called to be an evangelist or an itinerant minister. If you are called to be a pastor, you are called to live with your people.

In all of the varied pastoral ministries, outside of leading people to Christ and baptizing them, two functions stand out as most important—weddings and funerals. Nearly every family in the church will at some time need a pastor for weddings and funerals. When pastors stay at the same church for a long time, they have opportunity to make an indelible mark on the families of their church through weddings and funerals. If a pastor stays for decades, he will have the privilege of baptizing people, then marrying them, then dedicating their babies, leading their children to Christ, baptizing them, marrying them, and on and on.

Some pastors are involved in a family's life for several generations. It is impossible to estimate how much such a pastor will mean to these families. He will bury parents and grandparents and even little babies who die. He experiences the joy of climbing mountaintops with his people and the comfort of walking through valleys with them, especially the valley of the shadow of death.

Weddings

A pastor's wedding ministry should have several distinct stages. First is premarital counseling. Many churches have developed premarital courses, with the future bride and groom required to complete the course before the church can be used for their wedding ceremony. Some large churches have bride-and-groom Sunday school departments for engaged couples. Other churches have six-week courses that meet two or three times a year either during Sunday school or on Sunday evenings. The couples move out of the bride-and-groom department into the young married department when they marry. This is an effective way to build friendship and fellowship among young couples.

Once the pastor becomes involved and a date for the wedding is set, he should require the couple seeking marriage to meet with him several times before the wedding. The first session should involve asking several questions of both the future bride and the future groom. First, the pastor should ask each to give a testimony of his or her salvation. When did you accept Christ as your own personal Lord and Savior? Have you been baptized? When? Where? This is a marvelous time to lead to Christ those who have not had a personal experience with Christ.

This is important because the New Testament clearly teaches that a Christian may marry only another Christian: "Do not be unequally yoked together with unbelievers" (2 Cor. 6:14 NKJV). The pastor should not break this rule. Hopefully, he has been preaching this from the pulpit regularly. Premarital counseling can be a wonderful soul-winning opportunity. It can also be an opportunity to take a stand for biblical truth. A pastor should not marry a Christian to a non-Christian. Both bride and groom should be born-again believers.

In the counseling sessions that follow, the pastor should teach the young couple about the biblical role of husband and wife. This author, as a pastor, taught them Ephesians 5:22–33. He also included this passage in the wedding ceremony. The pastor should also refer the couple to a good book on sex in a Christian marriage. They can find help at any large Christian bookstore such as LifeWay or Family Christian Stores. The couple should be counseled that each should go to his or her physician for a physical exam in preparation for marriage. Their doctor may have a book on the mechanics of sex to prepare them for sexual intimacy. Check the bibliography in the back of this book for specific suggestions.

The pastor should also emphasize that the couple should keep themselves sexually pure before the wedding night. As the wedding approaches, it is only natural for them to be increasingly physically attracted to each other, but they should promise God and themselves to wait until their wedding night to have sex.

What If the Bride Is Pregnant?

If the couple has had premarital sexual relations and the bride is pregnant, go ahead and marry them. If they are going to live together, they should be married. When this author pastored a church in Fort Smith, Arkansas, his church had a ministry to Asian refugees brought to the relocation center at Fort Chaffee. The Vietnamese had their own pastor. Most of them were Christians when they arrived in the United States. The Laotians had a pastor, but most of them had a background of paganism before coming to the United States. They had been led to Christ by the young Laotian pastor. They had no Christian background at all. In Laos, if you wanted to become husband and wife you just started living together. When they arrived in the United

States and came to Christ, they wanted to have a Christian marriage ceremony. Most of these weddings were conducted in my study with the couple and their children present.

Some Christian young people love each other, become engaged to be married, and then the bride-to-be gets pregnant a month or two before the wedding. When a couple in this situation approached me, I encouraged them to have their wedding at the church. When their child was born a month or two earlier than the expected nine months, few people noticed. If they did, they graciously said nothing. In one sense, it is the intimacy of the couple and not the ceremony that marks the beginning of marriage. In Mexico and other countries, a civil ceremony is conducted before a church ceremony.

Sex before marriage is a sin, but it is a forgivable sin. A couple can be led to put this sin under the blood of Jesus, but they should be counseled to watch for a problem of mistrust if it arises after the wedding and to be prepared to deal with it. There was a time when a couple with a child out of wedlock had to get married to give the child a name. This is not the case today. Both parties should be marrying for love and commitment, not out of duty or for any lesser reason.

The Wedding Ceremony

A sample wedding ceremony is included in appendix 4. Some couples want to write their own ceremony and vows. If they do, the pastor should make sure it is biblical. During the beginning of the feminist movement, some brides did not want to promise to obey their husbands. I just told them that a promise to obey was both in the Bible and in my wedding ceremony. Pastors should not compromise their convictions to please those who do not agree with them.

The wedding ceremony should not be too long. By the time the parents are seated, songs are sung, candles are lighted, and the processional takes place, about ten or fifteen minutes has already passed. The actual pledging of vows and exchanging of rings should be not be more than seven to ten minutes. Add the recessional and the departure of the mothers, and the wedding will be about thirty minutes in length.

At the rehearsal go through the ceremony at least twice. Include instructions about handling the rings, saying the vows, where to stand, and so forth. Be sure to tell the couple not to lock their knees when standing. It is likely they will faint if they do. If small children are serving as ring bearers or flower girls, it is best to have them sit on the front row after the bride is presented and the wedding party faces the pastor. Hyperactive little children who cannot stand still for long have spoiled many weddings.

The pastor can read the ceremony, but it is much more effective if he memorizes it. He should smile, speak loudly and clearly, and thoroughly enjoy the ceremony himself. The wedding music should be Christian, not secular. It should be a happy time. Even Jesus enjoyed weddings (see John 2). The pastor should counsel the photographer not to use a flash for taking photos once the ceremony begins. The last picture taken with a flash should be the bride and her father coming down the aisle. Most photographers have cameras they can use from a distance during the ceremony without a flash. If the photographer is not a professional but a family member, this counsel is extremely important.

The pastor and his wife should attend the rehearsal dinner if at all possible. This is a wonderful time to meet family members who do not attend the church. Sometimes the family members can be reached for Christ and for the church beginning with the dinner. The pastor should not ask for an honorarium. If he is given one, he should receive it graciously and then give it to his wife to spend on wedding gifts for other church families in the future. He must also keep a record and report such honorariums as taxable income on his income tax return.

According to the etiquette books, it used to be appropriate for a pastor to wear to a wedding what he wears on Sunday morning. With the informality of church services today, that is no longer a good rule. The pastor should wear either a tuxedo or a dark business suit with white shirt and tie. If he preaches on Sunday in a robe, he may wear a robe when officiating at a wedding.

What About Divorcees?

The pastor needs to determine early in his ministry what his convictions are about marrying those who have been divorced. This is not a simple decision to make. A pastor may change his mind about what he thinks the Bible says about divorce, but he must come to some convictions about it.

When this author graduated from college and became an assistant to the pastor in his home church, his pastor had a rule that he would not perform the marriage of anyone who had been divorced. One of my best friends, a little older than I, came to me and asked if I would perform his wedding ceremony since the pastor would not. My friend had been through a whirlwind marriage as a high school student. His girlfriend had gotten pregnant. They were not in love, and neither wanted to marry the other. The honorable thing to do in those days was to marry and "give the baby a name," divorcing after the baby had been born and placed for adoption. During the pregnancy both lived at home with their parents. Now, after graduating from college, he had fallen in love with another girl and wanted to get married again.

I tried to tell him that I would not perform the ceremony, but I just could not bring myself to hurt my friend. I told him I would officiate at the ceremony. Evidently he saw the consternation on my face. A week later he told me that his wife had an uncle, a Methodist preacher, who had agreed to perform the ceremony. I was greatly relieved.

The next year I went to seminary and studied what the Bible says about divorce and learned that each situation must be decided on its own merits. We studied what Jesus said about divorce in Matthew 19. For the next ten years, when I was asked to marry a couple, I would ask if either had been married before. If either had, I would read to them Matthew 19:3–9 and ask if they felt they had biblical grounds for divorce and remarriage. For ten years the answer couples always gave me was yes. Then I moved to New Mexico, where people do not tend to tell you what they think you want to hear.

Our church, the largest in Albuquerque, was the only church in New Mexico that televised its services. I began to get frequent requests for "drop-in" weddings. These were people who had already bought a marriage license and just dropped in to the church to be married. One of those couples was in their fifties. Both had been married before. The woman was a Baptist from Oklahoma. The man was a native New Mexican who owned a bowling alley in the city. He said, "I wanted to go to a justice of the peace to be married, but she is a Southern Baptist and she just had to have a Southern Baptist pastor marry us."

I read Matthew 19 to them and asked if they felt they had biblical grounds for divorce and remarriage. Her first husband had left her for another woman, so it was easy for her to say yes. When I asked him, he said, "No. We just couldn't get along."

What probably took no more than a minute for me to make a decision seemed like an eternity to me. If I refused to "get my hands dirty" by marrying this unqualified couple, they would go to a justice of the peace, and she would never be able to get him inside a Baptist church again. I decided I would go ahead and marry them, acting as an agent of the state. But I felt guilty about my decision.

Word soon got around that there was a Southern Baptist pastor in town who would marry people who had been divorced, and I soon became the "marrying Sam" for divorced people in Albuquerque. Now I really felt guilty. One evening a deacon and his wife took me and my wife out to dinner. The woman was a highly skilled women's Bible study fellowship teacher in the city. She asked me a question I had never been asked before. "How is Jim Bryant the person doing?" Everyone had always asked me how the church was doing. The deacon was a long-time member of the Navigators. They were like Aquila and Priscilla in Acts 18, very capable of advising a preacher.

I shared with them the guilt I was feeling about some of the marriages of divorced people I had been performing. She told me about what was then a new book—*Divorce and Remarriage* by Guy Duty.[3] She indicated that she thought that book might help me work through my theology of divorce and remarriage. I bought the book. The heart of the book dealt with Matthew 19, the chapter I had been reading to divorced couples seeking to marry again.

I knew that Jesus in Matthew 19 was talking about the Mosaic divorce law found in Deuteronomy 24. I knew that in interbiblical times two different rabbinic interpretations of that divorce law had been expressed by two famous Jewish rabbis. I knew that this was perhaps the oldest written divorce law in existence. The Egyptians may have had such a law before Moses, but it has never been discovered. Moses' divorce law, for all practical purposes, was the first. Before then, if a man did not want to keep his wife, he just sent her away. She could not take the children or any possessions with her. She could not marry anyone else because she was still considered married to her first husband. I knew all of that.

Moses said, "When a man takes a wife and marries her, and it happens that she finds no favor in his eyes because he has found some uncleanness in her, and he writes her a certificate of divorce, puts it in her hand, and sends her out of his house" (Deut. 24:1 NKJV). Rabbi Hillel focused on "she finds no favor in his eyes" and interpreted Moses as allowing divorce for any and every cause. His list of possible reasons for divorce included such minor things as her burning the bread while preparing a meal for her husband. The Pharisees who brought up the issue of divorce to Jesus in Matthew 19 phrased the question according to this interpretation. "Is it lawful for a man to divorce his wife for just any reason?" (Matt. 19:3 NKJV).

Rabbi Shammai focused on "some uncleanness" and concluded that a man could divorce his wife only if she had committed fornication with another person. Jesus aligned Himself with this view and said very clearly, "I say to you, whoever divorces his wife, except for sexual immorality, and marries another, commits adultery" (Matt. 19:9 NKJV). Now, that's pretty clear, isn't it?

Well, it is as far as it goes. Why I had never read the Mosaic divorce law in its entirety, I do not know. Guy Duty pointed out in his book that Moses went on to say that when she left his house, she was free to marry another (see Deut. 24:2 NKJV). In other words, the guilty party was free to remarry. This was the whole purpose of the divorce law.

When Jesus began to answer the question about how to interpret the Mosaic divorce law, He did not go to Deuteronomy 24, but to Genesis 1:27 and 2:24, and then He added, "Therefore what God has joined together, let not man separate" (Matt. 19:6 NKJV). This sounded like Jesus allowed no divorce at all. The Pharisees blurted out, "Why then did Moses command to give a certificate of divorce, and to put her away?" (Matt. 19:7 NKJV). Jesus, in the next verse, corrected their choice of words. God did not "command" divorce. He only "permitted" it because of the hardness of heart brought on by sin. "From the beginning it was not so" (Matt. 19:8 NKJV). In other words, God's glorious ideal was one man and one woman for life, but that was before sin entered the world. After sin, God "permitted" divorce. Why?

In Genesis 2:18 God concluded about Adam, the first man, "It is not good for the man to be alone." So he created Eve, the first woman, as a helper who was comparable to Adam. If it was not good for man to be alone before woman was created, it was not good for him to be alone after she was gone. Jesus taught that if a spouse is unfaithful, caught up in fornication of some sort, God permits divorce. That is the only reason. But it is assumed that he or she may remarry. Divorce, in the Bible, is a sin (Mal. 2:16), but it is a forgivable sin. The only unforgivable sin is blasphemy of the Holy Spirit (Matt. 12:31).

When I began pastoring a church in Arkansas, I followed a pastor who would not perform the marriage of anyone who had been divorced. The church had built a large ministry to single adults. Among them was a man who had been a deacon in his church in Florida before moving to Arkansas. His wife had left him for another relationship. He had transferred with his company to Arkansas to begin a new life. He was one of the leaders of the older single adults. In his Sunday school department was a woman whose husband had left her with three babies. She had raised them alone. They were beautiful, godly teenage girls. All of us could see that this man and this woman would make a wonderful couple.

In time, they made an appointment with me. He had asked her to marry him. But she thought the Bible taught that she could never marry again or she would be living in sin. She had heard this all of her life in Baptist churches. I taught her what I had learned about the Mosaic divorce law and Jesus' teachings. She wept. I asked if I could give their testimony at their wedding. It was attended by a large number of our church members since they were such a popular couple.

At their wedding—the first that had been performed for divorcees in the relatively new sanctuary—I explained that the couple had given me permission to share their testimony about marriage and divorce with the congregation. I stated that both had been divorced on biblical grounds. I further explained that both believed divorce is a sin, but they had asked God to forgive them and put it under the blood of Jesus. They had, in writing, asked their former spouses to forgive them for any part they may have had in the failure of their previous marriage. They had even asked their children and their parents to forgive them because they knew their divorces had hurt their families as well.

They also wanted to ask the church to forgive them, and they intended to illustrate in their new relationship God's glorious ideal of one man and one woman together for the rest of their lives. The congregation wept. It was as if they said, "Your church forgives you."

Every pastor should be allowed by his church to follow his own conscience and his own understanding of the Bible's teaching about divorce and remarriage. Every pastor needs to wrestle with the issue and come to his own convictions about divorce and remarriage. In the kind of world in which we live, divorce and remarriage are realities. Pastors should deal with these matters from the pulpit with great sensitivity.

Drop-in Weddings

Sometimes a couple comes to the pastor with a marriage license in hand. In these cases the pastor needs to counsel with the couple to determine if they are both Christians and, if they are divorced, whether or not their divorces meet the pastor's biblical convictions about divorce and remarriage. Many churches, at their pastor's request, have adopted a policy against drop-in weddings. If the church has such a policy, the pastor or his secretary can hand the couple a copy of the printed policy, explaining that the church requires several weeks of counseling before a wedding can occur.

Other pastors consider themselves like justices of the peace or agents of the state and perform these drop-in weddings. This author did that at one time, as noted above. It is not a good and godly thing to do. Some argue that the state licenses ordained ministers to perform such weddings as his contribution to the state. Some states require pastors to register and get a state number to put on the marriage certificate. If a pastor moves to another state, he should check into the state's requirements. Most state laws authorize judges, justices of the peace, mayors, and ordained ministers to sign marriage certificates. No state requires a minister to officiate at a marriage that he does not approve.

With "family" being redefined legally in some states today, a pastor needs to defend the integrity of marriage and the family as established in the Bible. Marriage is between a man and a woman, period. Same-sex marriages, as well as polygamy, are ruled out by the biblical definition of marriage in Ephesians 5:31.

Pastor, keep a journal or diary of the weddings you perform. This author did not do that, and he regrets it. A pastor should keep a journal of those who make professions of faith and are baptized by him as well. Keep a record of funerals and weddings at which you officiate. Keep a record of sermons you preach and when and where you preach them.

If you are a biblical preacher, you can sort these sermons by text. If you are a topical-biblical preacher, you can sort them by topic. If you do not keep a record of your preaching, you will most likely repeat yourself.

I knew one pastor who filed his sermon outlines in a box. After many years, he decided to sort them. He discovered that not only had he preached on the same passages time after time, but he had also written the same outlines over and over again.

Hospital Visitation

Hospital visitation is one of the key responsibilities of a pastor. A megachurch may have a separate staff member who visits people in the hospital. Even so, the pastor may be asked to make certain visits or he may want to visit key leadership when they or their families are hospitalized. In churches with multiple staff members, each staff member could be assigned a different day each week to visit the hospitals. Each staff member should represent the pastor when he or she visits. Both pastor and staff endear themselves to church members through consistent hospital visitation.

Hospital visits should be short. The patient may ask the pastor to stay longer, but he or she is probably just being polite. Visit briefly and then read a Scripture passage and pray. If a doctor or nurse comes in, the pastor should excuse himself immediately and tell the patient that he will be back another day. It is best for the pastor not to ask a woman why she is in the hospital. If she is there because of a female problem, she may be embarrassed to talk about it with a man. If the patient is a man, the pastor may ask, "Now what has the doctor said?" Always be uplifting and pray for healing, as the Bible tells us to do in James 5:13–14. Always leave a business card with the request that the patient call you if you can help in any way.

Sometimes family members of the ill need a visit from the pastor as much as the patient does. If family members are not in the room with the patient, the pastor should ask a nurse where they are. If they are at home, a follow-up phone call is in order. When asking the church to pray for people in the hospital, it is never wise to go into detail about the person's problem. Just indicate the seriousness of the illness without disclosing any details.

Funerals

Weddings are the happy assignments. Hospital visits usually are not. Funerals are the sad assignments, but they are still the responsibility of the pastor. Sometimes church members do not ask their pastor to officiate at the funeral of their loved ones. This can be very troubling to a pastor. Two suggestions can help keep him from being hurt when this happens. One, seal in your mind that there are two times when a church member should be free to select whomever he wants to officiate—weddings and funerals. An older minister or former pastor may have married family members before you arrived on the scene. He endeared himself to them, and it is natural for them to ask him to officiate at weddings or funerals for members of their family.

When this author became pastor of a large church, we had an assistant pastor who had been there for years and had married or buried many people. I asked him, if he were called upon to perform a wedding or funeral of a church member, that he suggest to the family that I be asked to assist him. This involved me in every wedding and funeral. In time families began to ask me to officiate at weddings or funerals and they asked the assistant to assist. This transfer of trust came very naturally. You have to earn peoples' trust.

A second suggestion is to attend the wedding or funeral even if you have not been asked to officiate. After all, these people are members of your church. You can attend the funeral just like other church members. This is a way for the pastor to practice humility. God will bless this show of respect for your people, and others will see that you love them even when you are not asked to be in charge.

The Death Call

Whenever the pastor receives notice that a church member has died, he should phone the home and arrange a time to visit. At that time he can determine whom the family wants to officiate at the funeral. If the family does not ask him, the pastor can ask, "Who do you want to preach the funeral?" If it is another minister, offer to assist him by reading a passage of Scripture or offering a prayer. Suggest they ask the minister to phone you if he wants you to be involved.

If the funeral home plans to schedule a time for visitation or view-ing of the body, the pastor and his wife should make a call at the funeral home at the beginning of the visitation. This is a good time to meet other family members, get to know them, and minister to them. W. A. Criswell, because of the size of the First Baptist Church of Dallas, was unable to visit people at home when there was a death. He went into the family room at the funeral home or the parlor at the church just before the funeral service and met each family member person-ally, going through the list of names on the obituary to make sure he knew how to pronounce their names. By phone, he had asked the most immediate member of the dead person's family to write out a page or so about the person. He read that eulogy at the funeral, explaining that the family had written it. That single thing made each funeral very personal.

The Funeral Service

A sample order of service for a funeral is included in appendix 5. The elements of a funeral service usually include music (religious, not secular), vocal and/or instrumental, reading of the obituary, a Scripture reading, prayers, and a brief message. The message should be no longer than fifteen minutes. The entire service should not be longer than twenty or twenty-five minutes. The gospel should be presented clearly. Our hope of heaven as believers should be presented. Encouragement should be given to those family members and friends left behind.

The pastor should ask the funeral director ahead of time what to do at the end of the service. In some funeral homes, the casket is open before the service begins for people to view the body if they wish, then closed before the funeral service begins. In some funeral homes, the casket is opened again at the close of the service for people to view the body or for just the family to have one last viewing. The funeral direc-tor can tell you where to stand. Usually the pastor leads the casket to the funeral coach. The funeral director will tell you where to park your car and where your car will be positioned in the funeral procession to the cemetery.

At the cemetery make sure you know the way to the grave. In some large cemeteries, more than one grave may be opened. Ask the funeral director for advice if you need it. Lead the casket to the grave. Stand to the side while the casket is being put in place over the grave. Then stand at the head of the casket.

The graveside service should be short, including a brief quotation of Scripture, prayer, and the benediction. It should last no longer than five minutes. After the final prayer, the pastor should shake hands with the family members who are seated on the front row by the grave and then wait outside the tent until the funeral director has taken the family members to their cars. If the family members linger and visit with those who have attended the funeral, the pastor is free to leave after greeting some of the guests.

If any family member asks, "What should I pay you for preaching the funeral?" the pastor should say, "Nothing. I'm just glad to help." If an honorarium is given, accept it graciously. Some pastors then write the family a thank-you note. If you make a practice of giving funeral honoraria to a church fund, you can indicate this in the note of thanks. Be sure to record the honorarium for income tax purposes. If the church or a Sunday school class is furnishing food for the family, the pastor may be invited to attend the meal. If he can attend, it is appropriate. If he cannot, that is fine too.

Pastor, keep a record of the funerals at which you officiate. A year later, send the widow, widower, child, or grandchild a note of remembrance. They will never forget this. They may forget your preaching, but they will never forget your pastoral care, whether it is good or bad. Of many a pastor it has been said, "He is a better preacher than he is a pastor." Or, "He is a better pastor than he is a preacher." Pray to God that both these things will be said about you.

TESTIMONY:

The Pastor
and His Counseling

Steve Hunter
Associate Professor of Counseling and Psychology
Criswell College, Dallas, Texas

According to "Lifeline for Pastors,"[1] 85 percent of pastors say their greatest problem is they are weary of dealing with problem church members. Ninety percent of pastors say the hardest thing about ministry is dealing with problem people and their problems.

Now, more than ever, pastors need a basic knowledge and understanding of counseling skills, crisis counseling, conflict management, and an up-to-date referral list. Most pastors who are fired or forced to resign leave the church not because they are theologically unsound or unable to preach eloquent sermons but because of their inability to deal with people and their problems. Both preaching skills and people skills are required for effective ministry.

It is your responsibility to care for those whom God has entrusted to your care. Good preaching will only carry you so far. Church members must know you care, and you must know how to care for them. A good preacher does not necessarily make a good counselor. Preaching and counseling require two different sets of skills.

This is why I'm so thankful to introduce this chapter on "The Pastor and His Counseling" written by two of my favorite ministers of all time—Mac Brunson and Jim Bryant. From this chapter you will glean words of wisdom on an important area of ministry. God bless you in your journey to becoming all that God desires you to be for His glory.

CHAPTER 14
The Pastor and His Counseling

Pastors make two front-end mistakes about counseling. Some pastors hate the very idea. They are like the young pastor whom I heard say, "I love people in groups. I just can't stand them one-by-one." What an unpastoral thing to say! When Jesus asked one of the first Christian pastors, Simon Peter, if he really loved Him, Peter affirmed (although weakly) that he did. Jesus then said, "Feed My lambs" (John 21:15). The pastor's first responsibility in the church is to feed the flock of God. This refers to his preaching. But when Jesus asked the question again and Peter affirmed that he did love Him, Jesus replied, "Shepherd [tend] my sheep" (John 21:16). A pastor cannot tend Jesus' sheep and neglect his counseling duties.

The second front-end mistake of some pastors regarding their counseling is the opposite extreme. Some pastors spend all of their time counseling people. By the way, if word gets around that a pastor will drop everything else when called upon to counsel, the entire community will line up at his office door.

Balance is the key to the Christian life. It is certainly the key to the pastor and his counseling. If a pastor spends too little of his time counseling his people, he is not tending the sheep. If he spends too much time counseling, he is not putting the first priority first—his study, prayer, and ministry of the Word of God. Acts 6:2 has implications for counseling as well as for meeting the physical needs of the congregation.

Learning the Secret of Micro Counseling

C. W. Brister first introduced the term "micro counseling" in his classic book, *The Promise of Counseling*.[2] That book, nearly thirty years old today, is still a wonderful book for pastors. John Drakeford has a chapter in Wayne Oates's classic book, *Pastoral Counseling*,[3] where he uses the term "brief counseling." All three of these men—Brister, Oates, and Drakeford—were trained in counseling and psychology and gave the major portion of their lives to teaching future pastors on the seminary level.

Both Brister and Drakeford refer to William E. Hulme, another pastoral counseling professor, who wrote *How to Start Counseling*.[4] Hulme emphasizes the importance of brief counseling. He discusses the length of each counseling session appointment (about thirty minutes), as well as the number of times to meet with a counselee. Most pastors do not meet more than five or six times with any counselee. It is my opinion that even five or six are too many times.

In my first pastorate, a small church, I poured my life into two couples who were having problems in their marriages. By God's help, both marriages were saved. But about a year later, one of the couples moved their membership to a nearby church. I was crushed. I had spent all that time with them, and they left for another church. When the second couple left, I visited them and asked why.

They replied that they loved me. They appreciated my help and counsel and credited God and me with saving their marriage. "But," they said, "every time you preach and touch on any problem that we had, we feel guilty and think you are talking about us. We know you aren't, but it brings up all that guilt again." I learned from this experience what W. A. Criswell later told me: "Don't let people pour out the sordid details of their sin to you. It may help them, but it will defile your mind, and eventually you will lose those people."

Micro counseling, or brief counseling, is not just an alternative for the busy pastor; it is a necessity. Wayne Oates says, "However we look at it, the fact remains that most pastoral counseling will be brief counseling."[5] There are several reasons for this.

First, time constraints on the pastor limit the amount of time he can give to counseling while also fulfilling the other responsibilities he has in the pulpit, in the church, and at home. Second, most pastors have limited training in counseling. A course or two just will not do! The pastor may be a minister by occupation, but he is likely a layman when it comes to counseling. Third, the legal liability of filling the role of a professional counselor is too great for the pastor and church to risk. Consequently, it is best for a pastor to give spiritual advice and leave the professional counseling up to those who are trained to provide it.

Wayne Oates notes three functions of what he calls "brief visits." First, a brief visit may help a counselee turn the corner. Talking helps. It helps a person to clarify things and map out a path to help solve problems. Second, brief visits are supportive counseling. It is good to know that someone is standing by to help. Third, brief visits can do no harm. In fact, a brief visit may be more advantageous than prolonged counseling, especially in a small town. "It is necessary too, for the pastor to remember that in a small community extended counseling is likely to be misunderstood."[6]

How to Refer

When I was a pastor and people came to me for counseling, especially about mental and emotional problems, I tried to give them the best biblical advice I could. But I always had three levels of referral I could use, explaining that I could help them spiritually but that I was not a trained counselor. A pastor may have to do some research, but he can find out where the community's trained counselors are and which of these professionals counsel from a biblical point of view.

The first level consists of licensed professional counselors. Usually the pastor's denomination will have a list of these people who are Christians. Sometimes large churches have professional counselors on their staff who will know other Christian licensed professional counselors in the area.

The second level consists of psychologists. The American Association of Christian Counselors will provide a list by geographical area of both licensed professional counselors and psychologists who are among their more than 50,000 members.[7] Going online and searching for "Christian Counselors" or "Christian Psychologists" will usually bring up local counselors and/or psychologists who identify themselves as Christian. An example of that in the Dallas, Texas, area is the Minirth Clinic,[8] founded by a Christian medical doctor, Dr. Frank Minirth. He has a network of Christian clinics across America and would be happy to provide information about those in your community.

The third level of referral consists of psychiatrists. Again, contacting someone like Dr. Frank Minirth mentioned above should enable the pastor to locate a nearby Christian psychiatrist.

One word of warning: there are counselors, psychologists, and psychiatrists who are Christians, but they use only secular approaches in their practice. John MacArthur, in the book he authored along with several faculty members at The Master's College, has an annotated bibliography in chapter 20 that gives a list of thirty-one basic resources for biblical counselors, along with seventeen basic theological resources for biblical counselors. It also includes an additional twenty-two suggested reading items and thirty-one sources the counselees could be given.

At the end of this bibliography are a number of recommended places that provide training for biblical counselors. Those places, spread across the country, could be contacted for a list of Christian licensed professional counselors, psychologists, and psychiatrists who approach counseling from a biblical perspective.[9]

Pastoral Counseling Basics

The pastor should be aware of the following basic principles for all pastoral counseling.

Counseling Women

Special caution should be observed by the pastor in his counseling of women. Bill Gothard[10] advises pastors not to counsel women but to counsel either couples or just the husband. Of course, not all women are married. Some have never married. Some are divorced and some are widows. The best advice ever given to me by older pastors was never to counsel a woman alone without either your wife or another person present. There are two reasons for this.

The first reason has to do with appearances. In chapter 16 we will advise a pastor never to be alone with any other woman except his wife. I knew a pastor who was accused of sexual harassment by a woman whom he was counseling. When he prayed with her, he held her hand. She misinterpreted this to be sexually oriented. Just the accusation literally ran him out of the pastorate. Some pastors leave the door to their study open while counseling a woman. I think it is best not to counsel a woman alone under any circumstances.

The second reason relates to the woman's marital status. If the woman is married, the pastor's counsel may come between her and her husband's counsel. I was studying 1 Corinthians 14 one day when a woman knocked at my study door and asked if she could come in and ask me a biblical question. My secretary was right outside the door, and I had arranged my desk so my secretary could see me from her desk in the outer office. The woman asked me a detailed question about the second coming of Christ. I told her I had just read 1 Corinthians 14:35 that says if a woman wants to know something she is to go home and ask her husband. Her husband was one of our younger deacons. I asked her to go home and ask him.

She laughed and said, "He wouldn't know anything about that!" I asked her to tell her husband that if he didn't know the answer, he should call me and I would tell him the answer that he could pass on to her. She indicated that it seemed a lot simpler for me just to tell her the answer. I asked her, "Are you telling me that your husband is not the spiritual leader in your home?" Her laughter changed to tears as she said, "If we ever pray at the table, I have to initiate it. If we ever pray as a couple, I have to initiate it. He is a wonderful husband, but he gives no spiritual leadership at home."

I told her to go home and tell her husband to call me. Then I would teach him how to be a spiritual leader in his home. The next day he called. We met for an hour once a week, not for counseling but for Bible study. Within six months his family had been transformed.

If a woman who asks for counseling is single, the pastor should ask his wife to counsel with her. Titus 2:3–4 clearly sets the pattern of older women in the church counseling the younger women. If a pastor is unmarried or if his wife is too young to take on this responsibility, he should enlist older deacons' wives to help him counsel women in the church.

More than one pastor and several staff members I know have been drawn into adulterous affairs with women whom they were seeking to counsel. It is best not to counsel with women at all. Two pastors of mega-churches whom I know have offices for their wives adjacent to their own offices. Their wives come in at least two or three days a week and are always present when women are in the offices for pastoral counseling.

Marriage Counseling

Marriage counseling begins in the pulpit. A pastor can preach on marriage and still preach through books of the Bible. If he is preaching through Genesis, there are multitudes of opportunities to preach on marriage. The entire creation story teaches the origin of marriage. No man could have thought of anything as wonderful as marriage. God was the divine architect of marriage (Gen. 2:15–25). The sovereignty of God in waiting on God's choice of a mate is seen in the story of the bride for Isaac in Genesis 24.

Ephesians 5:22–33 teaches the respective roles of husband and wife in marriage. Jesus' teaching about divorce in Matthew 19 yields several sermons on the duration of marriage. Second Corinthians 6:14 warns about dating and marrying people who are not Christians. In fact, expository preaching, faithfully done, wards off many future counseling problems that the pastor may face. John MacArthur notes, "The rise in psychotherapy and the decline of biblical counseling in the Church has paralleled a decline in biblical preaching."[11]

Marriage counseling moves to the church calendar. When any couple wants to place a wedding date on the church calendar, they should be required in advance to have an appointment with the pastor. During that appointment the pastor should determine that both are born-again Christians. He may be able to lead those who are not saved to Christ during the first marriage counseling appointment. If either of the marriage partners does not know Christ and refuses to accept Him, the pastor should refuse to perform the marriage ceremony, no matter how difficult this decision may be.

As a young pastor, I soon learned that when I married a couple with the promise from the unsaved one (usually the groom) that he would come to church and be open to accepting the Lord in the future, he would not keep his promise. I had created an "unequally yoked" couple, and I was at least partly responsible for the problems that came up in their home.

The wise pastor will lead his church to require six weeks of premarital counseling for any couple who wants to use the church for their wedding. Jim Henry, who wrote the introduction for chapter 13, has coauthored an excellent wedding manual, *The Two Shall Become One.*[12] This book, presented by the pastor to the couple he is counseling, can serve as the basis of their counseling sessions together.

One principle to follow in your marriage counseling is never to advise a couple to divorce. This cannot be emphasized too much. For one thing, God's glorious ideal is one man and one woman for life. Even though God does allow divorce and remarriage under certain circumstances in Deuteronomy 24:1–4 as interpreted by Jesus in Matthew 19:1–9, a pastor should never advise a couple to divorce. The legal liability alone should be enough to stop him from doing this. It is unthinkable that a couple should be able to say when they divorce that their pastor advised it. I have advised marital separation, especially in cases of physical abuse. The pastor should have available the locations and phone numbers of shelters for battered women in his area.

In a church I was pastoring, a woman came to me with black eyes and bruises that had been inflicted by her husband. She did not want to leave her husband and, like many abuse victims, said she was at fault for upsetting him. I told her she was in no way responsible and that she needed to go to the shelter for battered wives in our city. The abuse had been intensifying, and I assured her that it would only get worse. If she did not go to a shelter, he might even kill her. I called the shelter and handed the phone to her.

As you might imagine, her husband was furious with me. I told him not to waste his anger on me. Any man who would hit a woman is an abject coward. Through the weeks that followed, he was forced to deal with his own sinfulness. He came to realize that he had never been born again. He gave his life to Christ. He went for counseling at the shelter. In time his marriage was restored. If I had advised his wife to divorce him, he likely would never have come to Christ. It was unsafe for her to stay in an abusive situation. The shelter for battered wives was a godsend for the wife, the children, and ultimately the husband.

Bereavement Counseling

Chapter 13 dealt with death calls and funerals. A church member who loses a husband, a wife, parents, or children will need some follow-up after the funeral. Sometimes periodic phone calls help immensely. When the famous gospel singer, George Beverly Shea, lost his first wife, I called him about two weeks after her death. He asked, "Jim, how did you know I needed to talk to someone today? Ethel died two weeks ago. This morning the last of my children left to return to his home and I am all alone." Follow-up phone calls, coupled with a comforting letter sent on the first anniversary of a loved one's death, are good ways to tend to God's sheep.

Jesus referred to the Holy Spirit as another "Comforter [Counselor or Helper]" (John 14:16 KJV). That word in Greek means literally "one who comes alongside to help." The wise pastor will train his Sunday school teachers to comfort bereaved members. Deacons and their wives can be trained to minister to widows. In many churches, deacons plan an annual Valentine's banquet for the widows in the church. Churches with a Stephen Ministry will have trained people to walk with the bereaved for about a year. The pastor cannot do all the needed grief and bereavement counseling in a church, but he can see that it is done.

Assurance-of-Salvation Counseling

The pastor should always be alert to what I call "divine appointments." Many times people come to the pastor for counseling without knowing why they are there. When Paul James left Atlanta Baptist Tabernacle to begin Southern Baptist work in Manhattan, New York, decades ago, he opened an office on Fifth Avenue. A man came in one day to ask who Southern Baptists were. He had seen the sign on the door as he walked past each day on his way to lunch. James invited him in and began to talk with him about Christ.

The man listened intently but then said, "I will become a Christian if you can answer one question for me: where did Cain get his wife?" James, in telling this story, said that as they continued to talk it became clear that it was not Cain's wife who was the issue, but another man's wife with whom this man was having an affair. He felt guilty about it.

In time, James led this man to Christ. Always look for opportunities to witness for Christ in every counseling situation.

Every pastor should master some approach to leading people to Christ personally. Campus Crusade's *Understanding the Four Spiritual Laws*[13] is only one of many gospel tracts that can be used to lead people to Christ. Evangelism Explosion[14] has excellent similar materials. Many denominations have an evangelism department that will provide such resources free to member churches. Over the decades when I was a pastor, I used thirteen different training programs to train my laymen to lead others to Christ. The only one that really worked for me was Evangelism Explosion. I have used the EE approach all over the world. It is transcultural, and it is a great tool to use in leading people to Christ.

Counseling Children

In counseling children about salvation, pastors need to be very careful. Many times children can be led to repeat a prayer just to please their parents or the pastor. As a pastor I wrote a little booklet entitled *When God Speaks to You*. I never published it, just printed it in the different churches I pastored. It was a catechism, with questions and answers parents could use in teaching their children. Whenever a child under nine years old came forward during the invitation to accept Christ, I asked the parents to bring the child to my office for counsel. What I looked for was a knowledge and understanding of sin on the child's part. If we are going to be saved, we have to be saved from something.

Sometimes I was able to lead little children, who were under conviction of their sins, to accept Christ. Sometimes I was not; they were just too young to know what they were doing. In every case I gave the child this booklet and asked the parents to go through it together during the next month. I told the parents that if the child lost interest in working through the booklet, they should just drop the matter. But if the child persisted after they had finished their study, they should bring the child back to see me. Then we would talk about baptism and church membership.

Putting a distance between the original profession of faith and the child's baptism sealed in the child's mind forever the fact that there is a difference between being saved and being baptized. The booklet had four short chapters: "When God Speaks to Me About Being Saved," "When God Speaks to Me About Being Baptized," "When God Speaks to Me About Taking the Lord's Supper," and "When God Speaks to Me About Being a Good Church Member." The last chapter was about tithing, attending church regularly, living for Christ, and serving. Any pastor could write his own booklet like this to use in counseling children about salvation.

When counseling church members who doubt their salvation, I usually followed the same pattern. After hearing about their previous profession of faith, many of which were in early childhood, I would lead them to pray again to receive Christ as Lord and Savior and then advise them to be rebaptized. If, when they get to heaven, God says, "You did not need to do that. You were truly saved the first time," I doubt He will scold them. But if they did not make the second profession of faith and they found out in eternity that they were not really saved, how tragic that would be. Some people through counseling come to the conclusion that they really were saved when they made their profession of faith. Counseling people into assurance of salvation is a wonderful experience. They learn that they do not have to live with doubt anymore.

Suicide Counseling

Very few pastors will escape having someone in the congregation—or some person related to a church member—commit suicide. Pastors need to take seriously any threat of suicide. When asked if a suicide victim can go to heaven, the pastor needs to be alert. This question may indicate that the person who asks it is considering suicide.

In one of the cities where I pastored, a fellow pastor took out a full-page ad in the local paper advertising his sermon title that week: "Can a Suicide Go to Heaven?" In his sermon he pointed out that Roman Catholics do not believe that suicides can go to heaven because murder is a cardinal sin. The suicide victim has no time after the suicide to repent and ask forgiveness, so he could not go to heaven. He had a different view on this issue.

What he did not know was that I had been counseling a young woman who was toying with the idea of suicide. She had never asked me if I thought she could go to heaven, but she went to hear the other pastor preach. When she got home, assured that she could go to heaven, she took her own life with a handgun. I never told the other pastor about that event—but I have tried to be very careful ever since when dealing with suicidal people.

Sometimes you do not know if people are considering suicide, but you learn to watch for certain signs. In one of my churches, a college student came to me after the early church service on Sunday morning and asked if I would visit his father that afternoon. I asked what was wrong. He told me that his dad, going through his second divorce, just stayed in bed and cried. That is a sign of clinical depression. I suggested we go during the Sunday school hour, between the two morning services. He said that his dad had asked him to ask me to come about 2:00 p.m. that afternoon. I asked him if his dad had been talking about suicide. He replied that he had not.

When I got to the house, this man was dressed, expecting me. We went into his room and closed the door. He poured out to me how he had failed again at marriage and how his wife was threatening not to let him see their young children again. I tried to explain that the courts would make sure he had regular visitation rights, but he said, "You don't know my wife. She's mean."

This distraught man was a college basketball coach. He told me the new president at his school had told him that if he did not start winning some games, he was going to replace him. I tried to assure him that his favor and standing in the community would not allow this to happen. I suggested he go to the vice president for academic affairs the next morning and tell him he was clinically depressed and check himself into the hospital to get some help. He assured me he would do so. We prayed and I left.

The next morning he taught a math class. About 11:00 a.m. he saw his son, who asked if he wanted to go get a hamburger. He said he had an errand to run. He went to a pawnshop, bought a pistol, drove to a nearby lake, and shot himself. None of us saw that coming.

When his funeral was held, everyone seemed to be playing the "blame game." The family blamed his estranged wife. The basketball team blamed the president of the college. All of us were blaming ourselves for not seeing this coming ahead of time. As it turned out, his parents informed us that he had experienced problems with depression since he was sixteen years old, but he had always been able to overcome it.

God gave me a sermon from Matthew 7:1: "Do not judge, so that you won't be judged." I pointed out that we should not judge ourselves. All of us felt guilty that we did not realize what was happening until it was too late. The fact of the matter is we probably could not have prevented it had we known. I also pointed out that we should not judge others since this man alone was responsible for what he did. I suggested that just as he had chewed out his basketball team members when they did wrong, God had probably already had a good "chewing-out" session with him in heaven.

Finally, I pointed out that we should not judge the man who killed himself. I mentioned that he had fought the battle with depression since teenage years and had won up until now. We may never know how many times he fought the battle with suicide and won, until the last time. "Check his record," I said. "He won more than he lost."

The next morning that funeral sermon was on the front page of the sports section of the local paper. The headline read, "He Won More Than He Lost." The sportswriter had researched the man's high school and college games that he had played as a star player. He had checked his impressive record during his years as a coach, first in high school and then in college. He had won far more games than he had lost.

Counseling Moral Failures

A young couple came to me for counsel. The husband had propositioned another man at a local park. He turned out to be a police undercover officer, who arrested him. He vowed it was the first time he had done such a thing. He had asked his wife to forgive him, and she had tearfully done so. What should he do now?

I counseled him to come forward at the invitation the next Sunday and ask the church for forgiveness. An account of his arrest had appeared in the paper, so the church knew about his failure. When he and his wife came forward, I presented him to the church and said, "I think all of you know this man has had a moral failure. He has asked his wife to forgive him, and she has. He has asked God to forgive him, and He has. Now he wants you to forgive him. If you will, say 'Amen.'"

There was a loud chorus of "Amens." Then I asked the men in the church who knew him to come and kneel around him, lay their hands on him, and pray for him. Men flooded down the aisle and prayed with him and hugged him afterward. There was not a dry eye in the church.

I had also asked this man to resign the Sunday school class he had been teaching, to get into a young married class with his wife, and to stop singing in the choir for about a year in order to prove himself faithful. Then he could be restored. He did and he was.

Other Types of Counseling

There are many other types of counseling. Howard Clinebell has a book, *Basic Types of Pastoral Counseling*,[15] which is still good at defining the different types of counseling, although it is more than forty years old. Gary Collins's book *Christian Counseling: A Comprehensive Guide*[16] outlines the various types of counseling a pastor may be called upon to provide. His book is grouped by issues.

Identity issues include topics such as self-esteem, inferiority complexes, illness, grief, singleness, and choosing a mate. *Family issues* involve premarital counseling, pregnancy, family, divorce, and remarriage. *Personal issues* include topics such as anxiety, loneliness, depression, anger, and guilt. *Interpersonal issues* involve relationships, sexuality, homosexuality, violence, and abuse. Under *other issues*, he includes mental problems, alcoholism, addiction, financial problems, and vocational problems. Under *concluding issues* he covers spiritual issues, specialized problems, and he includes a good section on "Counseling the Counselor." (See appendix 1 on that topic.) *Developmental issues* include the various stages of life.

Concerning the adult developmental stages of life, Gail Sheehy has one of the best books available on this subject. It is not a Christian book, but it seems very accurate in describing the various stages of adulthood. She speaks of Provisional Adulthood, ages eighteen to thirty; First Adulthood, thirty to forty-five; Second Adulthood, forty-five to eighty-five (the Age of Mastery is forty-five to sixty-five, and the Age of Integrity is sixty-five to eighty-five). She then speaks of the Tryout Twenties, the Turbulent Thirties, the Flourishing

Forties, the Flowering Fifties, the Serene Sixties, the Sage Seventies, the Uninhibited Eighties, the Noble Nineties, and the Celebratory Centenarians.[17] These stages will help the pastor understand himself as well as his people who come to him for counseling.

The pastor should be equipped spiritually and professionally to do counseling within the framework of a pastoral setting. He should not attempt to counsel people with problems beyond his training and ability. He should develop his own directory of counseling services for the different levels of referral. He should train his congregation to help one another in the spirit of Romans 15:14: "Now, my brothers, I myself am convinced about you that you also are full of goodness, filled with all knowledge, and able to instruct [or counsel] one another."

TESTIMONY:
The Pastor and Finances

John D. Morgan
Senior Pastor, Sagemont Church
Pasadena, Texas

Pastors need to be reminded of the words of Jesus, "If you have not been trustworthy in handling worldly wealth, who will trust you with true riches?" (Luke 16:11 NIV). We are to be stewards of the Word and stewards of money. The emphasis of our ministry should be on giving and not getting because again Jesus reminds us, "It is more blessed to give than to receive" (Acts 20:35).

Satan delights in seeing pastors preach Philippians 4:19, "My God will supply all your needs according to His riches in glory in Christ Jesus," and then get themselves and their churches in financial bondage, which greatly decreases their effectiveness in serving the Lord. God's people should be certain that their handling of money makes God, not themselves, look good. Credit often is borrowing what you do not have, to buy what you do not need, to keep up with people you do not like. Prosperity is having everything you need and the capacity to enjoy it, not having everything you want.

As you give attention to how to handle God's money, remember 2 Chronicles 16:9, "The eyes of the LORD range throughout the earth to show Himself strong for those whose hearts are completely His." If you lack head knowledge, heart knowledge, and discipline in the financial area of your personal life and ministry, every other area will be affected and significantly weakened.

CHAPTER 15
The Pastor and Finances

Personal finances, church finances, and stewardship are all important to the pastor. In the 1960s *Time Magazine* every year issued small cards with a slogan that expressed the mood of the times. One year they issued a card that read, "Money is not the most important thing in life." On the back of the card they added, "but it is way out in front of whatever is in second place." Most pastors do not want to talk about money, but if they do not, they do not preach and teach the whole counsel of God. There is a lot about money in the Bible.

The pastor's attitude toward money will be reflected in his church's attitude toward money. He needs to practice a biblical balance about money. If he talks about it too often, some people will think that money is all he is interested in. If he never talks about money, he robs his people of the opportunity to discover God's financial plan.

The Pastor and Personal Finances

W. A. Criswell, former pastor of the First Baptist Church of Dallas, Texas, for nearly fifty years, gave young couples seeking marriage some good, biblically balanced advice about handling their money. It is good advice for pastors as well. He told them to give the first 10 percent of their money back to God. Leviticus 27:30 tells us that the tithe is holy to the Lord. First give God His tithe. Then give yourself the next 10 percent. Put this in savings. If a pastor does these two things consistently, he will capture the biblical balance about handling money in his personal finances.

The pastor should be above reproach in his personal finances. One of the biblical qualifications of a pastor is that "he must have a good reputation among outsiders, so that he does not fall into disgrace and the Devil's trap" (1 Tim. 3:7). One of the ways a pastor fulfills this responsibility is by paying his bills on time. Although we live in a credit economy, the wise pastor will not borrow money except for appreciating items, such as a house or land. The possible exception to this rule is the purchase of a car. Many pastors now pay cash for their new or used vehicles. How do they do that? By saving in advance to pay cash or by leasing. Leasing a car is a way of staying out of debt for a depreciating item.

Bob Eklund was a pastor for many years before entering denominational service to assist churches in the area of raising funds for building programs. After retiring from the Baptist General Convention of Texas, he organized Eklund Financial Ministries to broaden financial assistance to all denominations. He shares this testimony and advice with us, in his own words, about a personal financial plan for pastors. He calls it the "10-70-20 Plan."

God gave me the 10-70-20 financial plan in 1975. Here is the way it works. Determine your gross income. Then take out your tithe. Next take out your IRS taxes (plus state and city if any). The remainder is your 10-70-20 working income.

- Use 10 percent of the working income to set up two funds. (1) An emergency fund equal to three times your monthly income, (2) a cash-buying fund to avoid future problems with overextended debts.
- Use 70 percent of the working income to take care of family expenses. Both your house mortgage and car payment should come from this category.
- Use the 20 percent category for two things: (1) Eliminate all debts with the exception of your house and car. Use the 20 percent to pay off credit cards and other debts. Use any extra money you have each month to pay above the minimum payments. Don't add to these debts. Work diligently at paying off each debt as quickly as possible. (2) After debts are paid off, stay with the 10-70-20 plan. The last 20 percent

can be used in various ways. Consider the following suggestions: (1) mission projects and needs, (2) children's education, (3) retirement savings, (4) pay off house, (5) pay cash for cars, (6) investments, (7) trips, gifts, etc.

The long-range goal is to become debt free in every area of family finances. Be sure, as you move through the process, that you are seeking God's leadership in your finances.[1]

Increasingly, young pastors are not depending on their wives working outside the home in order to make ends meet. If a pastor's wife does not work outside the home, she can assist him in his ministry in many ways. She will be free to make visits with him. She will be free to care for their children and even perhaps home school them, if God leads in that direction. If a church is too small to pay the pastor adequately, he should consider asking its members to allow him to become bivocational. Many pastors can become substitute schoolteachers to supplement their income if necessary. Paul did this with tentmaking more than once during his missionary journeys.

The Pastor and Church Finances

A pastor should have a written agreement about his salary and benefits before he accepts the call to a church. In that agreement should be his base salary, his car allowance, his health insurance, and a retirement benefit. Almost every denomination has a pension board that publishes help for churches on how to provide adequately for their pastor. GuideStone Financial Services, owned and operated by the Southern Baptist Convention but available to pastors of all denominations, has excellent materials to help churches know how much and how to pay their pastors and staff members. They have studies of churches of all sizes to show average salaries paid for pastors and other staff members.

For many centuries Jews have agreed that a minimum of "ten righteous men" was required in order to begin a synagogue. If each of the ten men gives a tithe of his income to the rabbi, then the rabbi will always be paid an average of what his people make. As the synagogue grows beyond the ten, money becomes available to build buildings, start programs, and so forth. For pastors, this model means that it takes only ten families who are tithing to plant a church. It may start off in someone's living room. As the group grows beyond ten, the pastor is still paid an average salary of those who are tithing, but the giving of additional people provides money for renting a building and eventually for building a worship center.

The wise pastor will not handle church funds himself. He should get a finance committee to do that. The church should have a treasurer. All checks should be cosigned, but the pastor should not be a cosigner. Most churches ask their pastor to cosign checks, but this is not wise. The pastor should not make the weekly offering deposits. Gifts that are mailed to the church should be opened by two people and then delivered to the church treasurer to make the deposit. The pastor can lead the church to write and adopt a financial policies and procedures manual to outline exactly how money should be handled, from receipts to disbursements.[2] Every church should have a finance committee, a church treasurer, an annual budget, regular financial reports, and an annual audit.

When the pastor is spending church funds for approved items in which he is involved, he needs to keep careful records and give a complete report with copies of receipts to the finance committee. He should remain above reproach in financial matters.

The Pastor and the Church Budget

The first item in the church budget should be its gifts to missions. The largest item in the missions budget should be the church's denominational missions program. If the pastor wants to teach his people to tithe their personal finances, he should be willing to tithe the church's finances. Numbers 18:26 sets forth the principle of tithing the tithes. The priests were commanded to tithe the tithes given to them by the people.

A pastor's salary is paid out of the people's tithes and offerings. He should tithe those tithes by giving at least 10 percent back to the church budget. Then the church can follow the same principle by budgeting at least 10 percent of undesignated receipts to missions. By leading the church to tithe the tithes of the people, the people can be led to tithe.

But what about all the other needs of the church? Matthew 6:33 promises to people and church alike, "Seek first the kingdom of God and His righteousness, and all these things shall be added to you" (NKJV).

Teaching God's Plan for Managing God's Money

At least once a year, the pastor should teach his people about biblical stewardship. God has a biblical plan for managing His money. This special teaching can be used to promote the annual church budget or a special building program. Many churches can be led to pay for a new building the church has voted to build with cash and/or three-year pledges. God's people need to know that God's financial plan will work for their own lives as well as for their church.

God's plan for managing money begins with the tithe. Tithing, giving 10 percent, is older than the Bible. A thousand years before Moses began to write the first five books of the Bible, Abraham was already a tither. In Genesis 14:20 we read that Abraham gave "a tithe of all" (NKJV) to Melchizedek, the priest of Salem (Jerusalem). When God gave the law to Moses, tithing was made the financial basis of Jewish giving. Moses commanded it in Deuteronomy 14:22. Jesus commended it in Matthew 23:23, assuming that while there were weightier things such as justice and mercy, His followers should keep on tithing. Tithing is the starting point of Christian stewardship, not the goal. God says that the tithe is holy to Him. In Malachi 3:8 the Lord says failure to tithe is actually a way of robbing Him.

God's plan for managing money advances to sacrificial giving above the tithe. In a sense, we do not "give" our tithes to God; we "owe" them to the Lord. One doesn't give what he owes; he pays what he owes. We pay our tithes to God. We only begin to "give" when we give above the tithe. Paul in 1 Corinthians 16:2 said that Christians should "lay something aside" (NKJV) on the first day of the week (Sunday). He was not talking about tithing, but sacrificial giving, because he stated that this kind of giving is to be done based on one's financial ability.

Tithing is not based on financial ability. It is based on duty and obedience. Sacrificial giving, on the other hand, is based on ability. The 10 percent is a fixed and fair amount for every child of God. Many affluent Christians could afford to give an additional 10 percent or more, while poor Christians could not, but some do anyhow. From the example of the widow who gave everything she had, we know that God does not judge a person by how much he gives but by how much he has left over after he gives (see Mark 12:41–44).

J. M. Kraft, founder of Kraft Cheese, had only one delivery wagon, and it broke down. Kraft took this breakdown as God's message to him to begin tithing. The rest is history. Another layman invented the Caterpillar earth-moving machine, sold the patent, and then set out to live on 10 percent of his income and give God 90 percent. He became a very wealthy man. He discovered that you can't out-give God.

God's plan for managing money culminates in supernatural giving. In 2 Corinthians 8, Paul motivated the church at Corinth by using as an example the churches of Macedonia, a province in ancient Greece. Those Macedonian churches were poor and persecuted, yet they gave liberally. Paul said they not only gave according to their ability, but "beyond their ability" (2 Cor. 8:3 NKJV). That was supernatural giving. One might refer to this level of giving as "revelational giving." The Macedonian Christians asked God to reveal to them how much they should give, and He evidently told them how much. If God tells us to give above our ability, He must have some plan of blessing us that we do not know about. We trust Him and do as He leads.

When God's people manage God's money according to God's plan, the result is always abundance—for His house and for ours. Malachi 3:10 relates the giving of our tithes to the opening of the windows of heaven's blessings. Some people say, "I would give more if I had more." They have it backward. If they would give more, they would have more. That is the way it works, according to Jesus. "Give, and it will be given to you; a good measure—pressed down, shaken together, and running over—will be poured into your lap. For with the measure you use, it will be measured back to you" (Luke 6:38).

When we do not follow God's financial plan, we are not under His umbrella of protection. Without His protection we leave ourselves open to all kinds of financial difficulties. "You have planted much but harvested little. You eat but never have enough to be satisfied. You drink but never have enough to become drunk. You put on clothes but never have enough to get warm. The wage earner puts his wages into a bag with a hole in it" (Hag. 1:6). Have you ever worked hard but just did not seem to have enough money? Have you ever had difficulty feeding or clothing your family? ~~Have you ever had month left over at the end of the money?~~ Have you ever prayed and asked God to provide your needs but there was still not quite enough?

Are you managing God's money according to God's plan? Perhaps you earn enough, but unexpected expenses come up every month and eat up what you have. Haggai 1:6 reports God's people earning wages and then putting those wages into a bag with holes in it. Are you constantly in the hole? "Think carefully about your ways" (Hag. 1:7).

Contrast your difficulties with the promised blessings of Malachi 3:10 where God provides "a blessing for you without measure." Are you living in Malachi 3:10 or in Haggai 1:6? Consider your ways. Are you managing God's money in God's way?

God wants to bless us, if only we will follow His financial plan. It is a plan of blessing. First, recognize that everything we have, including the money we earn, belongs to God, not us. Second, begin tithing to the church. Take that first step of Christian stewardship. Third, respond to your church's appeal for projects that must be funded by additional, sacrificial gifts. Fourth, ask God what He wants you to give even above the tithe and sacrificial gift, and be obedient to the heavenly vision. Then He will pour His blessings on you. If the pastor does not follow God's plan of financial giving, how can he expect to teach his church to do so?

Mary Crowley was a single mother, trying to make a living for her family. She was saved and baptized in the First Baptist Church of Dallas when George W. Truett was pastor. She was taught to tithe, even though she was having a difficult time making ends meet. Then she learned about sacrificial giving and supernatural giving. God gave her an idea for a business that she could organize and run. She called it Home Interiors and Gifts, Inc. It was designed to help women have parties in homes where home gifts and accessories would be sold.

The first bank Mary approached to borrow the five thousand dollars needed to start the business turned her down. They said her plan would never work. Today that business, international in scope, is one of the most successful businesses for women in the world. Mary is in heaven now. But her testimony of giving still lives on.

For decades Mary wore an intriguing custom-made piece of jewelry. It consisted of two little silver shovels. One was smaller than the other. She enjoyed explaining, "The little shovel is mine. The big shovel is God's. Whenever I give Him a shovel full, He gives me a shovel full right back. But His shovel is bigger than mine. You can't out-give God." Mary epitomized Luke 6:38. She gave to get to give. She started with giving and ended with giving. The getting was only for the purpose of giving. That is God's plan for supernatural, revelational giving.

God's primary purpose is His own glory. In Haggai 2:6 God makes clear that the purpose of His house being built is to shake things up so that "all nations . . . shall come to the Desire of All Nations [Jesus], and I will fill this temple with [My] glory" (NKJV). When we manage God's money according to God's plan, God gets the glory and nations come to Christ.

God's secondary purpose is our own personal peace. The Lord says, "The final glory of this house will be greater than the first . . . . I will provide peace in this place" (Hag. 2:9). Learning to manage God's money in God's way is one of the most satisfying things in the world. If He is in control of our lives and our fortunes, we do not have to be afraid of declining economies and failing businesses. When we do things God's way, He will provide for our needs and give us peace. The pastor, church members, and the church will live in peace when they practice God's financial plan.

TESTIMONY:

The Pastor and His Ethics

Jerry A. Johnson
President, Criswell College
Dallas, Texas

This may be the most important chapter in this book. While preaching and sermon preparation are important, it may not matter how skilled you are in the pulpit or how much time you spend in the study. If you fail morally, your effectiveness will be limited and your ministry may even come to an end.

In terms of pastoral ability, preaching is the one essential competency. The apostle Paul wrote in 1 Timothy 3:2–7, "A bishop [another word for pastor] must be . . . able to teach" (NKJV). But fifteen other requirements are also given in this passage for the pastor—and they are about moral character. For example, the pastor must "be blameless . . . of good behavior" (NKJV) and "have a good testimony among those who are outside" (NKJV). A preacher's ethical behavior is to be above reproach lest his lifestyle discredit his messages.

A pastor's marriage and family life can make or break his ministry. Pride, alcohol, and the love of money can also disqualify a pastor from office. All of us can name well-known and lesser-known preachers who are no longer fit for ministry because of sin. This does not have to be your fate.

Paul instructed the young pastor Timothy to be an example to the believers "in conduct" and "in purity" (1 Tim. 4:12 NKJV). Pray that God will enable you to be a moral and spiritual example to others as you read this chapter on "The Pastor and His Ethics."

The Pastor and His Ethics

CHAPTER 16

There are personal ethics and professional ethics. The pastor should practice both. In the Bible, people in leadership positions were called upon to have higher ethical standards than the other people of God. The pastor should never see how close he can come to the line between what is ethical and unethical, but he should stay as far away from it as possible.

Personal Ethics

If the Bible teaches anything, it teaches absolute truth and absolute ethics. Integrity is like pregnancy: a person either is or is not. There is no "almost." You are either honest or you are not. Many pastors have ruined their ministries by compromising personal ethics. Just in the past year, the press has reported pastors who committed adultery, sexually abused minors, lied on their résumés, and embezzled money from their churches. One cannot help but wonder if such pastors are even saved, let alone called to preach. Their moral failures have hurt the reputation of all pastors and all churches. Christ Himself will deal with them at the judgment.

James 1 traces the progression of lust, temptation, and sin in the life of any believer. "Blessed is a man who endures trials, because when he passes the test he will receive the crown of life that [the Lord] has promised to those who love Him" (James 1:12). While some interpreters equate temptation with being tested, the context clearly shows that James is talking about being tempted to do evil, not just some hardship. Hardship often comes from God. Temptation does not (see James 1:13). Temptation occurs when one's own desires go unchecked. Lust is desire run wild.

Martin Luther is said to have remarked that a person can't keep birds from flying over his head, but he can keep them from making a nest in his hair. Passing, glancing thoughts of evil pop into a pastor's mind just as if he were any ordinary man. After all, pastors live in the sinful environment of the world just like everyone else. Pastors were born sinful just like all mankind since Adam and Eve. Such evil thoughts ought to be brought into captivity to the obedience of Christ according to 2 Corinthians 10:5, regardless of the truth of Romans 7:23.

The regenerated person still suffers under the law of sin. He is still a sinner after he has been saved. But the Holy Spirit activates another law, the law of Christ, that enables the believer to deal with temptation quickly and to reject sin (see Rom. 7:25). Temptation is not sin; yielding to temptation is.

If the progression of sin in one's life begins with lust or desire, then moves to temptation, and finally to sin, the best place to deal with sin is at the beginning of this progression, not at the end. Committed sin can be forgiven, but the results of this sin are embedded in one's life until the end of time. If an athlete, on a skiing vacation, skied too close to a cliff, seeing how close he could come and still survive, he could be forgiven for breaking his leg, but it is likely he would see his athletic career come to an end. A pastor can do the same tragic thing. Perhaps this is why the Bible establishes a higher standard of ethical behavior for pastors—and a more severe judgment for breaking it—than it does for laymen.

Jesus said in Matthew 18 that if a brother sins against us, the first step is to go to him privately and try to salvage him. Paul said in 1 Timothy 5 that elders (pastors) who do well are to be honored, but those who are sinning are to be rebuked publicly. This warning should strike fear into the heart of every pastor when he is tempted. Be sure your sin will find you out.

The most serious sin into which a pastor can fall is sexual sin. He should go to extraordinary steps to guard himself from this sin. The first step should be to have a successful marriage (see chap. 5). In his wedding vows the pastor, like every other man, promises to remain faithful to his wife as long as they both live. The pastor should never close the door to his office with a woman inside unless his wife is present. This author has advised pastors not to counsel women. Let the pastor's wife or an older woman in the church do this. Titus 2:3–5 seems to outline the responsibility of older women in the church to counsel younger women. Titus was the young pastor of the church at Crete whom Paul was mentoring. Paul's advice is still good for young pastors today.

Billy Graham wrote in his autobiography that he never rode in a car with a woman alone. He never ate a meal with his secretary alone or rode in a car with her alone. He went on to cite several rules he followed throughout his ministry.

- Never be totally alone with a person of the opposite sex.
- Be careful about being in questionable environments.
- Be cautious about friendships that could be considered inappropriate.
- Be aware of the risk of emotional bonding.
- Avoid placing yourself in a position in which moral compromise could happen.[1]

Early in his ministry the wise pastor should write out his own code of ethics. Once a week he should review what he has written and evaluate himself, asking God for help in guarding his ethical life. Joe Trull and James Carter include an appendix—consisting of sample codes of ethics for pastors, associate pastors, pastoral counselors, and even military chaplains—in their excellent book on ministerial ethics.[2]

The most serious charge that can be brought against a pastor or staff member is clergy sexual abuse. Just the charge alone damages the pastor's reputation as well as the church's reputation. If Billy Graham's ethical rules itemized above are followed, such a charge should never be brought against the pastor. But how should the pastor respond to such a charge against one of his staff members?

First, he cannot ignore it. It must be investigated. If it is found to be true, the worst thing the pastor can do for the staff member and for the church is just to allow the person to relocate. The staff member should be led to confess the sin publicly to the church and resign. Trull and Carter have a detailed procedure that may be followed by the pastor and the church in the case of proven sexual misconduct. It is a procedure for responding to charges of clergy sexual abuse.[3]

A word needs to be said about the pastor and his secretary. The pastor should involve his wife in choosing his secretary. Wives have antennae that pick up signals that husbands miss. A pastor should never hire a secretary without his wife meeting her and approving his choice. He should never take his secretary out to lunch without his wife being present. He should never personally counsel his secretary on any matter without his wife being present.

The pastor's wife should not have to be channeled through his secretary to get permission to speak with him. Prior to cell phones, I advised young pastors to put in an extra, private, unlisted line in their offices, just for their wives to use.

The second most vulnerable ethical area of a pastor's life involves money. Pastors should avoid handling church funds as much as possible. Occasionally a church member will give an offering envelope to a pastor to deliver to the church. Every church that I pastored had the policy of making the pastor a cosigner of church checks. I always refused to do so. I was told that I might have a delay in getting checks cosigned if my signature was not on the bank's list of authorized signers. Usually the bookkeeper was one approved signature. The pastor and church treasurer or chairman of the finance committee would be other approved cosigners.

Sometimes we had to wait a day for the second signature, but I never allowed my signature to appear on a church check. The number of pastors who have ended their ministries under a moral cloud because of their misuse of funds is remarkably high. Stay away from the church's money.

It is better for a pastor to use his own credit card for church purchases and to be reimbursed than to have a corporate credit card. Under no circumstances should a pastor use a church credit card for personal purposes even if he reimburses the church at the end of the month. Most credit cards now apply interest from the time of purchase, not just from the time of billing. Let someone else handle the money.

Some pastors unintentionally separate themselves from their people by living in executive houses and driving luxury cars. Billy Graham has lived in the same house and driven older cars for decades. He did not allow people to give him automobiles. He did not allow local committees to furnish luxury automobiles for him during crusades. Guard against greed. It will do you in.

Rick Warren is a good contemporary example of guarding one's heart against greed. When his *Purpose-Driven Life* and *Purpose-Driven Church* books sold into the millions, he stopped his church from paying his salary. He promised God he would give 90 percent of his earnings to God's work and keep only 10 percent for himself. He continues to live in the same house, wear the same kind of clothing, and drive the same old pickup truck.

There was a time when most pastors were poor. Many still are today. Churches are to be commended for raising staff salaries as the membership and contributions have grown. But a pastor should not allow a well-meaning church to pay him an exorbitant salary. The pastor should not be the poorest member of the church. But neither should he be the richest member. The glory for a church's growth should go to God, not the pastor.

Personal Accountability

Many pastoral leadership publications suggest that every pastor should have an accountability partner, preferably another pastor, but possibly a godly layman. They should meet together regularly and ask each other hard questions about their ethical lives. If the pastor develops his own written ethical code, his accountability partner should have a copy of it and go over it with him each time they meet together. An accountability partner functions not as a judge or a policeman but as someone who watches your ethical back. He can keep you from walking too close to the edge. This person should be your best friend outside of Jesus and your wife.

Some wives function as accountability partners for their pastor husbands, but this puts them in the position of taking spiritual leadership in a relationship that belongs to the husband. Wives do have antennae that pick up things their husbands never notice, especially about other women. Pastor, always pay attention to your wife when she raises a question about someone in your life. Your wife should certainly approve any accountability partner whom you select. Don't choose someone who is exactly like you. Both of you may have the same blind spots.

One of the areas an accountability partner can help with involves what the pastor sees with his eyes. What kind of TV shows and movies is he watching? What Web sites is he visiting? There is computer software that can allow your accountability partner to review what Web sites you have visited. More pastors than you would imagine become addicted to pornography online. Church office computer networks should be equipped with periodic monitoring devices. All employees of the church should sign a statement giving permission for periodic monitoring of Web sites that they visit. An ounce of prevention is worth a pound of cure. More than one staff member or committee member should be authorized to monitor the church's computers at least quarterly.

Professional Ethics

Although the ministry is a calling and not a profession, there are professional or ministerial ethics that a pastor should observe. One involves being called to a church. A pastor should allow only one church at a time to consider him as pastor. If he violates this rule, he may find himself comparing one church with another rather than seeking God's will regarding the move. If a second church contacts a pastor when he is under consideration by another church—even if it is larger and more promising—he should inform the second church he is already under consideration by another church. If he decides it is not God's will for him to accept the first church, he can notify the second church and allow it to consider him. Both churches will appreciate his integrity.

Another matter of professional ethics involves how long the pastor stays at a church. The average time a pastor now stays at a church is only three years. If the church is of medium size or above, he can't even learn the names of all the members in three years. Stay if God and the church will let you stay. The grass always seems greener on the other side of the fence, but let me assure you that it is not. While some churches have problems that are more acute than those in other churches, the problems seem to be the same. Just the names and faces change. Tenure is power. Tenure is respect. Tenure is part of leadership. Look at the pastors who have successful churches. Most of them have been there a long time. Bloom where God plants you.

There is also an ethic involved in leaving a church. The authors of this book have never allowed churches to split over them. For a pastor to tell a disgruntled or difficult church member that he should leave the church is unthinkable. Jesus prayed in His high priestly prayer, "Those whom You gave Me I have kept; and none of them is lost except the son of perdition, that the Scripture might be fulfilled" (John 17:12 NKJV).

When a pastor leaves a church, he should do so with love and grace, not with hatred and bitterness, no matter what the circumstances of his leaving. But what if you are being forced out? Remember the words about Jesus, "He came to His own, and His own people did not receive Him" (John 1:11). If people rejected Him, why should we be surprised if they reject us?

It is unethical to use the pulpit to attack those who disagree with the way you are leading the church, even if you do not use their names. The president of the United States is said to have a "bully pulpit." The pastor should remember the implications of servant leadership and refuse to become a bully in the pulpit. The pulpit is where the Bible should be preached and where the people of God should be encouraged; it is not a place where attacks are launched against others.

Trull and Carter outline several "ethical obligations" that every pastor would do well to consider:

- education or competency
- autonomy
- service
- dedication
- ethics[4]

Under education and competency, they focus on an ethical obligation to prepare for the service to which God has called you (see chap. 2). If a man has the opportunity to go to seminary and does not take it, he has put a limit on his ministry. Treat education as an ethical obligation. The call to preach is a call to prepare.

Under autonomy, Trull and Carter discuss authority and decision making. The pastor must not be a hireling, controlled by any one person or any one group in the church. By protecting his own autonomy the pastor also protects the autonomy of his church.

Under service, these authors discuss following Jesus' example in John 13:1–16 when He washed the disciples' feet. That part of His Upper Room Discourse ends with something that all pastors should remember: "I assure you: A slave is not greater than his master, and a messenger is not greater than the one who sent him" (John 13:16).

Under dedication, Carter and Trull refer to the sense of obligation and debt that comes to any man who is called to be a pastor. To Paul, it was a universal debt that included all kinds of people—Greeks, barbarians, wise, and unwise. When you surrendered your life to preach the gospel, you dedicated your life to do exactly that.

Under ethics, they refer to the pastoral qualifications itemized in 1 Timothy 3:1–7. The list of sixteen qualifications begins with the word "blameless" (NKJV). There is a higher ethical standard for pastors than for other Christians. Some pastors complain that this is not fair. Whether fair or not, that is just the way it is. "Leviticus 19:2 is the *shema* of ethical belief: 'Be holy because I, the Lord your God, am holy.'"[5]

TESTIMONY:
The Pastor, Politics, and Moral Issues

Jerry Falwell
Senior Pastor, Thomas Road Baptist Church
Lynchburg, Virginia

As a young pastor, I kept waiting for someone to come to the forefront of the American religious scene to lead our nation out of moral, social, and political decline. Like thousands of other pastors, I kept waiting, but no leader appeared. The structure of American society makes political issues out of moral and ethical issues. The Supreme Court had legalized abortion on demand. Homosexual activists threatened to do further damage to the traditional family. Most Americans were shocked, but they kept hoping someone would do something about this increasing moral chaos.

In 1980 I stepped out by faith along with other pastors such as D. James Kennedy, Charles Stanley, and Tim LaHaye to call America's evangelicals to get involved in the social, moral, ethical, and political processes which were reshaping our nation and moving us further away from God. Today, more than twenty-five years later, it is time for us to stand up again.

As a pastor, I am convinced that our greatest national issues are spiritual in nature and that pastors need to lead the way. A national poll revealed that 84 percent of all Americans claim they believe the Bible, but only 11 percent read it regularly. It is time for pastors to come out of their ecclesiastical closets, preach the Bible, stand up for what is right, and be counted. We can have a better America, and we can have it now.

CHAPTER 17 The Pastor, Politics, and Moral Issues

In the 1970s, secular cultural think tanks redefined the term "privatization." Originally the term referred to taking a public agency and restructuring it as a private company. *Privatization* was redefined to identify the private sector and the public sector. In the public sector are politics, government, law, education, business, science, technology, work, and the economy. In the private sector are religion, values, ethics, pleasure, leisure, theology, and consumerism. The public sector is run by fact and is objective. The private sector is run by opinion or values and is subjective. A conclusion was drawn that never the two should meet.[1] Everything in the private sector should be kept private.

Added to this was the strange shift to interpret the separation of church and state—a long-cherished American belief held since the First Amendment to the U.S. Constitution was adopted in 1791—to mean the separation of religion and state, a questionable, if not blatantly false interpretation of the Bill of Rights.[2]

It is not the purpose of this chapter to argue against that misinterpretation but to point out its devastating results. Two of the results of that misinterpretation were the removal of the Ten Commandments and the removal of prayer from classrooms in our public schools. While not all pastors would agree that both ought to be restored to public school classrooms, all pastors would agree that the morals of America have steadily declined since that removal. This does not seem like a coincidence.

An even more devastating effect of interpreting the separation of church and state to mean the separation of religion and state has been the attempt by secular humanists to make moral issues nothing but political issues. For instance, abortion should not be discussed from the pulpits of America because abortion is a political issue, and therefore it resides in the public sector only. The church is in the private sector, so it should leave all political issues alone.

There is a strong movement today to make it illegal to speak against homosexuality from the pulpit since this is considered a "political" issue. In Canada, legislation has been passed that has resulted in more than one pastor being arrested for "hate speech" because he spoke out from the pulpit against homosexuality, pointing out that the Bible condemns it as a gross sin. This could happen in the United States if pastors do not take a stand on moral issues in the pulpit now.

The question about what a pastor may or may not say legally on political issues is very important. Legal foundations have been created to guide pastors and defend them legally if they act within the law but are attacked by the American Civil Liberties Union in court. Liberal judges frequently follow the politico-cultural idea of privatization. Some liberal state court judges have applied state law outlawing hate speech to pastors who take public stands on moral issues such as homosexuality. The American Civil Liberties Union, an atheistic organization, usually files such charges in courts of liberal judges.

New foundations, such as the American Center for Law and Justice,[3] have been created and now have representatives in almost every major city in the United States. First Amendment foundations, such as the Rutherford Institute[4] are now defending high school students who have been told by their schools that when they deliver the valedictory address at graduation, they cannot pray or mention the name of God or Jesus Christ.

Local school districts used to give in to demands made in any letter from the American Civil Liberties Union. Now they can expect a letter from the American Center for Law and Justice, clearly outlining the law and promising to bring suit in behalf of any student being discriminated against because he wants to give thanks to God or Christ in his speech. Very few First Amendment suits brought in defense of Christians by either of the above foundations have been lost in court. School boards have been forced to take a stand on these moral issues. Pastors should too.

What Is Legal and What Is Not?

It is important for the pastor to know what is legal and what is not when he addresses moral issues that are also political issues. In elections a pastor cannot—as pastor—endorse any particular candidate. A church cannot endorse any particular candidate. I think it is best not to have political candidates speak from the pulpit of any church at any time. If the pastor and church want to hear political candidates, hold a community meeting away from the church. This should be sponsored by church members as individual citizens.

That elections include moral issues is undeniable. In the midterm elections during the fall of 2006, the following moral issues were on the ballot in Texas:[5]

- a law to ban abortion except to save the life of the mother
- a law to protect workers from sexual orientation discrimination
- a law to legalize casino-style gambling
- a law defining marriage as limited to a man and a woman
- a law requiring public schools to present scientific evidence that supports intelligent design as well as evolution and present them as equally viable theories of the origin of life
- a law permitting embryonic stem cells to be used for therapeutic purposes

The question is, How can a pastor lay out before his people what the Bible says about these issues? Here are suggestions that fall within the limits of the law.

1. Preach a series of sermons on "the Bible and ethical questions" long before an election is scheduled.

2. Emphasize the importance of all qualified citizens registering to vote, especially eighteen-year-olds. It is perfectly legal to set up tables in the church with voter registration forms and voter guides available.

3. Get from Dr. James Dobson's Web site information consisting of "Guidelines for Political Activities by Pastors and Churches."[6] He has links to family policy councils both national and statewide that focus on social issues such as abstinence, bioethics, sanctify of life, constitution and government, education, gambling, pornography, marriage and the family, and so forth.[7]

4. Select from Focus on the Family links a "Voters' Guide"[8] that has solicited and recorded politicians' stands on moral and ethical issues being considered on the ballot. These can be made available to church members at the voter registration tables. A pastor may not be able to tell his people to vote a certain way, but he can make them aware of the moral issues at stake in elections. Judicial elections are extremely important. In the Voters' Guide referenced above, questions asked judicial candidates included the following.

- Do you support, oppose, or are you undecided on a judge's display of the Ten Commandment in his or her courtroom?
- Should the code of judicial conduct for judges include protection of people on the basis of sexual orientation?
- Do you support legalized homosexual marriages?
- Do you support Roe vs. Wade?
- Would you allow athletes to gather on the field and pray before a football game? Would you allow prayer over the loudspeaker at such games?

All of these are moral issues, not just political issues. It is important for the pastor and his people to know what politicians seeking their vote believe about these moral matters.

The Ethics and Religious Liberty Commission of the Southern Baptist Convention has made available online a list of "Legal Do's and Don'ts" for pastors in regard to elections.[9]

Is That Legal?

Good question! Many pastors are confused about what is and what is not legal because of the IRS restrictions on political activity by tax-exempt organizations. While it is impossible to lay out a definitive list of do's and don'ts since the IRS interprets what is and isn't legal, the resource on the next page is offered for general guidelines:

Legal Do's and Don'ts	Pastor
Preach on moral and social issues and encourage civic involvement?	Yes
Endorse candidates on behalf of the church?	No
Engage in voter registration activities that avoid promoting any one candidate or particular political party?	Yes
Use church funds or services (such as mailing lists or office equipment) to contribute directly to candidates or political committees?	No
Distribute educational materials to voters (such as voter guides), but only those that do not favor a particular candidate or party and that cover a wide range of issues?	Yes
Permit the distribution of material on church premises that favors any one candidate or political party?	No
Conduct candidate or issues forums where each duly qualified candidate is invited and is provided an equal opportunity to address the congregation?	Yes
Use church funds to pay fees for political events?	No
Set up a political committee that would contribute funds directly to political candidates?	No
Allow candidates to solicit funds while speaking in a church?	No
Invite candidates or elected officials to speak at church services? (Churches that allow only one candidate or a single party's candidate to speak can be seen as favoring that candidate or party. No candidate should be prohibited from addressing a church if others running for the same office have been allowed to speak. Exempt from this are candidates or public figures who may speak at a church, but they must refrain from speaking about their candidacy.)	Yes

Do Not Confuse Personal Belief with Party Alignment

The pastor needs to recognize that every candidate in the same political party may not believe the same way on moral issues. A serious challenge for American Christianity has to do with the identity of right-wing Christianity with the Republican Party. While one political party may have policies more consistent with evangelical moral beliefs, each individual candidate should be evaluated to see where he or she stands individually on the issues.

Whatever political party the pastor prefers, he needs to know what every candidate believes morally. The claim that a politician can hold to a moral belief personally but not politically is hypocritical. To believe personally that abortion is wrong but to support it politically comes out of the 1970s redefinition of privatization. Moral relativism must be exposed for what it is.

Preach About Moral Issues, Not Political Candidates

The wise pastor will not talk about political parties or political candidates, but he must preach about moral issues. There is an old saying that all that is necessary for evil to triumph over good is for good men to do nothing or say nothing about the evil. The same logic that tries to convince a pastor not to address moral issues is the logic that led to an attempt early in the Clinton administration through OSHA to make it illegal for anyone to wear religious jewelry in the workplace, or to carry religious literature to work, or to send out religious cards to fellow workers, or to talk to anyone about religion in the workplace. Thank God, the new congressmen elected that term found out about this and stopped it through a congressional committee.

My point is that privatization will not only say "don't ask and don't tell" to the issue of homosexuality in the military, but it will also say "don't ask and don't tell" to the Christian anywhere in public. Pastor, take a stand for Christ in the public sector as well as in the church. As you do, remember that Jesus advised us to be as wise as serpents and as harmless as doves.

Develop a Christian Worldview

Every pastor needs to develop not only sound doctrine but also a thoroughgoing Christian worldview. The whole gospel of Jesus Christ is for the whole world and for the whole man. Because of the Social Gospel movement of the early twentieth century, many evangelicals shied away from social issues altogether. Thank God, the evangelical pendulum is swinging the other way. Hunger, poverty, homelessness, disease, and the environment are as much moral issues as abortion, euthanasia, and homosexual marriage. Political liberalism tried to co-opt those issues as their agenda, accusing conservatives of capitalistic greed and not caring.

The Bible has much to say about feeding the hungry and helping the poor. Jesus identified Himself as the Messiah, among other things, by preaching the gospel to the poor without charge (Luke 4:18). He healed people without charging them. He delivered them from demon possession without charge, and He even fed them in large numbers without taking up an offering beyond the leftovers (John 6:1–13).

One of God's first commands to mankind was to have dominion over the earth and subdue it (Gen. 1:28). That has great ecological implications for Bible believers. The Great Commission that Jesus gave to the church before He ascended into heaven includes teaching as well as baptizing (Matt. 28:19–20). The modern missions movement established hospitals and schools all over the world in response to the Great Commission. A Christian worldview is a biblical view of everything in the world.

Every pastor needs to ask himself, What does the Bible say about every view in the world, including all moral issues? What does the Bible have to say about abortion? euthanasia? embryonic stem cell research? family? homosexuality? divorce? racial prejudice? hunger? poverty? homelessness? illegal aliens? ecology? the environment? sex outside of marriage? gambling? use of wealth? taxes? respect for government? Are there biblical implications about disease, death, and burial?

For too long these issues have been co-opted by liberal politicians as strictly political issues. They accuse conservatives of greed and neglect. Yet when conservative evangelicals speak out on hunger, poverty, and disease, the liberals are surprised and even question whether the conservatives are trying to take over their issues for political purposes. And when we speak out against issues they disagree with us on, they cry foul. Those are political issues, they say; therefore, the church should be silent on them. Pastor, do not let the liberal press or politicians intimidate you into silence. Apply the Bible to all of life.

Should a Pastor Run for Public Office?

On the one hand, every American who qualifies for a specific office should be free to run for that office. Some of us can remember when the question was asked, "Can a Roman Catholic run for president of the United States and be elected?" John F. Kennedy answered that. Another question was, "Can a divorced person be elected president?" Ronald Reagan answered that. Now the questions are, "Can a black person be elected president?" "Can a woman be elected president?" Those questions may be answered sooner than we think.

What about a pastor? Why should that question be any different from the others? Yet when a well-known ordained Southern Baptist minister announced he was running for president, the press raised such a stink that he felt compelled to give back his ordination papers. He may have lost anyhow, but he lost my vote when he renounced his ordination. An ordained Southern Baptist minister was elected governor of Arkansas without renouncing his ordination, and he may run for president of the United States. Why should a pastor not run for public office?

On the other hand, the Bible says, "God's gracious gifts and calling are irrevocable" (Rom. 11:29). To me, the step from being a pastor to becoming the president of the United States would be a step down. Most pastors have been intimidated by the liberal press into thinking that the pulpit does not influence people very much. Yet Bill Gothard,[10] who has worked with pastors for over forty years, constantly reminds them in pastors conferences that the pulpit is more powerful than either the press or the government.

Think about it. No one knows the name of the English judge who put John Bunyan in the Bedford jail for fourteen years for contempt of court in the 1600s, but we know John Bunyan. English law required religious dissenters like Bunyan to have his babies baptized in the Anglican Church and required him to take communion in the Anglican Church at least once a year. He was a Baptist, and he felt that his conscience would not allow him to do either. For fourteen years he wrote his sermons in jail, and his deacons read them to the church on Sundays. He also wrote *Pilgrim's Progress*,[11] which probably did more to bring about religious liberty in England than any other writing.

John Leland was a Baptist pastor in Virginia when the United States Constitution was adopted and sent to the states for ratification. He complained that it did not spell out religious liberty or the separation of church and state. Through his preaching he gained the ear of Thomas Jefferson, who said that a Bill of Rights should be added to the Constitution as amendments. Congress kept dragging its feet on the matter. Leland threatened to run for election to the ratifying convention and oppose ratifying the constitution in Virginia. Benjamin Franklin agreed to support the Bill of Rights if Leland would withdraw from the race.[12]

The pulpit is more powerful than you can imagine. A pastor does not have to run for public office to influence public policy.

Go Back in History

When the New Testament was written, slavery, polygamy, and homosexuality were prevalent in Roman life and culture. Although Paul the apostle encouraged slaves who had become Christians not to seek freedom but to serve Christ by serving their masters, he did take a stand against slavery in his letter to Philemon. Paul had led a runaway slave to Christ in a Roman prison setting. He sent him back to his master, Paul's friend Philemon, in Colosse, with the letter that appears in our Bibles. He urged Philemon to treat Onesimus as a brother and not as a slave. Tradition tells us that Philemon freed Onesimus.

Polygamy was usual in New Testament times in Roman culture. Just by telling Timothy and Titus not to ordain anyone who was a polygamist as a pastor, elder, bishop, or deacon, he set an example for the church to follow. In about three hundred years, polygamy almost disappeared from the Roman Empire. Laws were written prohibiting it. Paul's strong teaching against homosexuality in Romans and 1 Corinthians had almost the same effect on homosexuality. It became known as a perversion and a gross sin, yet one from which people could be delivered. The pulpit is powerful!

Slavery was abolished in England because the pulpits thundered against it. John Newton, a former slave ship captain who had been converted, confessed it as a sin. His close friendship with William Cowper, the hymn writer, indirectly caused William Wilberforce to reflect on British slavery after he became a Christian, by reading one of Cowper's hymns. It was Wilberforce who convinced Parliament to abolish slavery in Great Britain.

In America, the Civil War was launched against the South because northern pulpits thundered against slavery. The pulpit is a powerful place! Remember that God told young Jeremiah when He called him to preach, "I have filled your mouth with My words. See, today I have set you over nations and kingdoms to uproot and tear down, to destroy and demolish, to build and plant" (Jer. 1:9–10).

Pastor, you do not have to hold public office to influence public policy. In fact, one of the most effective things a pastor can do is to preach the truth, apply the Bible to life, and equip his laypeople to know how to apply a Christian worldview to their decisions. Win a single person to Christ, disciple him and teach him, and if he becomes a public servant at any level of government, his pastor has had an effect on public policy not by leaving the pulpit but by staying in it.

Encouraging Church Members to Get Involved in Politics

One of the most effective things a pastor can do to influence public policy on moral issues is to encourage his laypeople to get involved in politics at every level. It is by Christians being elected to serve on state school textbook committees that our public education can be influenced greatly. The secular humanists have long dominated most state school textbook committees. It is only there that history books that ignore the religious foundation of our country can be rejected. When they are rejected because of this, all publishing houses will correct their history textbooks. On textbook committees Christians can insist that science textbooks present intelligent design as a legitimate alternative to evolution as a theory of the origins of life. It is only at the textbook committee level that health textbooks that assume all high school students are sexually active can be replaced by books that teach abstinence.

Many health textbooks present homosexuality as an alternative lifestyle that must not only be accepted but also lauded, with teachings of how to go about it. Some health textbooks even encourage oral sex as a way to prevent pregnancy. It is only on textbook committees that Christians can reject social studies textbooks that redefine family as any group of people living together rather than a man and woman with children.

It is a sacrifice when a pastor encourages one of his leading lay-people to go into politics. This usually means that he or she will not be as active in church as before. But what a difference it can make when Christians get involved in public policy. Many public servants have a strong sense of calling to their service. Pastors and churches can plan an annual public servants appreciation day and invite local, state, and national public servants to attend. The pastor should introduce each and tell what he or she does in government. Then he can have a prayer for all of them in the spirit of 1 Timothy 2:1–3. A good sermon can be given from Romans 13:1–7. A service like this would also give the pastor an opportunity to encourage his people to be involved in politics.

Pastor, preach the Bible, apply it to every area of life, encourage your people to be good citizens, and lead them to use their votes to influence this nation for good.

Three American presidents quoted from <u>Alexis de Tocqueville,</u> the French historian who said after he visited our country in the 1800s: "I sought for the greatness and genius of America in her commodious harbors and her ample rivers—and it was not there . . . in her fertile fields and boundless forests—and it was not there . . . in her rich mines and her vast world commerce—and it was not there . . . in her democratic Congress and her matchless Constitution—and it was not there. Not until I went into the churches of America and heard her pulpits flame with righteousness did I understand the secret of her genius and power. America is great because she is good, and if America ever ceases to be good, she will cease to be great."[13]

Government, commerce, education, the press, Hollywood, television—these do not guard America's goodness and greatness. This is done by our churches. Pastor, take a stand, preach the Bible, and keep America good and great.

TESTIMONY:
The Pastor Changing Churches

Steve Gaines
Senior Pastor, Bellevue Baptist Church
Memphis, Tennessee

The only thing that does not change in life is the fact that everything changes, except the Lord and His Word. From the moment we are born, change becomes the norm. A person learns to walk, attends his first day of school, learns to read and write, begins to drive a car, leaves home, gets a job, gets married, has children, retires, experiences declining health, and eventually dies. Life is one successive change after another.

When a pastor begins his ministry at a church, he rarely considers that one day he will no longer be the leader of that congregation. That is probably a good thing. Why? Because transitioning from serving as the pastor of one church to another church, place of ministry, or even retirement can be a very taxing experience.

It is not easy to leave one church and go to another, but if God calls you, you must obey. He will help you go out with joy from your previous church and be led forth with peace to your new place of ministry a la Isaiah 55:12. The changes and transitions can draw you closer to the Lord, to your family, and in time, to the members of your new flock.

Remember, before you leave your present ministry, be sure God is in the move. If He is, take up your cross, follow Him, and joyfully sing, "Wherever He Leads, I'll Go."

CHAPTER 18 The Pastor Changing Churches

One could wish that the ordinary pastor would seldom have to read this chapter. In the eighteenth and nineteenth centuries among English Baptists, it was not uncommon for pastors to serve one church for their entire ministerial lifetimes.[1] Unfortunately, this is not true in America today. The average tenure of Baptist pastors has fluctuated over the past twenty years somewhere between eighteen months and three years. Ten years is thought to be a long time for Baptist pastors in most churches.

The exception to this rule is found in the megachurches. Rick Warren has been the only pastor of Saddleback Community Church in its twenty-seven-year history. W. A. Criswell served as the senior pastor of the First Baptist Church of Dallas, Texas, for nearly fifty years. John MacArthur, Charles Stanley, and Adrian Rogers are notable examples of pastors who stayed for a long time.

When this author served as W. A. Criswell's minister of evangelism and church organization from 1968–1973, he frequently recognized the visitors in the services. In those days visitors were asked to stand. One Sunday morning five men stood up, seated together, dressed in dark suits, white shirts, and ties. I leaned over to Dr. Criswell and said, "It looks like a pulpit committee to me." He laughed and at the beginning of his sermon told the church my comment. They laughed. Then Dr. Criswell said, "Would to God it were true! I haven't had a pulpit committee visit me since I became pastor of this church!"

The long tenure of Criswell and others mentioned above teaches us that a pastor has to stay a long time in order to build a large church. The tragedy of these past decades is that most pastors do not stay a long time. They change churches, change the types of ministry, or leave the ministry altogether. The reasons for their departure have already been cited in chapter 5.[2] Three of the seven reasons are family related: the need to give special care to his children and family, sexual misconduct on the pastor's part, and divorce or other marital problems. But the other four demand attention here: choosing a ministry other than in a local church, conflict with the congregation, conflict with his denomination, or becoming burned out or discouraged. Only the first reason is a pleasant one.

Going into Denominational Work

There used to be a saying among pastors that "those who can preach, do; those who can't go into denominational work." If that ever were true, it is not true today. Among Southern Baptists, all one has to do is listen to the preaching of denominational leaders such as Morris Chapman, Jimmy Draper, Jerry Rankin, Richard Land, and Bob Reccord to hear excellent preaching. The same could be said of seminary presidents such as Albert Mohler, Chuck Kelly, Danny Akin, Phil Roberts, Paige Patterson, and Jeff Iorg. Many seminary faculty members are excellent preachers. It is not unreasonable to expect pastors to enter denominational service in order to multiply their ministries by mentoring younger men.

From personal experience, this author can tell you how pleasant it is to teach and train future leaders of the churches. Besides, pastors who go into denominational work do not stop preaching. They are called on by pastors to supply their pulpits. They are called on by churches to hold interim pastorates. Leaving the pastorate to enter denominational service is not leaving the ministry. It is a pleasant stage in one's ministerial career and calling.

Conflict within the Congregation

The other reasons are very difficult. Conflict within the congregation is perhaps harder on the pastor than any other member of the church. This topic was dealt with in the chapter on the pastor and his leadership. Conflict management is a must course for the effective pastor. If he hasn't had a formal course in college or seminary on conflict management, he should read every book he can find on the subject. Often there has been a conflict between power groups within a church for years. There is a temptation for the pastor to take sides in a conflict within the congregation. One side may love and back the pastor. The other side may love him, but it will not back what he wants to do. It is so easy to spend one's time with positive people and ignore those who are negative. This is unwise.

The pastor needs to take sides on moral issues but not on personal issues. There are some leadership techniques for getting through conflict that are dealt with in chapter 7. Often, it is when a congregation begins to grow that conflict arises for one of two reasons.

First, the devil doesn't like church growth and does everything in his power to stop it. Conflict, at heart, is a spiritual matter that involves spiritual warfare. Frank Peretti's book *This Present Darkness*[3] is a classic novel about this issue. It is important for the pastor to recognize spiritual warfare and to use the spiritual armor described in Ephesians 6 to fight it. Just be sure you do not fight people. We wrestle not against flesh and blood.

The second reason for conflict in a congregation that is growing is that new members sometimes are considered a threat to the existing control group. New members tend to be loyal to the pastor rather than to the group of laymen who have controlled the church for years. The control group may not even realize why they are opposing the pastor, but it is probably because they feel like they are losing control. Getting a congregation to face this is difficult. There is an old saying that one should stay close to his friends and even closer to his enemies.

Splitting the church is not the answer. Dissension breeds dissension. The pastor who allows a church to split over his leadership is teaching the group who stays with him how to split again if they ever disagree with his leadership. A church split is a terrible testimony to a community. Most denominations have counselors in the field of conflict resolution who will work with a pastor and a church in conflict. Call on them for help.

Burnout or Discouragement

More than we imagine, pastors who leave the ministry do so because of burnout or discouragement. There is an old joke about a man who got up one Sunday morning and told his wife, "I'm not going to that church this morning."

She replied, "Oh yes, you are. Now get up, get showered, put your clothes on, and go."

He responded, "Nobody there likes me and I don't like anybody there. Just give me three good reasons why I should go to church this morning."

She answered, "One, God expects you to do it. Two, your family expects you to do it. And three, the church expects you to be there. After all, you're the pastor."

Burnout is a terrible thing. How does a pastor avoid burnout?

Keeping the Fourth Commandment

So often we brush over the fourth commandment that tells us to remember the Sabbath day to keep it holy. As Christians we don't worship on the Sabbath, the seventh day of the week. We worship on Sunday, the first day of the week. The earliest Christians were Jewish Christians. They kept the Sabbath day as holy. They did not work. They did not cook. They did not travel except to go to the synagogue. The Sabbath lasted from sundown Friday to sundown Saturday. When it ended, they cooked and they came together as Christians to worship Jesus.

After Christianity broke with Judaism when mostly Gentiles began to be saved during Paul's missionary journeys, their calendar did not begin the day at sundown as did the Jewish calendar, which was based on a literal interpretation of "the evening and the morning" in Genesis 1. The Gentile day began at sunrise. The pagan weekly day of worship was the first day of the week just like the Christian Jewish day, only the Gentile Christians began to worship on Sunday morning rather than Saturday evening. By the third century Sunday worship was fixed in the Christian church.

For pastors, Sunday is not a day of rest. Yet the principle in the fourth commandment is still there: work for six days and rest for one. The pastor must take another day of the week, preferably not Saturday, for rest. If he does not, he not only breaks the intention of the fourth commandment, but he also breaks himself on it. Pastors need a regular schedule just like anyone else. Pastor, you cannot do all that God has called you to do in seven days, but you can in six. Take a day for rest and relaxation. If you do not, you will burn out.

Dealing with Discouragement

Many pastors deal with discouragement by eating. This is probably why there are so many overweight pastors. An obese pastor gives a terrible testimony to his congregation and his community. He is supposed to be a disciple of Jesus. How can you be a disciple without discipline? Face your obesity as a spiritual problem.

When this author was a young pastor, he gained about seven to ten pounds a year. By the time he was thirty-two, he carried almost 250 pounds on his 5'10" frame. He did not have enough willpower to stop eating. He blamed it on his metabolism. His doctor told him that a person's basic metabolism is established in his first year of life. If his mother overfed him in the first year of his life, he would gain weight easily the rest of his life. I took that as an explanation for why I would always be fat.

But other things in my life began to make me doubt that excuse. I bit my fingernails down to the quick. I couldn't stop doing it. A woman in one church I served gave me a bottle of Thumb, the hot medicine they put on babies' thumbs to keep them from sucking their thumbs. I would just lick it off, a little at a time, and go on biting my nails. On top of that, my devotional life was in shambles. I would start having daily devotionals and then stop.

Finally, I put it all together. It was a matter of spiritual discipline. I recognized that being overweight was a poor testimony. When I made the issue of being overweight a spiritual matter, I was able to discipline myself and bring my weight under control. An interesting thing happened. Suddenly, without trying, I stopped biting my fingernails and started having regular devotions. All these problems came together when I faced them as spiritual issues.

W. A. Criswell was an admirer of the nineteenth-century British Baptist preacher, Charles Haddon Spurgeon. He had every book Spurgeon had ever published, and he studied Spurgeon's life and ministry extensively. I asked Dr. Criswell one day what Spurgeon died from. He answered, "He ate himself to death." Spurgeon became obese and died at fifty-seven years of age. Dr. Criswell's answer may have been an overstatement, but the truth is still there: Pastor, no matter how successful you are, keep your weight under control.

Exercise is another important ingredient of emotional as well as physical health. Some pastors may play too much golf, but I never met a pastor who played golf regularly who left the ministry because of burnout. Even Paul recognized that "bodily exercise profits a little [literally, for a little while]" (1 Tim. 4:8 NKJV). Younger pastors can run. Older pastors can walk. Jesse M. Hendley, the old scholar-evangelist, had a daily regimen of exercise he did in motel rooms well up into his eighties. He never burned out. It is not God's will that we burn out any more than it is that we rust out. We may wear out for the sake of the gospel, but that is commendable. Burning out is not.

The rest of Paul's verse on exercise contrasts bodily exercise with the exercise of godliness. He adds, "But godliness is beneficial in every way, since it holds promise for the present life and also for the life to come" (1 Tim. 4:8). It has been said that an ounce of prevention is worth a pound of cure. This is certainly true in the exercise of godliness.

David had a melancholy temperament and was subject to discouragement and depression. All you have to do is read his psalms to realize this. Every pastor who is prone to discouragement or depression needs to memorize Psalm 42. David asked, "Why am I so depressed? Why this turmoil within me? Put your hope in God, for I will still praise Him, my Savior and my God" (Ps. 42:5). David was going through a dry and thirsty period in his life. Every pastor has dry and thirsty periods. David had been crying. Pastors certainly understand that. The pastorate is a lonely place. David was suffering from what the medieval mystics called "the dark night of the soul." How did he get out of what John Bunyan called "the slough of despond"?[4] How did he escape what

Winston Churchill called "the black dog"? How does he escape discouragement and depression?

David remembered the mountaintop experiences he had experienced with God (Ps. 42:6). He remembered what God is really like (Ps. 42:6, 8). He remembered how prayer in the lonely nights changes into a song (Ps. 42:6, 8). He remembered God's mercy, His lovingkindness, His stability, and His smile (Ps. 42:5–6, 8–11). Depression and discouragement should lead the pastor to a fresh seeking and finding of the face of God. Do you remember the song that says, "Whatever it takes to draw closer to You, Lord, that's what I'm willing to do"? Do you really mean that?

Clinical Depression

Some pastors may have hormonal deficiencies that bring on clinical depression. How do you know when you are suffering from clinical depression that should be dealt with medically? Use the calendar test. Depression sometimes lasts only two hours. Sometimes it will last two days. But if it goes beyond two weeks, you are clinically depressed and need to see a doctor who specializes in treating clinical depression.

Some pastors mistakenly feel that the pastor should be able to treat himself. After all, he counsels his members all the time. If a pastor is not willing to face his personal need of help, he has first of all a spiritual problem—pride. If you break your arm or leg, you go to a specialist for treatment. Why should you not do the same if you break your nerves? It is nothing to be embarrassed about to admit that you need help. Appendix 1 has a list of resources for the pastor who needs counseling himself. There are plenty of books dealing with depression, but if you have clinical depression you do not need a book. You need clinical help. Do not be too proud to seek it.

Staying Where You Are

Often pastors ask, "When do I know God is calling me to another church?" I asked a pastor that question once. He had been pastor of the same church for forty-two years and eight months before he retired. I asked him if he ever thought of taking another church during that time. His reply was humorously profound. He said, "When I wanted to leave, no other church asked me. When other churches asked me, I did not want to leave." If all pastors found the question that simple, there would be far fewer pastors changing churches.

The rule of thumb is to stay where you are if you can. As one minister told me, "At least I know what the problems are in my church. I don't know what they are in another church." One pastor's wife noted that the problems are the same in every church. Just the faces change. There is a lot of truth in that. The grass always looks greener on the other side of the fence. But it isn't.

The secret to staying where you are is twofold. First, just say no. If a church asks for your résumé, just say no. If God really wants you at that church, they will come back to you. When pastors send out their résumés on a regular basis, they become double-minded, and this leads to instability (James 1:8). Second, recognize the eighteen-month rule (the time varies depending on which book you read). This rule says that every relationship tends to reach a plateau about every eighteen months. This is true of marriages, families, jobs, and churches. In other words, adjustments need to be made to enable you to continue moving forward. This is why organizations have strategy planning meetings at least every year or two.

A wise pastor will review his relationships at least every eighteen months. Could it be that one of the reasons there are short pastorates is that the pastor does not recognize the eighteen-month rule? About every eighteen months he will run into opposition. If it is not opposition, it will be lethargy. The relationship between a pastor and his church is much like a marriage. He must find ways to improve this relationship or it will stagnate. That leads to ineffectiveness at the least or conflict at the worst. Adjustments must be made if you want to stay.

The pastor's preaching can be adjusted and improved. The Stephen Olford Institute in Memphis, Tennessee,[5] is designed to help pastors improve their preaching. Many seminaries offer continuing education courses to help the pastor do the same with his administrative skills. There are seminars on church growth. Many megachurches have annual pastors conferences to help pastors learn how not only to survive, but also how to prosper in their calling and career. An alternative to leaving a church is to improve yourself and your relationships.

Some pastors say, "But I want a larger church." Then grow your own. Almost any church can grow, regardless of its location or history. Stay with it. Tenure is power in leadership. The longer a pastor stays at a church, the more the leadership of the congregation will belong to him.

Called to Another Church

When a pastor is asked to consider accepting the pastorate of another church, how does he know God's will in the matter? Charles Spurgeon told of a harbor with three lighthouses. When a captain was able to line up the three lighthouses, one directly behind the other, it was safe to enter the harbor. There are three lighthouses in a pastor's life that should line up in determining the will of God: the Word of God, circumstances, and the inner voice of the Holy Spirit.

First, there is the lighthouse of the Word of God. There is a lot in Scripture about determining the will of God. One powerful point is, "Everything that is not from faith is sin" (Rom. 14:23). While the immediate context has to do with eating meat sacrificed to idols, the principle behind it is applicable to the will of God in anything. If a pastor does not believe it is God's will for him to accept another church, he would be wise to turn it down. It is always unwise to act out of "unfaith." In fact, Paul says that such an act is sin. Applied to this situation, it would be a sin for a pastor to accept a pastorate without fully believing it is God's will. The Word of God gives us this guidance.

Second, there is the lighthouse of circumstances. God does guide through circumstances. Sometimes these circumstances have to do with remuneration. It is uncomfortable for a pastor to talk with a prospective church about salary. There is a way to leave money out of the consideration until the very end of the process. If a pastor senses that God is leading him to consider the church, when he is asked about his salary he could reply, "Let's not talk about that now. Let's wait until the committee and I agree that we should pursue the matter further." Of course, you will have to talk about it before you preach in view of a call.

Most churches vote on calling a man as pastor and on his initial salary in the same action. If you are invited to come to a church and preach in view of a call, you can say, "If I were single, I could just take whatever the church has budgeted for my salary. But I have a wife and children to think of. This is what I am being paid where I am." If the committee replies that they cannot afford to match your present salary, you should think a long time before accepting that church. How the church deals with you initially is how they will continue to deal with you financially.

When this author had just graduated from seminary, a church in another state, five or six times larger than his first little seminary church, asked him to come and preach in view of a call as pastor. My wife and I spent a long weekend with the church. When they showed us the parsonage, the carpet in the hallway was worn through to the pad beneath. They explained that the former pastor had little children who abused the carpet with their tricycles. When asked if it would be replaced, they replied that it would not. There were window air conditioning units in each room. They explained that these belonged to the former pastor. I would have to provide my own. Even though I received a 90 percent affirmative vote from the congregation, I did not accept that church. The circumstances told me it would be an unhappy place for my family.

Another circumstance is the strength of the call. This author's conviction is that the pulpit committee should be unanimous in recommending him as pastor. Not every church has this rule in its bylaws, but the pastor can have it as his rule.

This author withdrew his name from consideration of the pastorate of a megachurch some years ago when one woman on the pastor search committee voted against him. She then offered to change her vote and make it unanimous, but I did not think that wise. I had already seen several power groups struggling in the church. Her negative vote let me know that God was not in the call. If a pastor cannot get a 100 percent vote by the pastor search committee, he should think seriously about withdrawing his name from consideration by the church.

What percentage represents a strong call from a congregation? Some churches have a 90 percent requirement. Even if they do not, that is a good rule of thumb. I suppose if you got an 89 percent vote, you might still want to consider accepting, but if the call were no more than 75 percent this should tell you the church has fellowship problems. Unless God has gifted you in the ministry of reconciliation, you should pray long and hard about accepting a divided church.

The third lighthouse is the inner witness of God's Spirit. God's Word never changes. Circumstances are usually fairly evident. It is the inner witness of God's Spirit that is sometimes difficult to ascertain. This is the third lighthouse that must line up. Is God leading you to this new assignment? No one can tell you how to ascertain this. In the several times I changed churches, no discernible pattern of this inner witness emerged. This is why pastors must have a close walk with the Lord. This inner urge must come from Him. "Whenever you turn to the right or to the left, your ears will hear this command behind you: 'This is the way. Walk in it'" (Isa. 30:21). If you do not have this inner leading, you had better stay where you are.

Here is where it pays to believe in the sovereignty of God. If you believe in this biblical doctrine, God will not let you make a mistake about something as important as what church you serve as pastor. It is Jesus who is the Great Shepherd. Even if you belong to a denomination where a bishop assigns pastors to churches, it is ultimately Jesus who makes the assignments.

A pastor moving to a new church needs a firm belief in the sovereignty of God and the wisdom of Jesus in making the assignment. This does not mean every assignment will be pleasant. Think of Jeremiah. He was assigned to serve in Jerusalem when it was under siege and when the people were rebellious and disobedient. What makes us think that every assignment must be pleasant? I knew a minister once who thought that his happiness was the barometer telling whether he should stay at a church. But God's happiness is the barometer—not ours.

Leaving Where You Are

When you are called to another church, tell your church leaders along the way what is happening. They will appreciate your integrity. If you accept another pulpit, give your present church at least two weeks' notice. That will give them time to say good-bye in an appropriate manner. You can take unused but earned vacation after you leave and have a family vacation between the two assignments. On your last two Sundays, preach Christ-exalting, uplifting messages.

Assure the church you are not being called away from them as much as you are being called to another assignment. Assure them that God will give them a wonderful pastor to take your place and that you will be praying for them.

When Is It Time to Leave?

When is it time for a pastor to leave a church? In chapter 20 we will deal with the pastor and his retirement, but here we are asking about a pastor who is not retirement age. It is generally wise that a pastor should not resign until he is called to another church. There are several good reasons for this.

First, it is very difficult for a pastor who does not have a church at present to get one. People wonder why he left the previous church with no place to go. If relationships deteriorate between a pastor and the leaders of his church, it would be far better for him and the church if the leaders would allow him to relocate. His denomination should be able to help him. He may not go to a church as large. He may take a cut in salary, but he will not have on his résumé that he left without a place to go. Nor will the church have on its conscience the forced termination of a pastor.

A church can be led to write a constitution and bylaws or revise its bylaws to deal with the severance of a pastor in the same article that guides the church in electing a pastor. In that article could be a paragraph that says something like this:

> If conflict arises between a pastor and his leaders or his people, every attempt will be made to resolve the conflict. If it cannot be resolved, the pastor should be given ample time to relocate to another church. If he is unsuccessful at relocation and the relationship becomes increasingly worse, the deacons are responsible to lead the attempt of reconciliation. If they cannot be reconciled, it would take at least a 75 percent vote of the deacons to recommend to the church that the pastor be dismissed. (This requirement will protect the church and the pastor from a small power group within the deacons.) If 75 percent of the deacons recommended dismissal, it would take only a 50 percent vote of the church

to accept the deacons' recommendation. (If the pastor can't get a 50 percent vote from the church, he will not be able to function as pastor anyhow.) In the event of his dismissal he should receive at least three months' severance pay and be allowed to stay in the parsonage during that time. (This will protect the pastor's family and the church's reputation. Even if the pastor has been dismissed because of a moral failure, his family still needs to be helped. How a church deals with dismissing a pastor will speak volumes to any future pastor about the love, grace, and mercy of that church.)

If a pastor is dismissed, he has no choice but to leave. It goes without saying that once these termination actions begin to surface, the pastor needs to relocate. If God does not open up another church, what does the pastor do? The gifts and calling of God are without repentance. If you are a God-called pastor, you need to keep preaching. You may have to become a "tentmaker" like the apostle Paul. You may have to get a secular job to feed your family, but you can still preach in prisons, nursing homes, even on the streets without pay. After all, you did not get into the ministry for money in the first place. You got into the ministry as a response to God's call.

One out of every four pastors in America will either be fired or asked to resign during his lifetime. The effect on the pastor, his family, and the church is horrible. If the church has in place a termination policy as suggested above, the agony of it is relieved a little by the severance package. Many denominations now have counseling programs for terminated pastors. Some megachurches have assistance programs for pastors who have been terminated. Appendix 2 has a list of who to call for help.

Avoiding Bitterness

It is important for the pastor to guard himself and his family against bitterness when asked to leave a church. One pastor was asked to leave a large church by a small group of members after nearly seven years during which the church had grown, a new building had been built, and many people had been won to the Lord. They had no charges to bring against him. They just thought it was "time for a change in the pulpit."

The pastor had no warning this was going to happen. The local denominational leader phoned him on a Wednesday afternoon and informed him that a motion would be brought in the quarterly business meeting that evening to declare the pulpit vacant. The pastor was shocked. The denominational leader suggested he resign before they could bring the motion. The pastor discovered who was leading the small group and phoned him to ask that he call off the group and give the pastor from three to six months to relocate. The man did call off the group but reported to them that the pastor promised to be gone in three months. He had not, but that is what was reported.

No opportunity opened up for the pastor, and at the next quarterly business meeting the motion for his dismissal was brought before the church. There were church members in attendance whom the pastor had never seen. They had not attended during the entire seven years of his ministry. The vote failed 40 percent to 60 percent. The group said they would try again to dismiss him in another three months. If they failed again, they would leave the church.

During that time the personnel committee asked for a meeting with the pastor. They indicated that they could not bear watching him hurt any longer. They were not asking him to resign or even suggesting it. They did promise that they would support him if he should stay, but they would recommend six months of full salary and benefits if he chose to resign in order to keep the church from splitting.

The pastor asked them to recommend that he be made minister at large. He would keep his study at the church during those six months that he was paid unless they called another pastor before then, in which case he would move his study to his home. The church asked during the business meeting if that was what the pastor wanted. He said it was. Naming him minister at large would protect his reputation and the reputation of the church. He was in another ministry before the six months were finished.

The same group that had tried to dismiss the first pastor made an attempt to fire the next pastor after only three years. That pastor split the church and took a large number of people with him to establish a new church. When the church called another pastor, he led them into a 2 Chronicles 7:14 revival. During a service of public confession, the church, on a Sunday morning, voted unanimously to ask the pastor whom they had first tried to fire to forgive them. He wrote back that they were forgiven long ago, but if it would help, he would say it again. Then he said that if it took the heartache he and his family went through to bring revival to the church, he would be willing to go through it again. He had avoided bitterness.

When this pastor was asked how he kept from becoming bitter, he told how he was praying all night one night before one of the business meetings. He cried out to the Lord to reveal anything that was wrong about him that was causing the trouble. The Lord said, "You are not perfect, but this isn't about something you have done." The pastor sobbed, "Lord, they are hurting Your prophet." He said that it was not an out-loud voice, but Jesus clearly said to him, "If they crucified Me, why would you be surprised if they want to crucify you?" The pastor sobbed, "But Lord, it is Your people who are doing this." Jesus answered, "Who do you think it was that crucified Me?"

The pastor said that suddenly he was filled with joy as well as peace. For the first time in his life and ministry, he had the privilege of entering into "the fellowship of His sufferings" (Phil. 3:10). It was the first time he had ever been counted worthy to suffer for Jesus. It is one thing for a pastor to suffer because he has been wrong or unwise. "But if anyone suffers as a Christian, he should not be ashamed, but should glorify God with that name" (1 Pet. 4:16). That is how this pastor kept from becoming bitter.

A Happy Leaving

The best change of churches comes when there is no reason for the pastor to leave where he is. He is happy. The church is happy. Yet somehow God in His providence has another assignment elsewhere. Leaving one church to go to another should be a hard thing to do. Read Acts 20:17–38 to see how it ought to be when a pastor and a church are separated. The Ephesian elders—all of them—wept freely and fell on Paul's neck and kissed him when he said they would see him no more. That's the way a parting should be. A pastor should not look for a call to leave the church where he is, but he should wait for a call to go to another congregation.

God calls a pastor to a church for specific tasks to match the pastor's specific gifts. I am not talking about his preaching but his leadership. Some pastors are gifted to plant churches from the beginning. This author's wife had an uncle like that. He would start a church from scratch, get it organized, get it going and growing, and then leave to start another church. We lost count of how many times he did that. The apostle Paul was like this.

Other pastors are "turn-around" pastors. They are challenged by the need to turn a declining church around. When it is turned around and growing again, God moves them on to another assignment.

Still other pastors are designed to stay with a church as it grows or until it dies. There was a church in Atlanta, Georgia, like that years ago. When the church began to decline, the deacons built a large savings account. They calculated that whichever ran out first—the aging pastor or the money—this would tell them when to disband the church. As it turned out, the pastor ran out of energy first at seventy-eight years of age. The church sold its building, gave some of the money to the retiring pastor and the rest to their denomination's mission fund. Had the church called a "turn-around" pastor, he probably would have led them to relocate and reach a new community for Christ.

Some pastors are challengers. They push the people to do better for Christ. When such a pastor reaches the point where his people cannot or will not be pushed any further, he usually goes to another church. It is the unusual pastor who can adjust his leadership style to meet a church's changing needs. When that kind of pastor is found, he usually has a long pastorate with a church that grows and grows and grows.

Pastor, stay at your church if you can. Leave if you must. Follow the Word of God and the will of God for your life and for the church. Remember that the call is for a lifetime, but the assignment may change. Most pastors should probably stay a longer time rather than a shorter time at a particular church. Love the church as much as Jesus loved it, and it is likely you will stay a long, long time.

TESTIMONY:
The Pastor
and His Denomination

John Sullivan
Executive Director, Florida Baptist Convention

My life and ministry are products of my denomination. I was saved, baptized, and called to preach in a church started with denominational assistance. The Arizona Baptist Convention largely paid for my education for four years when I attended Grand Canyon College. I received at Southwestern Baptist Theological Seminary a quality seminary education, subsidized by the Southern Baptist Convention. I have great reason to love my denomination.

Within the denomination are vital organizations: the church, the association, the state convention, and the national convention. Local Southern Baptist churches voluntarily relate to all and maintain control over all. There is no connectionalism. The SBC is not made up of state conventions. State conventions are not made up of associations. All three levels of cooperation are composed of and controlled by the local churches.

In 1925 Southern Baptists established the Cooperative Program, a giving program that embraces Southern Baptist missions, evangelism, and education on state, national, and international levels. The Cooperative Program makes it possible to take all of the gospel, to all of the world, all of the time, at the same time.

Pastors must love the church that Christ loves and for which Christ died. We should also love the denomination that allows us freedom to be as missionary as we desire and to be educated in schools that offer the finest education for doing the work to which God has called us.

CHAPTER 19 The Pastor and His Denomination

U nless a pastor serves a nondenominational church, he needs to relate to his denomination. If he is in a denomination that assigns pastors to churches, this is an obvious statement. However, even in a free church denomination, such as Baptist, he needs to relate to his denomination. In fact, in a free church denomination it is extremely important that he relate to his denomination.

The Origin of Denominations

In the history of Christianity there were no denominations before 1054 when the Greek Orthodox Church split off from the Roman Catholic Church. Ecclesiology in the patristic era, AD 100–451, shows that there was a consensus among all Christians that the church was one. The Latin word for such a church is *catholic*, which means literally "universal." There was a hierarchy, but it was regional, usually headed by a bishop, an *episcopos* in the Greek New Testament. Not until AD 325 did the bishops assemble in what is known as the first ecumenical church council.

In the late 300s, an African presbyter or elder by the name of Donatus threatened to split the African church from the Roman Church. Augustine devoted a decade of his life trying to keep the church from splitting over what to do with bishops who willingly had handed over their Bibles and books to be burned in the last Roman persecution. When the persecution ended, Donatus did not want to let these bishops back into the church, let alone into leadership.

Augustine appealed to Simon Peter's denial of Christ (see John

18:15–27) and his subsequent repentance and restoration, along with the parable of the wheat and the weeds, where Jesus said to let them (the wheat and the weeds) grow together until the harvest at the end of time. Then God would separate the wheat from the weeds (see Matt. 13:24–30). Up until this time *catholic* meant only "universal." Augustine began to talk about Catholics and Donatists, lining out Catholics as a denomination, although it was the only denomination at that time.[1]

In these early Christian centuries, theology was being done in two different languages in several different geographical areas. In a broad sense, the division between the use of Greek and Latin was between the Eastern Church and the Western Church.

Theology was first done in Antioch, Syria, and it was done in Greek, the language of the New Testament. That center of Christian theology then moved in the fourth century to Capadocia, a Roman province in Asia Minor. Ultimately, the patriarch of Constantinople, present-day Istanbul, became the head of the Eastern Church, the Greek Orthodox Church. He still is today.

A second center of theological debate was in Alexandria, Egypt. Originally, Alexandrian theology was done in Greek, but it soon changed over to Latin, although Alexandria was in the East and not in the West.

The third center of theological debate was in Carthage in northwest Africa. Latin was the language used from the beginning. It was in this area that scholars such as Augustine were located. In time, Alexandrian Latin theology merged with that of Carthage. The center of Western Christianity soon moved to Rome, Italy. Even in early Christian times the bishop of Rome was the titular head of the Western Church. From the fifth to the eleventh centuries the two leaders, of equal importance, were the bishop of Rome and the patriarch of Constantinople.

Beginning around the ninth century the Western Church wanted to insert a word into the Nicene Creed that would give a slightly different belief to the doctrine of the Holy Spirit than was stated in the creed and believed by the Eastern Church. Patriarchs of Constantinople for nearly two hundred years corresponded with their counterparts, the bishops of Rome, begging them not to write the change into the creed. In 1054, Rome did exactly that. Then the Roman bishop sent a legate to Constantinople to excommunicate the patriarch from the Roman Catholic Church, who promptly excommunicated the legate and the Roman bishop from the Eastern Orthodox Church. Thus, in 1054, the first separate denominations arose: the Roman Catholic Church and the Greek Orthodox Church.

For nearly five hundred years these were essentially the only two Christian denominations. Then in 1517, Martin Luther nailed his Ninety-Five Theses to the church door in Wittenberg, Germany, and began the Lutheran Reformation. About the same time, reform was coming to the Roman Catholic Church in Switzerland as well. Ulrich Zwingli in Zurich and later John Calvin in Geneva led the Swiss Reformation. Luther never intended to separate his church from Rome, but Rome excommunicated him and would have killed him had not the German princes intervened.

Not knowing what to call these Lutherans, Rome first labeled them evangelicals, literally "gospelizers." Later, when fourteen German princes issued an official protest about how the churches in Germany were being treated, they were called Protestants. In Switzerland they were called The Reformed. Out of the Swiss Reformation came the Anabaptists and other free churches.

Since the sixteenth century, there have been Roman Catholic, Greek Orthodox, Protestant, Reformed, and Anabaptist churches. Other free church denominations such as the Mennonites, the Brethren, and the Quakers sprang up in Europe. In 1534, Henry VIII of England separated the Anglicans from Rome. Under the Puritans the Anglican Church became clearly Protestant. Some of the Puritans separated from the Anglican Church and formed dissenting groups such as the Congregationalists. From Scotland and John Knox came the Presbyterians.

The early English Congregationalists, Baptists, Anglicans, and Presbyterians migrated to America in the seventeenth century. Under John Wesley in the eighteenth century, the Methodists came into being in England and America. Baptists, Methodists, Presbyterians, Episcopalians, and Lutherans split into several different denominations in the nineteenth and twentieth centuries. Denominations are a reality to be reckoned with.

Denominational Identification

Most pastors will have to identify with a specific denomination. Some denominations still require pastors to receive a minimum of denominational education, although that has declined in recent years. In free churches that call their own pastors, denominational education is no longer a prerequisite. This presents a problem.

A pastor needs to understand the denomination with which his church is identified. For that reason, it would be advisable for a pastor to receive some education in a denominational seminary. Some churches require this. If it is not a written requirement, it is an unwritten understanding on the part of the congregation that the pastor they are considering is fully committed to the denomination to which their church belongs.

It is wrong for a pastor without a denominational loyalty to become pastor of a denominational church and then move that church out of the denomination. This is true both doctrinally and practically. If a pastor's theology changes to the point where he is outside of the parameters of belief of his denomination, he should have the integrity to resign his church. It is tantamount to "stealing" a church to take it out of a denomination. It is certainly unethical.

Denominationalism occurs on three levels: local (often called the association), regional (often called the state convention), and national. When denominations on any level depart from the historic belief of the denomination, a serious problem occurs. Rather than pull out of a denomination, it is better for the pastor to find a way to function within the denomination. Baptists, Methodists, and Presbyterians, among others, have formed new national denominations that adhere to the traditional belief of their denominations when their denominations departed from traditional belief. New associations have been formed. Even new state conventions have been formed. And, of course, new national conventions have been formed.

Such a split is not pleasant, but it is sometimes preferable to leaving a troubled denomination altogether. The problem with this approach is that it leaves the old denominational entity in the hands of those who are not consistent in their beliefs with the historic beliefs of that denomination.

J. Frank Norris, pastor of the First Baptist Church of Fort Worth, Texas, left (some would say he was forced to leave) the Tarrant Baptist Association, the Baptist General Convention of Texas, and the Southern Baptist Convention to form the Bible Baptist Fellowship in the first part of the twentieth century. When Norris was an old man, a Southern Baptist pastor's mother and father died within a week of each other. Norris had his chauffeur drive him out to the Southern Baptist pastor's home to express his condolences. He was too weak to go in, so the Southern Baptist pastor came out and sat with Norris in his car. At the end of the meeting Norris called the man by name and said, "Don't leave the convention. When I left I lost my influence. Stay in it and try to change it from the inside."

That is good advice. Twenty-five years later, the conservative movement within the Southern Baptist Convention, which had begun to drift to the left theologically, brought their denomination back to where it had been historically. It took twenty-five years to make all the necessary changes, but they have been made because pastors chose to stay and reform their denomination from the inside.[2] An interesting development occurred when the historic First Baptist Church of Fort Worth in recent years reunited with the Southern Baptist Convention because the Convention had returned to its original conservative Christian beliefs.

Supporting Your Denomination

A pastor should support his denomination on all three levels. Locally, he should attend the meetings of his association. The association is the oldest organization of Baptist churches. It began in England, and it was called an association because of Cromwell's New Model Army. Cromwell enlisted soldiers for his army by establishing what he called associations, established in the various burroughs or counties. The Baptists followed the same nomenclature and geography. When English Baptists migrated to America, they established associations long before they established either state or national conventions.

A pastor should support the regional or state convention. He should also support his national denominational convention. In Southern Baptist churches, the pastor should ask the church to budget for sending him and his wife to all three annual meetings of these organizations. Through the support of their denomination at all three levels, pastors ensure that the denomination will remain anchored to its historic beliefs. Since the pastors and staff members are the only people in their churches who are trained theologically, they are responsible for assuring that their denomination's colleges and seminaries remain doctrinally sound.

A pastor's denomination will provide him with continuing education, publications, and guidance in many different ways. Most denominations are involved in helping place pastors and other church staff members in churches. Most denominations have counseling services for pastors, their wives, and their churches for those situations when conflict arises. Most denominations have health insurance and retirement programs available to churches, pastors, and staff members. Churches can be led to provide for the denominational retirement program for pastor and staff in the church budget.

Leadership conferences, family conferences, Bible study conferences, and a variety of training conferences for pastors, staff members, and lay leadership are also available. A wise church will budget for its pastor and staff to attend some of these events every year. The wise pastor will ask for the church to make provision for him to attend these events.

A Wider Fellowship

With the emergence of Billy Graham as the leader of what came to be known as "evangelicals," a wider fellowship beyond a specific denomination was made possible. It was Billy Graham who separated what is now known as Evangelicalism from Fundamentalism. Bob Jones Sr. and John R. Rice criticized Graham for allowing a liberal Methodist pastor to lead the invocation in his crusade in Greenville, South Carolina, in the 1940s, and they boycotted his crusades.

About that time Billy Graham began a theological journal that he called *Christianity Today*. Originally it was designed to look like and compete with the liberal *Christian Century*, the leading liberal Protestant theological magazine. Carl F. H. Henry was the first editor of *Christianity Today*. He also became one of the first and most important evangelical theological writers. About the same time Harold Ockenga, pastor of Park Street Congregational Church in Boston, Massachusetts, coined the term "neo-evangelical" to describe evangelicals in contrast to the narrow-minded and mean-spirited fundamentalists, although their doctrines were not that much different. The primary difference between the two groups is in their approach to biblical education.

The fundamentalists did not want any critical study of the Bible. The evangelicals recognized the value of lower criticism in contrast to the liberal higher criticism. The latter treated the Bible as if it were only a human book. The former asked legitimate questions dealing with authorship, dating, recipients, and background of the various biblical books. Evangelicals were also open to serious theological dialogue with those who held other viewpoints. The fundamentalists were not. Harold Ockenga and Charles Fuller united to form a new evangelical seminary, Fuller Theological Seminary, in Pasadena, California.

Billy Graham gave evangelicals within various denominations the opportunity to come together in large crusades for the purpose of reaching their cities for Christ. He gave them a magazine. His support of various conservative, Christian, interdenominational colleges; his worldwide radio and television broadcasts; his Christian movies; and his news magazine—all of these brought evangelicals out of their denominations into a wider evangelical fellowship. National organizations such as the National Evangelical Alliance, the Council of Christian Colleges and Universities, the Evangelical Council on Financial Accountability, and the National Religious Broadcasters, along with international organizations such as the Evangelical Theological Society, have created support for a continuing wider fellowship for evangelicals.

Add to this many national and international agencies such as those of James Dobson and Pat Robertson, along with pastors of megachurches, and the tie that binds evangelicals together becomes wider and stronger. Some people have even suggested that we now live in a postdenominational era. But some denominational distinctives are important enough to maintain even within the wider evangelical community.

Unfortunately, many pastors seem to be losing their loyalty to their denomination. This author encourages denominational loyalty. We can do more for Christ together than we can do separately, particularly in missions. Few churches would be able to support even one missionary family. But together churches within a denomination can support thousands. The wise pastor will educate his church in his denomination's missionary program. Most denominational mission boards will provide missionaries as speakers for local churches, even for small churches. If a missionary in person is not available, video presentations are a good stand-in. With the expanding use of the Internet, pastors can link their churches with overseas missionaries who can provide up-to-date prayer requests and praise items to the congregation on a weekly basis.

Denominational colleges and seminaries will provide speakers and singing groups to their member churches. Denominational agencies are glad to send churches printed materials and other resources to explain and promote their work on behalf of the denomination.

TESTIMONY:

The Pastor
and His Retirement

Jerry Vines
Former Pastor of the First Baptist Church
Jacksonville, Florida

"You are out of the will of God retiring. Nowhere in the Bible does it give a preacher the right to retire." That's what one brother wrote me upon my announcement that I was retiring as pastor of the First Baptist Church of Jacksonville, Florida. I don't think the brother read the entire announcement about my retirement. I thought I had made it clear that I was not retiring from the ministry; I was just moving to a new phase of the ministry to which God was calling me.

It is important for the pastor to retire in such a way that his church will be benefited, his successor will be helped, and the cause of Christ will be extended. I have felt for some time that it is far better for a pastor to retire from his church at a time when it can accomplish those ends. Far better for the people to be saying, "Why did he?" rather than "Why doesn't he?" Be your successor's best friend and your former church's greatest prayer warrior.

The retiring pastor needs to be sure that his final months are productive. I would urge the retiring pastor to have a carefully planned schedule of study. He needs to keep his preaching fresh and up-to-date. Work on staying as physically fit as possible. Try to be a mentor and friend to younger pastors. Go to glory in a blaze of glory!

The Pastor and His Retirement

Perhaps no subject is more controversial among pastors and congregations than a pastor's retirement. A familiar theme heard in pulpits across America—especially in churches where there is a growing number of older people—is, "Retirement is not a word that is found in the Bible." This is usually said to keep older adults active in the church, but it may convey a subliminal message that a pastor does not want to retire, especially if he is serving a large, prominent church.

Many pastors fear retirement, and they hold on to their last church too long. Pastors who stay too long at a church will tear down what they worked so hard to build up. The church will decline and the average age of the congregation will rise. It is not what happens when a pastor retires that should concern him but what will happen to the church if he stays too long. That certainly is not finishing well.

What Retirement Means

Contrary to what many people think, the word *retire* as well as the concept of retirement for ministers is found in some of the newer translations of the Bible. The Holman Christian Standard Bible translates Numbers 8:23–25 like this: "The LORD spoke to Moses: 'In regard to the Levites: From 25 years old or more, a man enters the service in the work at the tent of meeting. But at 50 years of age he is to *retire* [italics added] from his service in the work and no longer serve. He may assist his brothers to fulfill responsibilities at the tent of meeting, but he must not do the work. This is how you are to deal with the Levites regarding their duties.'"

One could argue that people live longer today than they did in Old Testament times, but you will lose that argument quickly when you examine Moses' age at death (120). One could argue that Moses did not retire at fifty and he was of the tribe of Levi. He did not even begin his ministry until he was eighty years old. Why then these instructions from the Lord to the Levites?

There are two principles revealed in these verses. First, the nature of the service of Levites was to change at fifty. No longer was the priest required to do the hard work (killing and dressing the animals). The principle was that he was to turn over the more difficult tasks to the younger men. The exact age was given to the Levites. This principle may be applied in modern terms. The ministry should not be getting older but younger. When a pastor turns fifty, he should try to surround himself with younger men on his staff. If he is a secure person, he can even share the preaching responsibilities.

This biblical principle will actually work at any age. When this author was in his late thirties, he hired a youth director who was in his midtwenties. He was not only excellent with young people, but he was also a very good, evangelistic preacher. After about a year, I asked him to start preaching on Sunday evenings. I was more of a teaching preacher. He was more of an evangelist.

Sunday evening attendance increased, and many young people came to Christ on Sunday evenings. Instead of feeling jealous, I believe God gave me a sense of vicarious satisfaction. After all, I had found this young man, I had hired him, and I had asked him to preach on Sunday evenings. When I listened to his preaching each week and then stood at the front of the church during the invitation to receive those who came forward to accept Christ and join the church, I felt as if I had done this myself.

One of the deacons said to me, "Pastor, thank you for being secure enough to let him preach every Sunday evening. With your deep Bible preaching on Sunday morning and his evangelistic fervor on Sunday evenings, it is like a double-barreled gospel shotgun!" Pastor, surround yourself with younger staff members. It will keep you and the church young. Someone once said that if you want to stay young, stay around young people. (If you want to die young, try to keep up with them!)

Mentoring younger staff members is a great privilege. They are a lot of fun. As they mature, many of them will become pastors of their own churches and you will remain their mentor for decades. If you can keep your eyes on the kingdom of God and not just on your particular church, what a wonderful life! Someone has said that there is no limit to what a person can accomplish in the kingdom of God if he doesn't care who gets the credit.

What Does a Retired Pastor Do?

A further principle found in the Levitical retirement is that a minister does not leave the ministry, just the more difficult aspects of it. When a pastor retires, he is not retiring from the ministry but only from his ministry at a particular church. There are many opportunities for a retired pastor to continue in the ministry.

One widening opportunity is what is called an "intentional interim." Many denominations, such as the Southern Baptist Convention, have training programs for intentional interim pastors. Usually they involve contracts not longer than two years. They usually require three days a week plus Sundays. If the church is not near the retired pastor's home, the church may furnish a parsonage or apartment. Small to medium-sized churches are encouraged to pay the interim the full salary they have budgeted for the position, if he gives them five days a week. If he gives three, the salary should be two-thirds of the budgeted amount. If he gives only weekends, he should be paid one-third of the budgeted amount.

Many foreign mission boards now have two-year appointments for retired pastors to serve English-speaking churches abroad. Home mission boards are constantly looking for retired pastors to move to a pioneer area and plant a church, turning it over to a younger man after two years. Many larger churches look for retired pastors to do pastoral care or to become senior adult directors.

How to Retire

If a pastor is in a large church, he should inform the church six months to a year in advance of his retirement plans. By law, a man cannot be forced to retire from any job, but the pastor's position is more than a job. And he is not retiring from the ministry, only from a particular church. He may want to consider it a career change within a given field of work. A year's notice will allow the church time to organize for his replacement.

It is essential that the retiring pastor not be involved in selecting his replacement. But he can lead the church, according to its bylaws, to select a pastor search committee to start looking for God's new man for the church. The First Baptist Church of Jacksonville, Florida, the third largest Southern Baptist church in the nation, was given six months' notice of his retirement by Jerry Vines, its pastor of twenty-four years. They were able to call a new pastor, Mac Brunson, within a month after Jerry Vines retired.

As a rule, the retiring pastor should move his membership to another church, even if the church from which he retires asks him to stay. He may want to be helpful, but more often he becomes a problem to the incoming pastor. There are exceptions to this rule, but they should be very rare.

The author of this chapter followed a pastor who retired after more than forty-two years as pastor of the same church. The church gave him the parsonage and made him pastor emeritus. He stayed a member of the church until he died. He told the new pastor that watching someone else pastor the church was like watching someone else live with his wife and not being able to do anything about it. This former pastor as well as the church would have been better off if he had moved to another church.

As a member of another church, the retired pastor should never serve as a deacon but should serve as a "fellow elder" to his new pastor, whom he should love, support, and advise only when asked for advice. A retired pastor should view himself as having moved off the playing field into the stands. He should be the most consistent encourager of his new pastor. He should never allow any church member to pull out of him anything but praise for his replacement.

Preparing for Retirement Financially

When should a pastor begin preparing for retirement financially? The answer is, as soon as he begins his ministry as a pastor in his very first church. Social Security is a federal retirement program almost all wage earners are forced into.[1] Prior to 1935, there was no Social Security. Families and churches took care of their aging members. When Social Security was established, the retirement age was set at sixty-five. In 1935, very few people lived that long. The average lifespan was in the fifties. Today the average lifespan is in the seventies, but the retirement age is still sixty-five, although it is in the process of being raised to sixty-seven.

Because people are living longer, the great challenge to our federal government is how to "fix" Social Security. At the present rate of payment to retirees, the fund will be depleted in twenty years or so. Many men under forty years of age are preparing their own retirement investment programs, not depending on Social Security alone.

As denominations began to establish pension funds for ministers and church staff members, they did so because some retired pastors had no children to care for them when they were no longer able to work. Insurance actuaries tell us that ministers and Supreme Court justices have a longer average lifespan than any other group. The Southern Baptist Convention began what was first called the Southern Baptist Relief and Annuity Board[2] in 1914, before Social Security was established. The goal was for churches to establish a retirement fund into which they would deposit regularly an amount equal to 10 percent of the minister's salary. Upon retirement, he would have a pension to take care of him and his family.

Every denominational pension board publishes materials that pastors can pass on to their churches to show them how to set up this much-needed benefit. If a young pastor asks his first church to provide this benefit, he can also do the same with other churches to which he may move.

Some denominations will add a minimal amount to a minister's retirement fund with their pension board if the local church is doing so as well. The funds should be fully vested in the minister's name from the beginning. If a pastor's first church refuses to pay into a retirement fund, he should set up his own account with his pension board and use at least 10 percent of his pre-taxed salary to fund the account.

If a retiring pastor has both a pension fund and Social Security upon which to draw at sixty-five, his retirement income is likely to be about the same or even more than the salary at his last church. Denominational pension boards issue charts to show a pastor how much he needs to deposit in order to keep his annual pension in retirement growing to overcome annual inflation expected in his retirement years. The key to financial preparation for retirement is to begin early.

Finishing Well

One of the dangers a pastor in his sixties must guard against is retiring psychologically when he turns sixty. Some pastors become fearful of upsetting anyone this late in their careers. They just want to hold on. They stop leading and start following. This is disastrous for the church. It subjects the church to power struggles within the congregation, and it renders the church incapable of obedience. The Bible commands churches to follow their spiritual leaders (Heb. 13:17). The pastor must continue to lead, or the church will become disobedient and unruly.

There is a pastor in Mobile, Alabama, who has served the same church for almost fifty years. He was in his seventies when some of the younger men in the church asked him to lead the church to relocate. It was in a dying community. He had faced the need to relocate twenty years before, but he thought he was too old then and many widows who lived near the church begged him not to move the church. He decided he would let the next pastor deal with the problem. But the next pastor never came. He was still the pastor of the church twenty years later. Now the church was declining and the need to face the question of relocating had come up with the new generation. Most of the members had long since moved to new areas of the city. Most of the widows who did not want the church to move had died.

As this pastor shared his problem with this author, I urged him to lead the church to relocate. Because of his long tenure and the love of the people for him, the church would follow his leadership. They did. The church is now growing again rather than declining. How did this pastor "keep on keeping on" into his seventies and still lead the church? He did not retire psychologically, as many older pastors do. He continued to work and lead.

My grandfather died when my father was just thirteen years old, so I did not know him. But my father taught me something my grandfather had taught him. I taught it to my two sons as they were growing up, and all three of us practice it to this day. My grandfather said a simple but profound thing: "When you work for someone else, pitch a full shovel with a little on the handle." In other words, *work*. As you get older, don't just work harder; work smarter. But above all, work—pitch a full shovel with a little on the handle.

Remember, you work for the Lord. The church may pay your salary and you do have a responsibility to the congregation. But God is the one who employed you in the first place when He called you to preach. Paul said it well in Colossians 3:17, "And whatever you do, in word or in deed, do everything in the name of the Lord Jesus." When you think that no one appreciates or even knows about all the hard work you do as a pastor, just remember that God knows and He keeps careful records.

As you near retirement, a good verse to memorize is Hebrews 6:10: "For God is not unjust; He will not forget your work and the love you showed for His name when you served the saints." The One who needs to know, knows—and He does not forget. Keep on keeping on!

TESTIMONY:
The Pastor and His Reward

W. A. Criswell (1908–2001)
Former Pastor of the First Baptist Church,
Dallas, Texas

Late one afternoon, I entered that great sanctuary of First Baptist Church of Dallas. No one sat in the twenty-seven hundred seats nor stood against the walls or in the hallways. Even the choir loft was empty. The organ was silent, and the instruments of the orchestra were all locked away. The television cameras and microphones were covered. The red glow of a Texas sunset illuminated the auditorium in pale pink light as I sat in the front row looking up at the great carved pulpit that had been my home these many years.

How long, Lord, I wondered silently, *before I open my Bible and preach the Word in this great place for the very last time?*

God was silent, but He was there, for I could feel His loving, sympathetic presence.

"Lord," I whispered, "You know that dying holds no fear for me. To rush from this world into Your open arms will be a moment of triumph and praise. But, dearest Father," I continued, "there are times when I wonder if all of heaven could hold the joy that preaching Your Word has brought to me. Is there anything in eternity, Lord, that even compares to kneeling beside someone at this mourner's bench who is finding forgiveness for sin and accepting Jesus as Lord and Savior?"

As I sat alone in the quiet sanctuary, God answered my question. There is only one joy greater than preaching or teaching the Word, and that joy is this: One day soon we will see the Author of the Word face to face. God Himself will hold us in His arms and take us home. In the meantime, all He asks of us is that we go on loving the Word and sharing it in our own ways, that we remain faithful to the Word, that we win the lost to Christ. And when our trials come, when we feel pain and suffering, when our tears flow again, it is our joy and comfort to lift our faces heavenward and to go on standing on the promises of God.[1]

CHAPTER 21 The Pastor and His Reward

E very pastor thinks about appearing some day in heaven and giving an account as an undershepherd to the Great Shepherd of the sheep, the Lord Jesus Christ. There is much in the Bible about giving an account some day. Pastors who turn to Hebrews 13 as they call on their people to follow their leadership mention that some day pastors will have to give an account of how their members have done on earth. "Obey your leaders and submit to them, for they keep watch over your souls as those who will give an account, so that they can do this with joy and not with grief, for that would be unprofitable for you" (Heb. 13:17).

This verse is an admonition to church members to follow the spiritual leadership of their pastors. However, hidden like a land mine in this verse is an admonition to the pastor himself. He will have to give an account to the Chief Shepherd of his work as an undershepherd. That is an awesome thought.

The word *pastor* appears only once in the English New Testament (Eph. 4:11), where the favorite word for the office of pastor is "elder."[2] But the elders are told to shepherd or pastor the flock of God (1 Pet. 5:2). At the judgment seat of Christ every Christian will "be repaid for what he has done in the body, whether good or bad" (2 Cor. 5:10). This is not a judgment of eternal destiny. That is decided when a person gives his heart to Christ in salvation. This is a judgment of rewards, or the lack of them.

This is both good news and bad news for a pastor. The good news is that Jesus will compliment and even reward the pastor for all the good things he has done. This author's wife often says, "You do so many things that nobody ever knows about." My reply is always, "The One who needs to know does know about them." Ultimately, what every pastor wants is for Jesus to say, "Well done" (Matt. 25:21). That's the good news.

The bad news is that at that same judgment seat of Christ, they may see a frown instead of a smile on the face of Jesus. This is what Paul talks about in 2 Corinthians 5:11 when he refers to the "fear of the Lord." In his first Corinthian letter (1 Cor. 3:10–14), Paul speaks of God giving us a foundation of faith in Christ Himself upon which we build our lives and ministries. Some pastors build with gold, silver, and precious stones. The fire of God's personal presence will purify their works. Others build with wood, hay, and stubble. Their works will burn up before their eyes. That's the bad news.

While the word *pastor* appears only once in the English New Testament, it does appear in the King James Version of the Old Testament, particularly in the book of Jeremiah. Jeremiah 10:21 is one of the most convicting verses in the Bible for a pastor. In the King James Version it is translated, "The pastors are become *brutish*" (italics added). In the New King James Version the last word is translated "dull-hearted." In the Holman Christian Standard Bible it is translated "stupid." Sometimes pastors remark humorously about how stupid sheep are, but this verse is about stupid pastors.

The Hebrew word comes from a prime root, *ba-ar*, which means literally "to consume" as by fire or by eating. It can also mean "to burn" and more specifically "to be kindled by self-combustion." The burning bush that caught Moses' attention did not burn out. It kept on burning. Sometimes the fire in pastors seems to burn out. Even the lost world understands the word "burnout." If a pastor burns out, his future reward is in jeopardy.

Regardless of the translation, the cause and the result are given clearly: "For the shepherds . . . have not sought the LORD; therefore they shall not prosper, and all their flocks shall be scattered" (Jer. 10:21 NKJV). How does a pastor avoid brutishness, dull-heartedness, or burnout in the pulpit? Recognize the symptoms and do something about them.

Passion for God

God says in Jeremiah 10:21, "they don't seek the Lord." In early days American pulpits were on fire for God. Most of us have either read or heard the words attributed to Alexis de Tocqueville quoted in a previous chapter. The famous French historian said this about his visit to discover America's greatness: "I visited America's factories seeking the secret of her greatness. I walked through the halls of her great universities. I frequented the business houses on Wall Street and sat solemnly in her houses of Congress. But it wasn't until I visited her churches and saw their pulpits aflame with truth that I discovered the secret of America's greatness."[3]

Are America's pulpits still aflame with truth today? Pastor, are you still on fire for God? Do your messages move you, let alone those who hear you? Do you pray? Do you have a family altar? Are you leading a godly life? Are you separated unto the Lord? Do you practice the presence of God? Do you have a reverence for and fear of the Lord? Are you witnessing and winning souls to Christ?

The pulpit that is on fire is still the most powerful platform in America and the world if the pastor fears no one but God, hates nothing but sin, and stays aflame for Jesus without being consumed. "But those who trust in the Lord will renew their strength; they will soar on wings like eagles; they will run and not grow weary; they will walk and not faint" (Isa. 40:31). The church and the world need pastors who will go to the pulpit from their knees, who will seek the Lord for themselves first, and then challenge others to seek Him. Pastor, don't lose your passion for God.

Passion for God's Word

If a pastor puts everything else first and studies in his spare time, he is in danger of burnout, dullness of heart, and brutishness. Matthew 6:33 needs to be applied by every pastor to his study of the Word of God: "But seek first the kingdom of God and His righteousness, and all these things will be provided for you." Many pastors fall into the trap of studying the Bible only homiletically and rarely devotionally.

Every pastor should be on a program of daily Bible reading that will take him through the Bible every year. A pastor found an old Bible in a used bookstore. When he opened it he realized that a bookworm had eaten its way through the entire Bible. Every pastor should be like that bookworm, devouring the Word of God.

Harry Ironside was pastor of the Moody Church in Chicago. He became one of the great expositors of the Word of God in the twentieth century. He tells of taking the train from Chicago to see his widowed mother in California. When he got to his mother's house overlooking the Pacific Ocean, he saw a tent on the back of her property. She had permitted an old Welch preacher, who was dying of what people called "consumption" in those days, to put up his tent by the sea. The climate helped his consumption. Wanting to meet the old preacher and to make sure he was harmless, Ironside went out to the old man's tent.

The old preacher was sitting on a log by a campfire. He said to Ironside, "I understand you are going to make a preacher." Ironside laughed. After all, he was pastor of one of the elite pulpits in the world. "Sit down beside me, and let me share with you some of the things God has taught me," the old man told Ironside. He took his Bible and for over an hour shared some of the most beautiful and powerful truths from the Scripture Ironside had ever heard.

When the old man ran out of breath and stopped, Ironside asked him where he got those wonderful truths. Where did he go to school? What books did he read? The old man replied, "Nay, but on a sod floor in Wales, kneeling before an open Bible God taught me these things."[4] Pastor, never lose your passion for God's Word.

Passion for the Lost

Psalm 126:6 contains this promise: "He who continually goes forth weeping, bearing seed for sowing, shall doubtless come again with rejoicing, bringing his sheaves with him" (NKJV). When this author was a young pastor attending the Southern Baptist Convention each summer, he heard Baker James Cauthen, for many years president of the Southern Baptist Foreign Mission Board.[5] Each year he warned the Convention that if we did not do what God wanted us to do in reaching the lost for Christ, God would raise up another group of His people to reach them. The same is true of an individual church and of a pastor. God will not fail to reach those who are ready to believe in Him. Every pastor should be on fire for souls. He may not have the gift of an evangelist (see Eph. 4:11), but he is commanded to do the work of an evangelist (see 2 Tim. 4:5).

When this author graduated from Wheaton College, he and a friend covenanted to pray together for each to be a daily witness and try to win to Christ one soul each day for the next year. As an assistant pastor for that year between college and seminary, I discovered that a pastor can do a lot of church work and not do the Lord's work. I fell behind on my evangelism. I became so discouraged that I quit counting. I recorded in a diary the results of my preaching, but I wanted to lead someone personally to Christ each day. At the end of the year, I added up those who had been won both personally and through my preaching. To my great amazement, God had given me 365 decisions for Christ that year. Would to God I had prayed that prayer every year! Pastor, do not lose your passion for the lost.

Who Pastors Are

The Hebrew word *baw'ar* is translated either "shepherd" or "pastor." The latter translation comes directly from the Latin and French translations of the word. When the Hebrew Old Testament was translated into Greek about 280 BC, the Greek word *poimen* was used. It is translated in our English Bibles as "shepherd." It is the title assigned to the preacher in an evangelical church. After His resurrection Jesus three times asked Simon Peter, "Simon, son of Jonah, do you love Me?" Peter answered, "Yes . . . I love You." Jesus then said, "Feed My lambs . . . tend My sheep . . . feed My sheep" (John 21:15–17 NKJV).

Above everything else, a pastor is a shepherd. God issues a stern warning to all of us who are pastors, "Woe to the shepherds [the pastors] who destroy and scatter the sheep of My pasture" (Jer. 23:1 NKJV). He goes on to say in verse 9 that His heart is broken because of His prophets. They have been telling people their dreams and their thoughts instead of feeding them the Word of God. The pastor's chief job is feeding the sheep. But a pastor is also a prophet of God. If a pastor loses his passion for the Lord and God's Word, he will inevitably feed God's sheep straw instead of grain.

The Holman Christian Standard Bible is graphic in its translation of Jeremiah 23. "What is straw compared to grain? . . . Is not My word like fire . . . and like a sledgehammer that pulverizes rock?" (Jer. 23:28–29). Then God lodges a charge against His prophets who are not seeking Him and waiting upon His Word. They become pulpit plagiarizers. "Therefore, take note! I am against the prophets . . . who steal My words from each other" (Jer. 23:30). Pastor, maintain such a passion for God and His Word that you dig out your own sermons from the Bible. Do not take another man's sermons and preach them. God hates that and will let you know on the day of judgment how much He hates it. A pastor is a prophet of God who loves God and seeks the Lord for himself, waits upon God's Word, and then faithfully delivers it to others.

The WD Award

God's reward for faithful pastors is spoken of in several ways in the Bible. In 2 Timothy 4:8 Paul speaks of it as a "crown of righteousness." It is spoken of as if God had already fashioned the crown and put Paul's name on it. Yet Paul would not receive it until he completed his ministry on earth. Is it possible for a pastor to lose his crown that already has been prepared for him? How do you keep your name on God's crown of righteousness? Paul says there are only three rules to keep, three things to do, three disciplines to cultivate as a pastor.

Fight the Good Fight

Being a pastor is hard work. You will not serve without opposition. You have to stay in shape. There is a battle to be won. There is a battle with one's own flesh. What pastor has not read Paul's desperation in Romans 7 and cried out, "I understand"? Who among us has not had to struggle with carnality? How often have we done things we don't want to do and not done things we ought to do? Pastors can be "wretched men" just as Paul said he was in Romans 7.

There is a battle with the world. How long has it been since you dared to preach a message on worldliness? Is it because you are worldly?

None of us likes to live in a fishbowl, but the truth is that the pastor is held to higher moral standards than other church members. This issue was addressed in chapter 16 on the pastor and his ethics. One of the oldest pastors who ever lived counsels us, "Do not love the world or the things in the world. If anyone loves the world, the love of the Father is not in him" (1 John 2:15 NKJV).

There is a battle with the devil. If you are not under attack from the devil, you should look carefully at your life as a pastor to make sure you are doing what God called you to do. If a pastor is pleasing God, the devil will attack him, his family, and his church. Pastors need to recognize spiritual attacks and know how to wage spiritual warfare. Ephesians 6:10–18 should be a memory requirement for every pastor. "Do you have those six pieces of spiritual armor plus the secret weapon?"[6] Do you know how to put on the whole armor of God and how to wage spiritual warfare?

Finish the Race

Too many pastors do not finish the race. Some have a great start, a mediocre middle, and they fail to finish. A pastor is a steward of the grace of God. Paul tells us the number one qualification of a steward: "Moreover it is required in stewards that one be found faithful" (1 Cor. 4:2 NKJV). Seeing an old pastor who is still preaching is like seeing an old couple who have been married to each other for fifty years. When a couple in the church celebrates fifty years of marriage, this in itself is like fifty sermons on the permanence of marriage. When a pastor stays with it through thick and thin, one can almost hear Jesus saying, "Well done, good and faithful servant." That's the WD Award—"well done." Pastor, don't give up. Finish the race.

When the young W. A. Criswell became pastor of the First Baptist Church of Dallas, Texas, in 1944, an old pastor in the city by the name of Wallace Bassett took the young pastor to lunch. Bassett was pastor of Cliff Temple Baptist Church in Dallas for forty-eight years. He asked Criswell about his conversion experience.

Criswell told him that when he was ten years old, his home church in west Texas had a two-week revival, then known as a "protracted meeting." The evangelist stayed at the Criswell home. Each evening, after the service, the evangelist would sit down in the kitchen for a glass of buttermilk. Young W. A. would pull his chair up beside the evangelist and listen to him talk about Jesus. On the second Thursday morning, in the morning service, W. A. gave his heart to Jesus.

Bassett asked if Criswell remembered the name of the evangelist. Criswell replied, "I remember it well. It was John Hicks. I never heard of him before or since." Bassett's mouth fell open. Just the Thursday before, a nurse who belonged to Bassett's church had phoned in the middle of the night asking if he would send a deacon to the hospital. She was caring for an old evangelist who had never married. He had no relatives. He was dying and he was all alone. The nurse thought someone else ought to be with him when he died.

Bassett went to the hospital himself. The old evangelist told him, "Dr. Bassett, I'm not afraid to die. I know Jesus. I know I'm going to heaven. My only regret is that I don't have many souls to take with me. All of my meetings were in small country churches. I never won very many to Christ."[7] His name was John Hicks.

The reason the judgment seat of Christ occurs at the end of time is that it will take that long for all the credits to work out in God's economy. John Hicks may not have won many people to Christ, but he won W. A. Criswell. Consider how many people Criswell won and how many other men surrendered to be preachers under Criswell. It goes on and on and on. Pastor, Jesus says, "Be faithful until death, and I will give you the crown of life" (Rev. 2:10). And that is enough.

Keep the Faith

One of the tragedies of the ministry is pastors who fall from the faith. Some fall morally. This has been addressed already in this book. Some fall emotionally. They burn out. But some fall spiritually. They literally lose their faith. Faith is both personal and propositional. Personal faith is trust. Some pastors go through all the trials of the pastorate and quit trusting in God. Jesus clearly reveals Himself as our friend. In Him we have a personal, loving, purposeful, all-powerful, all-knowing friend. What a friend we have in Jesus!

If the pastor does not watch his attitude, when he goes through difficult times he may not think Jesus is a good friend. In all of the inevitable sufferings and trials of life, the pastor must keep his trust in Jesus. The arm of flesh may fail, but the arm of Jesus will not. Real friends do not have to explain themselves. Sometimes Jesus tells us what He is doing. Sometimes He does not. Like Job of old, the pastor must say to the Lord and to himself over and over again, "Even if He kills me, I will hope in Him" (Job 13:15).

A Pastor Must Keep the Faith Doctrinally

A pastor must also keep the faith doctrinally. There is a minimal content to the gospel. Paul outlines this in 1 Corinthians 15:1–4. The minimal intellectual content of the gospel is belief in the death, burial, and resurrection of Jesus Christ. A person cannot be a Christian and doubt the death, burial, and resurrection of Jesus. Nor can a pastor be a gospel preacher and neglect these gospel truths. Always put the gospel in every message you preach. If you cannot fit the gospel into a sermon, there is something wrong with the sermon. Keep the faith.

A pastor also has a responsibility to keep the faith denomination-ally. If his denomination has either a creed or a confession of faith, he has a solemn duty to keep his church's faith. Some pastors have shipwrecked their ministries by losing their denomination's faith. If a pastor finds himself outside of the parameters of his denomination's beliefs, he should resign.

The modern American Baptist missionary movement was started by two men, Adoniram Judson and Luther Rice, who were under appointment by the Congregational Missionary Society. On the ship going to India, while reading the book of Acts, they came to the con-clusion that the New Testament teaches believer's baptism and not infant baptism, as the Congregationalists believed. When they arrived in India (later going to Burma), they asked the English Baptist mis-sionary, William Carey, to baptize them. The first letter they wrote back to the United States was to resign as missionaries for their send-ing board. They had become Baptists. Adoniram Judson asked Luther Rice to go back to America to raise support for their missionary work among Baptist churches. Pastor, keep your denomination's faith.

It is in fighting the good fight, finishing the race, and keeping the faith that the pastor proves himself worthy of a reward. An humble pastor said once that he did not want any crowns. He did not do his work as a pastor for that. But remember what we are going to do with our crowns. We are going to cast them at the feet of Jesus over and over again in eternity. We will join the twenty-four elders in Revelation 4:10 in casting our crowns before the throne at the feet of Him who lives forever, saying, "You are worthy to receive glory and honor and power" (v. 11).

The reward of the pastor is the glory of Christ. It is good for every godly pastor to say what children used to recite in Vacation Bible School: "I will do the best I can with what I have for Jesus' sake today."

APPENDIX 1 | Where Does a Pastor Go for Personal Counseling?

Almost all denominations have a counseling service available to their pastors. LifeWay, a Southern Baptist Convention agency, has such a service for ministers and their families regardless of their denomination. It is called LeaderCare. Consider it your partner in ministry. You can e-mail them at leadercare@lifeway.com. Their Web site is www.lifeway.com/leadercare.

The various LeaderCare ministry venues include:
- Career assessments
- Compassion fatigue training
- Counseling network
- Dealing with forced termination
- Executive leadership course for pastors
- Ministers' families
- Ministers' wives
- Ministers' marriages
- Stress management
- Team-building retreat for church staff
- Health screening

Periodic LeaderCare retreats are offered free of charge to all pastors and their wives. There is even scholarship assistance available to assist couples in covering their travel expenses to and from the conferences. Go to their Web site to find the schedule, location, and nature of the various conferences.

There is a toll-free, confidential phone number available for ministers and their families: 1-888-789-1911.

Perhaps the most complete service offered to evangelical pastors belongs to Focus on the Family, an interdenominational ministry led by Dr. James Dobson. H. B. London, vice president for pastoral ministries at Focus on the Family, directs a Web site called "The Parsonage" at www.parsonage.org.

This very extensive Web site contains information vital to pastors and their families. There are online resources as well as free e-mail subscriptions to bimonthly and weekly briefings plus listings of professional counseling available from a conservative evangelical perspective, listed by states. These "Caregiving Ministries" include:

- Leadership and conflict consultants
- Financial and legal consultants
- Reflection and relaxation providers
- Rest and renewal retreat centers
- Restoration and counseling retreat centers
- Psychologists, psychiatrists, and counseling offices
- Treatment centers, clinics, and hospitals
- Online Web site ministries

A pastoral care line is available toll-free at 1-877-233-4455.

Where Does a Pastor Go for Help When He Is Fired?

Most mainline denominations now have help for pastors who have been either fired or forced to resign. When I was a young pastor, a friend of mine was fired by his church. There were no agencies then to help. As I reached out to him by mail, he responded, "My emotions are terminal!" I could only imagine. The incredible statistics today reveal that one out of every four ordained ministers will either be fired or forced to resign at some time in his ministry.

There are at least two agencies available for ministers who have been fired. One is a nondenominational agency, Focus on the Family. The other is a denominational agency, Southern Baptists' LifeWay LeaderCare. Both are open to pastors or church staff members from all evangelical denominations.

The LifeWay agency may be reached at leadercare@lifeway.com. The phone number is 615-251-2953. They also have a 911-type help line at 888-789-1911 for ministers and their families. Periodic LeaderCare retreats are provided for forced-termination ministers and their families, with all expenses covered by LifeWay. Scholarship assistance is also available to assist couples in their travel expenses to attend these retreats. This testimony from a pastor appears on their Web site: "I had just resigned under pressure after nearly five years. As a fifty-one-year-old with nearly twenty-six years of pastoral experience, I was devastated. The situation led me to question my abilities and personal worth. The retreat, however, gave me great encouragement and good insights. I will now wait for God to open a door for a pastorate, or some ministry."[1]

Focus on the Family also has a Web site for pastors: www.parsonage .org. Pastoral ministers are available at 719-531-3360 and at pastors@ family.org.

There is a third ministry owned and operated by Sagemont Baptist Church in Houston, Texas. They have a Restoration Ministry where several times a year they bring in ministers and wives who are either under stress in the ministry or who have been fired. This is a small ministry, limited to ten couples at a time. All expenses including travel expenses are paid for this week-long conference in Houston. Over the years, this local church, through this Restoration Ministry, has ministered to more than seven hundred ministerial couples from eighteen different states and four different countries.

I have seen tapes of one of these conferences, and it is wonderful. John Morgan, pastor of Sagemont, had this ministry going before denominations began to get involved in ministering to ministers who had been fired or forced to resign. Web sites include www .sagemontchurch.org and stress-in-the-ministry.org. Phone numbers include 281-481-8770 and 713-991-4910.

APPENDIX 3 How Does a Pastor Build His Personal Library?

D avid Allen,[1] a long-time professor of expository preaching, made the following suggestions about the pastor's library by e-mail to the author.

1. Start now.
2. Buy quality, not quantity.
3. Build a broad-based library with works in every area of theological studies and beyond. For example, have books in historical theology and systematic theology. In systematic theology have books that cover the major doctrines: revelation and inspiration, theology proper (the doctrine of God), anthropology, harmartiology, Christology, soteriology, pneumatology, ecclesiology, and eschatology. Books in other theological studies would include hermeneutics, apologetics, philosophy, biographies, prayer, the Old Testament, the New Testament, missions, evangelism, and comparative religions. Also buy theological dictionaries and encyclopedias.
4. Seek to own at least three commentaries on every book of the Bible.
5. Consult annotated surveys and guides to biblical commentaries.
6. Buy used books when possible. Visit used bookstores and look for discarded biblical treasures.
7. Scan the Internet for new and used theological books.
8. Watch for library sales from theological and public libraries.

9. Watch for retired pastors selling or even giving away some of their books.

I would add to his suggestions that you ask your church members periodically to bring discarded books to you and let you dispose of them. I picked up a set of *Great Books of the Western World* this way.

Please note that neither Dr. Allen nor I suggest that you buy commentary sets first. Often young pastors ask me what set of commentaries to buy. Sometimes relatives offer to buy a set of commentaries for a young pastor. If you want a set of Old Testament commentaries, I suggest Keil and Delitzsch's *Old Testament Commentary*. For the New Testament, I suggest Barclay's *Commentaries on the New Testament*.

Beyond that, you can build your commentaries as you preach through individual books of the Bible. If you plan to preach through books of the Bible, start a year in advance collecting commentaries on the particular book through which you plan to preach.

One other suggestion from Dr. Allen and me involves the following specific books on preaching that we recommend.

Books on the History of Preaching

Brooks, Phillips. *Lectures on the History of Preaching*. New York: Sheldon, 1876.

Dargan, Edwin Charles. *A History of Preaching*. Vols. 1–3. Grand Rapids: Baker, 1954.

Larson, David L. *The Company of the Preachers*. Grand Rapids: Kregel, 1998.

Webber, F. R. *A History of Preaching in Britain and America*. Milwaukee: Northwest Publishers, 1952.

Wiersbe, Warren W. *Listening to the Giants*. Grand Rapids: Baker, 1980.

———. *Walking with the Giants*. Grand Rapids: Baker, 1976.

Books on Biographies of Preachers

Capill, Murray A. *Preaching with Spiritual Vigor: Lessons from the Life of Richard Baxter*. Fearn, UK: Mentor, 2003.

Drummond, Lewis A. *Spurgeon: Prince of Preachers*. Grand Rapids: Kregel, 1992.

Books on Sermon Preparation and Delivery

Broadus, John. *A Treatise on the Preparation and Delivery of Sermons*. New York: A. C. Armstrong & Son, 1870.

Brooks, Phillips. *The Joy of Preaching*. Grand Rapids: Kregel, 1885, 1987.

Bryson, Harold. *Expository Preaching*. Nashville: Broadman & Holman, 1995.

Chapell, Bryan. *Christ-Centered Preaching*. Grand Rapids: Baker, 1994.

————. *Using Illustrations to Preach with Power*. Grand Rapids: Zondervan, 1992.

Doriani, Daniel. *Putting the Truth to Work: The Theology and Practice of Biblical Application*. Phillipsburg, N.J.: P & R Publishing, 2001.

Draper, James T., Jr. *Preaching with Passion*. Nashville: Broadman & Holman, 2004.

Eby, David. *Power Preaching for Church Growth*. Fearn, UK: Mentor, 1996.

Greidenus, Sidney. *Preaching Christ from the Old Testament*. Grand Rapids: Eerdmans, 1999.

Hendricks, Howard. *Teaching to Change Lives*. Portland: Multnomah, 1987.

Kaiser, Walter. *Preaching and Teaching from the Old Testament*. Grand Rapids: Baker, 2003.

————. *Toward an Exegetical Theology*. Grand Rapids: Baker, 1981.

Kirksey, Franklin L. *Sound Biblical Preaching*. BookSurge, 2004.

Liefeld, Walter. *New Testament Exposition*. Grand Rapids: Zondervan, 1984.

MacArthur, John. *Rediscovering Expository Preaching*. Dallas: Word, 1992.

Mathewson, Steven. *The Art of Preaching Old Testament Narrative*. Grand Rapids: Baker, 2002.

Mawhinney, Bruce. *Preaching with Freshness*. Grand Rapids: Kregel, 1997.

McDill, Wayne. *The Moment of Truth.* Nashville: Broadman & Holman, 1999.

————. *The 12 Essential Skills of Great Preaching.* Nashville: Broadman & Holman, 1994.

Miller, Calvin. *The Empowered Communicator.* Nashville: Broadman & Holman, 1995.

Mohler, Albert R. *Feed My Sheep.* Morgan, Pa.: Soli Deo Gloria, 2002.

Morgan, G. Campbell. *Preaching.* New York: Fleming H. Revell, 1937.

Olford, Stephen, and David Olford. *Anointed Expository Preaching.* Nashville: Broadman & Holman, 1998.

Piper, John. *The Supremacy of God in Preaching.* Grand Rapids: Baker, 2004.

Robinson, Haddon. *Biblical Preaching.* 2nd ed. Grand Rapids: Baker, 2001.

Shaddix, Jim. *The Passion-Driven Sermon.* Nashville: Broadman & Holman, 2003.

Stott, John. *Between Two Worlds.* Grand Rapids: Eerdmans, 1982.

————. *I Believe in Preaching.* London: Hodder & Stoughton, 1982, 1986.

Streett, Alan. *The Effective Invitation.* Updated Ed. Grand Rapids: Kregel, 2004.

Unger, Merrill. *Principles of Expository Preaching.* Grand Rapids: Zondervan, 1955.

Vines, Jerry, and Jim Shaddix. *Power in the Pulpit.* Chicago: Moody Press, 1999.

Wiersbe, Warren. *Developing a Christian Imagination.* Wheaton: Victor, 1995.

————. *Preaching and Teaching with Imagination.* Grand Rapids: Baker, 1994.

————. *The Dynamics of Preaching.* Grand Rapids: Baker, 1999.

A Sample Wedding Ceremony

4

Any etiquette book may be consulted about the seating of family members of the bride and groom, the lighting of candles, and appropriate music before the ceremony begins. There is usually a solo during the seating of the parents. Sometimes the mothers of the groom and bride will light the candles that are on either side of a unity candle. The pastor, the groom, and his groomsmen may come to the front of the church from the side and stand in front of the platform. (The pastor mounts the platform and takes his place behind the kneeling bench, if one is used).

The bride, preceded by her bridesmaids and flower girl and/or ring bearer, will come down the aisle on the arm of her father to meet the groom at the front of the platform. The groomsmen and bridesmaids will go directly to their places as the bridesmaids arrive at the front. They will stand at an angle facing the congregation, so that they will see the bride as she comes down the aisle. The bride's mother, standing up as the bride comes down the aisle, will signal the congregation to stand as well.

As the bride comes to the base of the platform on her father's left arm, the groom will stand next to the bride's father. Then the pastor will ask, "Who gives this woman to be married to this man?"

The father will answer either "I do" or "her mother and I." Then the father will step back, placing the bride's right hand on the left arm of the groom. They will then ascend the steps leading up to the platform and stand in front of the pastor or kneeling bench, if there is one. As the couple mounts the steps, the wedding party will turn at an angle toward the couple. The bride's father will take his seat beside his wife. The pastor will say, "The congregation may be seated."

At this point the bride should pass her bouquet to the maid of honor. The pastor will say, "A wise man once said, 'There are three things which are too wonderful for me, yes, four which I do not understand: The way of an eagle in the air, the way of a serpent on a rock, the way of a ship in the midst of the sea, and the way of a man with a virgin' [Prov. 30:18–19 NKJV].

"We are gathered here together today (or tonight) to witness the exchanging of wedding vows between [groom's full name] and [bride's full name]. It is appropriate that this wedding takes place in the church because marriage is an institution ordained by God. No one except God could have thought of anything as wonderful as marriage. It was God Himself who placed that first man and woman together in the garden to love one another, to complete one another, and to provide that unique companionship found in the marriage union. In His wonderful book, the Bible, God tells us the duties and responsibilities of each marriage partner whereby they might have the blessing of God on their home.

"[Groom's name], to you God gives a wonderful assignment: 'Husband, love your wife, even as Christ loved the Church and gave Himself for her. . . . So the husband ought to love his wife as his own body; he who loves his wife loves himself. For no one ever hated his own flesh, but nourishes and cherishes it, just as the Lord does the Church' [see Eph. 5:25–29 NKJV].

"[Bride's name], God says to you, 'Wife, submit yourself unto your own husband, as to the Lord. For the husband is head of the wife, as also Christ is head of the church, and He is the Savior of the body. Therefore, just as the church is subject to Christ, so let the wife be subject to her own husband, in everything' [see Eph. 5:22–24 NKJV].

"As your lives are put together today in the legal and Christian manner, I pray that it is just the beginning of God taking two hearts and making them into one heart, which ought never to be broken, except by death.

"Now you have declared to me in private that there is nothing according to the laws of God or the laws of this state that would keep you from becoming husband and wife. You have made known to your family and friends gathered here together your intentions of giving yourselves each to the other as long as you both shall live. Now will you face each other and join right hands as you exchange these wedding vows.

"[Groom's name], will you take this woman, [bride's name], whom you hold by the hand as your lawful wedded wife? Will you love her tenderly, comfort her in times of sorrow, keep her in times of prosperity or poverty, sickness or health? Will you cherish her and keep her close to your side and to your heart as long as both of you live?" (The groom answers, "I will.")

"[Bride's name], will you take this man, [groom's name], whom you hold by the hand, as your lawful wedded husband? Will you love him tenderly, comfort him in times of sorrow, keep him in times of prosperity or poverty, sickness or health? Will you obey him and keep him close to your side and to your heart as long as both of you live?" (The bride answers, "I will.")

"Now each of you brings a ring as a sign and token of your love for each other." (The maid of honor and the best man should then place both rings in the pastor's hand. He will hold his hand with the rings out to the groom.)

"[Groom's name], please take your ring and place it on the third finger of [bride's name] left hand. Hold it there for a moment, look deep into her eyes and into her heart, and repeat these words after me: (The pastor will pause at the end of each line.)

"May this ring
Be a reminder
To you and to me
Of the love and devotion
I now pledge
This day to you."

"Now [bride's name], please take your ring and place it on the ring finger of [groom's name] left hand. Hold it there for a moment, look deep into his eyes and into his heart, and repeat these words after me: (The pastor will pause at the end of each line.)

"May this ring
Be a reminder
To you and to me

Of the love and devotion
I now pledge
This day to you."
(The couple then holds hands and faces the pastor.)

"Let these rings, circles of gold, mark the purity, the value, and the constancy of true wedded love. Let them be now and for the rest of your lives a twofold seal of the vows you have taken here before your family and friends and in heaven before God."

If there is a unity candle to be lit, a solo or organ interlude may be sung or played while the couple lights the unity candle and then returns to their place before the pastor. After the solo is over, the pastor says, "Now let us pray." The couple will kneel if there is a kneeling bench. Otherwise they will bow their heads as the pastor prays. Sometimes the Lord's Prayer is sung at this time. If it is, the pastor, at the close of the song will say, "Amen."

If the Lord's Prayer is not sung, the pastor will pray something like this: "Our Father in heaven, we ask you to bless [groom's name] and [bride's name] as they join hands together to climb the hill of life. May their blessings be doubled as two share them together rather than each alone. May the inevitable hardships of life be made bearable as two bear them together instead of each alone. If you bless this union with children, may they be raised in the nurture and admonition of the Lord. May Christ dwell at the center of the home that is hereby established today (or tonight). As [groom's name] and [bride's name] grow closer to Him, may they grow closer to one another than they ever felt possible. We pray this prayer in Jesus' name."

If the couple has been kneeling, they will stand. Then the pastor will say: "[Groom's name] and [bride's name], upon your solemn vows that you have made here today (or tonight), and upon your sacred pledge to love one another for the rest of your lives, in accordance with the laws of God and of this state, it gives me great delight to pronounce you husband and wife, in the name of the Father, and of the Son, and of the Holy Spirit. And what God has joined together, let no man put asunder. You may kiss your bride."

After the kiss, as the couple turns toward the congregation and the bride retrieves her bouquet, the pastor will say, "Ladies and gentlemen, may I present to you Mr. and Mrs. [groom's full name]."

The recessional takes place as rehearsed. The pastor will stand in place until the family members have been escorted from the church. Then he will either invite everyone to the reception and tell them how to get there, or he will simply say, "You are dismissed."

APPENDIX 5 A Sample Order of Service for a Funeral

O rgan music should play while guests are being seated. When the family comes in, the pastor should signal the congregation to stand while the family is being seated. Then he may ask the congregation to be seated.

SOLO

READING OF THE OBITUARY

SCRIPTURE READING
When committed to memory, John 14:1–6; 1 Thessalonians 4:13–18; 2 Corinthians 5:1–8; and 1 Corinthians 15:51–58 become a wonderful comfort to the family.

PRAYER

SOLO

MESSAGE
The message should be brief. The gospel should be made clear.

CLOSING PRAYER
The funeral director will tell the pastor what to do at the end of the service, where to stand, and so forth. At the cemetery, the pastor and funeral director will lead the casket to the gravesite. The pastor should stand at the head of the casket. When those attending have gathered,

the funeral director will signal the pastor to begin. The graveside service should be very brief. The pastor may say something like this: "I know the family appreciates so much all of you who are here today. Thank you for the beautiful flowers, the food you have brought by the house, and the many comforting words you have spoken. I know you will be praying for the family in the weeks and months ahead."

If the Person Is a Christian

You might say something like this: "Now as [person's name] committed his life to the Lord many years ago, we now commit his body to the earth from whence it was taken. 'Dust you are and to dust you shall return' (Gen. 3:19 NKJV). But even this committal is made not without hope. For we believe that Jesus is coming again. When He does, this grave will be opened, this body will be raised, glorified, and reunited with the beautiful person who is already with the Lord. And we who are alive and remain until that day will meet him [or her] in the clouds of the air and we will be together with the Lord forever. Against that day we place our hope. Now let us pray."

If the Person Is Not a Christian

You might say something like this: "Today we commit the body of [person's name] to the earth from whence it was taken. 'Dust you are and to dust you shall return' (Gen. 3:19 NKJV). We commit him [or her] to the God who made him [or her] and to His grace and mercy and justice. Now let us pray."

After the prayer, the pastor should shake hands with each family member seated by the grave and offer a word of comfort. Then he should wait to the side until the family leaves. Then he may leave.

Sample Staff Organization Charts

A Single Staff Member Organization

Many churches have only one full-time staff member, and that is the pastor. A second full-time staff member may be the church secretary. The rest of the staff will be either part-time or volunteer, but the pastor needs to meet with them at least once a month, even though they are a volunteer staff. Often it is called the pastor's cabinet or the church council, but it should function as the pastor's staff. Program planning and calendaring should be done through this group.

PASTOR———Church Secretary

Minister of Music	**Sunday School** Director	**Church Training** Director	**Chairman of** Deacons	**Director of** Women's Ministries	**Director of** Youth

A Church with Four Full-Time Ministry Staff Members

PASTOR———Church Secretary

Minister of Music	**Minister of** Education	**Minister to** Youth

As finances become available, an administrative assistant or secretary may be added to each of the three ministries. Until such time as funds are available, a church secretary may minister to all three of the ministry leaders above. Sometimes the minister to youth is placed under the supervision of the minister of education, who is usually the second in authority to the pastor and supervises any janitorial and office staff. As the church grows, ministerial assistants may also be hired.

A Church with Seven Full-Time Ministry Staff Members

PASTOR———Church Secretary

Minister of Education	**Business** Administrator	**Minister of** Music	**Minister to** Youth	**Minister to** Children	**Minister of** Recreation

In a church this size, each of the ministry heads should have an administrative assistant or secretary to help. The business administrator may have an office staff, including a bookkeeper. The minister of education usually supervises the ministers of youth, children, and recreation. He usually serves as an adult director, although as the church grows a retired pastor may be called as minister to adults or senior adult director.

A Church with an Attendance of More than 2,000[1]

SENIOR PASTOR———Administrative Assistant(s)
Research Assistant(s)

Executive Pastor———Administrative Associates
Receptionist/Calendaring
Computer/Phone Tech

Worship Pastor[2]	**CLF**[3] Pastor	**Connection Groups** Pastor[4]	**Evangelism & Missions** Pastor	**Communications** Director	**Business/ Facilities** Administrator	**Center Stage** Pastor[5]

The Pastor's Résumé

It is important for a pastor to develop a résumé. There are books and Web sites available to give guidance. Contemporary advice regarding résumés is that they should be only one page in length. This would be fine for an introduction sheet just to introduce the pastor were he speaking somewhere else besides his church. However, if he were asked to submit a résumé to a Pastor Search Committee, it would need to be more extensive. Both kinds of résumés are included on the following pages.

INTRODUCTION SHEET
FOR DR. JAMES W. BRYANT

Dr. Bryant has been preaching the gospel since he was sixteen years old. He is a native of Atlanta, Georgia. He and his wife, Ruby, have two sons and two grandchildren.

For more than forty years, he has served churches in the Southern Baptist Convention. His pastorates include Hoffmantown Baptist Church in Albuquerque, New Mexico; Sagamore Hill Baptist Church in Fort Worth, Texas; and the Grand Avenue Baptist Church in Fort Smith, Arkansas. Before the above pastorates, Dr. Bryant served for five years at the First Baptist Church in Dallas, Texas, as Minister of Evangelism and Church Organization, under Dr. W. A. Criswell. During that time, Dr. Bryant became the Founding Dean of the Criswell Bible Institute, now the Criswell College.

Dr. Bryant received the Bachelor of Arts degree, with honor, from Wheaton College in Wheaton, Illinois. He also holds the Master of Divinity and Doctor of Theology degrees from Southwestern Baptist Theological Seminary in Fort Worth, Texas. In 1999, The Criswell College awarded him the honorary degree, Doctor of Divinity.

From 1991 to 1993, he was the Executive Vice President, then President of the Luther Rice Seminary in Atlanta.

From 1993 to 2002, Dr. Bryant taught at the University of Mobile's School of Religion in Mobile, Alabama, where he held the rank Professor of Religion.

In August of 2002, Dr. Bryant became the Vice President for Academic Affairs at The Criswell College in Dallas, Texas. Since August of 2004, he has served teaching full time as Senior Professor of Pastoral Theology.

In August of 2002 Dr. Bryant became the Associate Teacher of the McLaughlin Bible Class at the First Baptist Church in Dallas, Texas. Since September of 2003 he has been the Teacher.

Revised September 4, 2006

DR. JAMES W. BRYANT
Senior Professor of Pastoral Theology
The Criswell College
4010 Gaston Avenue
Dallas, Texas 75246
(214) 818-1352
jwbryant@criswell.edu

PERSONAL
1. Born September 24, 1936, in Atlanta, Georgia.
2. Married Ruby Ann Garland August 14, 1959, in the First Baptist Church of Elmhurst, Illinois.
3. Two sons and two grandchildren.

EDUCATIONAL
1. Graduated from Southwest High School, Atlanta, Georgia, in May of 1954.
2. B.A. from Wheaton College, 1958.
3. B.D. (later changed to M. Div.) from Southwestern Baptist Theological Seminary, 1963.
4. Th.D. from Southwestern Baptist Theological Seminary, 1968.
5. D.D. (honorary) from The Criswell College, 1999.

SPIRITUAL
1. Raised in the Gordon Street Baptist Church in Atlanta, Georgia.
2. Converted to Christ in a citywide revival in Atlanta, Georgia, 1951.
3. Called to preach in that same revival meeting.
4. Baptized by the Colonial Hills Baptist Church in East Point, Georgia.
5. Present church membership: First Baptist Church of Dallas, Texas.

MINISTERIAL

1. Ordained to the gospel ministry by the Colonial Hills Baptist Church in East Point, Georgia, 1958.

2. Served as Associate Pastor of the Colonial Hills Baptist Church in East Point, Georgia, under Dr. Paul R. VanGorder for fourteen months between college and seminary, 1958-1959.

3. Served as Associate Pastor of the Sagamore Hill Baptist Church in Fort Worth, Texas, from 1960 to 1964, under the late Dr. W. Fred Swank.

4. Served as Pastor of the Burton Hill Baptist Church in Fort Worth, Texas, from 1964 to 1968. A new auditorium was constructed during these years.

5. Served as the Minister of Evangelism and Church Organization of the First Baptist Church of Dallas, Texas, under Dr. W. A. Criswell from 1968 to 1973. Directed the evangelism and educational programs of the church. Presided over the entire staff. During this time, the Sunday School grew from a little under 5,000 in average attendance to a little over 6,000. The staff increased from 75 to 150 persons. Supplied the pulpit in Dr. Criswell's absence. Organized the Criswell Bible Institute, now The Criswell College, and served as its first Academic Dean. Organized and directed the annual School of the Prophets, a weeklong school for pastors and church staff members.

6. Served as Pastor of the Hoffmantown Baptist Church in Albuquerque, New Mexico, from 1973 to 1977. During those years, the church grew from 550 average Sunday School attendance to more than 900, and the church averaged baptizing between 100 and 200 converts annually. The annual budget income tripled.

7. Served as Pastor of the Sagamore Hill Baptist Church in Fort Worth, Texas, from 1977 to 1983. During those years the church baptized between 100 and 200 converts each year, grew to an average of 1,500 in Sunday School attendance, and reached a membership exceeding 4,000.

8. Served as Pastor of the Grand Avenue Baptist Church in Fort Smith, Arkansas, from 1983 to 1989. A new Adult Education and Administration Building was completed during those years. Average annual baptisms were between 150 and 200 converts. At the high

point, the Sunday School averaged almost 1,600, with annual giving exceeding two million dollars.

9.   Became Minister-at-Large of the Grand Avenue Baptist Church in Fort Smith, Arkansas, on November 15, 1989, in order to devote full-time to holding revivals, Bible conferences, and seminars.

ACADEMIC ADMINISTRATION AND TEACHING

1.   Organized, served as Academic Dean, and taught in the Criswell Bible Institute (now The Criswell College) from 1970 to 1972, while serving on the staff of the First Baptist Church of Dallas, Texas.

2.   Served at Luther Rice Bible College and Seminary in Atlanta, Georgia, from 1991 to 1993, first as Executive Vice President, and then as President. Also served as Professor of Philosophy of Religion.

3.   Served as Professor of Religion in the School of Religion of the University of Mobile at Mobile, Alabama, from 1993 to 2002, specializing in Biblical Studies, Theology, Baptist History, and Apologetics.

4.   Beginning August 2002, served as Vice President for Academic Affairs at The Criswell College in Dallas, Texas. Since August 2004, has been serving as Senior Professor of Pastoral Theology.

PROFESSIONAL ORGANIZATIONAL MEMBERSHIPS

Evangelical Theological Society
Near East Archaeological Society
Biblical Archaeology Society
Christian History Society

DOCTRINAL POSITION

Dr. Bryant endorses the 2000 Baptist Faith and Message Statement of the Southern Baptist Convention and believes in the plenary, verbal inspiration of the Bible, accepting it as the final rule of faith and practice, and takes it to be inerrant in its original manuscripts.

(References furnished upon request.)

Revised November 2006

APPENDIX 8 The Pastor's Salary and Benefits

Before accepting the call to a church, the pastor should get *in writing* a church-approved salary and benefits schedule. There should be a base salary, a housing allowance, an automobile allowance, a book allowance, a retirement benefit, and insurance benefits. If the pastor is covered under Social Security, many churches add on to the salary a figure equal to one-half of the pastor's self-employment (Social Security) tax. (Other church employees not ordained have this benefit from the church.) This agreement should also spell out annual vacation, sick days, and church-sponsored attendance at denominational meetings for both the pastor and his wife. In addition, it would be helpful if the church could provide one personal developmental conference for the pastor each year.

There is an excellent online resource offered by GuideStone Financial Resources, a Southern Baptist Convention agency, available to almost any minister, regardless of his denomination. GuideStone handles both insurance and retirement funds for pastors. They recommend that a church provide a figure equal to 10 percent of the total of a pastor's annual base salary and housing allowance, to be put in a fully vested retirement fund. GuideStone also offers to churches and their finance committees a sample schedule of salary and benefits. Their Web site is www.GuideStone.org. On their Web site, click "Resources." Then click "Church Resources." There you will find several topics and subtopics, including:

- Retirement Plans
- Annual Ministers Tax Guide
- Planning Financial Support Workbook

- Southern Baptist Convention Church Compensation Study
- Federal Reporting Requirement for Churches
- Ministers Tax Questions and Answers
- Financial Checklist for Ministers
- The Minister's Housing Allowance
- Insurance Coverage Solutions

These resources, available online, can be placed in the hands of the church personnel committee and finance committee.

9 Journaling and Filing

The best resources I have found on the pastor journaling and filing are two books by Donald S. Whitney[1]—*Spiritual Disciplines for the Christian Life*[2] and *Simplify Your Spiritual Life.*[3]

Journaling

In the first book, the author has an entire chapter on journaling. He explains what a journal is, discusses its value, and outlines various ways of going about journaling. The bulk of the chapter is about the value of keeping a journal. He suggests several ways in which keeping a journal will help a pastor in his spiritual life.

- Help in self-understanding and evaluation
- Help in meditation
- Help in expressing thoughts and feelings to the Lord
- Help in remembering the Lord's works
- Help in creating and preserving a spiritual heritage
- Help in clarifying and articulating insights and impressions
- Help in maintaining the other spiritual disciplines[4]

While Whitney prefers a loose-leaf notebook for each month (if you lose it you will never lose more than a month), he recognizes the electronic ways of preserving journals. If you journal electronically, I would suggest that you do it on a floppy disk, CD, or DVD rather than leaving it on your hard drive. I wish I had had access to Whitney's ideas when I was a young pastor. I started out keeping a journal, but because I could not seem to be able to write in it daily, I finally gave up. Whitney points out that there is no need to write daily, just regularly.

In the second book referenced above, the author has a section on simplifying your journaling. This section is excellent. He reviews the journaling of the old divines such as George Whitefield, Jonathan Edwards, and John Wesley. Whitney recounts the ten spiritual questions Whitefield kept in the flyleaf of his journal. Whitney also shares thirty-one topics from which he journals throughout the year.[5]

Filing

I had never thought of filing as a spiritual discipline, but Whitney presents it that way. He covers the subject of filing under the section, "Simplifying and Your Time." He keeps two sets of files: biblical and topical. Some items are copied and filed in both places. The biblical file has sixty-six folders, one for each book in the Bible. The topical files may be doctrinal or ethical or illustrative in nature. He gives examples of topical headings: Abortion, Baptism, Christ, Church, Cross, Discipleship, Evangelism, Fellowship, and so forth.[6]

As long as I was a pastor, I kept a file that contained copies of every letter I had ever written. Such files can be kept efficiently today electronically and can include e-mail correspondence as well as hard copy correspondence. There have been times when I consulted those files in reconstructing the past, especially in regard to my service on denominational boards or committees.

Every pastor ought to keep files of his preaching. Sermon files can be arranged by books of the Bible and by verse, if he preaches through books of the Bible expositorally. Under each sermon should be recorded the date, place, and time that specific sermon was preached.

Every pastor should keep a chronological file of his church services Sunday by Sunday, filed year by year. In this file should be the text and title of the sermon preached, morning and evening, the attendance, and the response. The names of each person joining the church and being baptized should be listed. One of our Southern Baptist missionaries, who had grown up in one of the churches I pastored, suddenly died overseas. I did not know her husband and children, but I did know her parents. I had been their pastor when their little girl made a profession of faith in Christ and was baptized. I was able to tell them the very day she made her profession of faith and when she was baptized. That meant so much to the family.

Every pastor should keep a file of funerals he has preached. Again, date, time, place, text, and title of the sermon should be listed. This file can be used to send annual follow-up letters to the surviving family members. Such thoughtfulness will endear a pastor to families through the generations.

Files may also be kept on the various programs of the church. Copies of printed programs can be kept as well as advertisements promoting attendance. As a pastor moves from one church to another, these program files become invaluable resources. As Whitney says, "File it for the sake of your soul."[7]

APPENDIX 10 | The Baptist Faith and Message, 2000

I. The Scriptures

The Holy Bible was written by men divinely inspired and is God's revelation of Himself to man. It is a perfect treasure of divine instruction. It has God for its author, salvation for its end, and truth, without any mixture of error, for its matter. Therefore, all Scripture is totally true and trustworthy. It reveals the principles by which God judges us, and therefore is, and will remain to the end of the world, the true center of Christian union, and the supreme standard by which all human conduct, creeds, and religious opinions should be tried. All Scripture is a testimony to Christ, who is Himself the focus of divine revelation.
Exodus 24:4; Deuteronomy 4:1–2; 17:19; Joshua 8:34; Psalms 19:7–10; 119:11,89,105,140; Isaiah 34:16; 40:8; Jeremiah 15:16; 36:1–32; Matthew 5:17–18; 22:29; Luke 21:33; 24:44–46; John 5:39; 16:13–15; 17:17; Acts 2:16ff.; 17:11; Romans 15:4; 16:25–26; 2 Timothy 3:15–17; Hebrews 1:1–2; 4:12; 1 Peter 1:25; 2 Peter 1:19–21.

II. God

There is one and only one living and true God. He is an intelligent, spiritual, and personal Being, the Creator, Redeemer, Preserver, and Ruler of the universe. God is infinite in holiness and all other perfections. God is all powerful and all knowing; and His perfect knowledge extends to all things, past, present, and future, including the future decisions of His free creatures. To Him we owe the highest love, reverence, and obedience. The eternal triune God reveals Himself to us as Father, Son, and Holy Spirit, with distinct personal attributes, but without division of nature, essence, or being.

A. God the Father

God as Father reigns with providential care over His universe, His creatures, and the flow of the stream of human history according to the purposes of His grace. He is all powerful, all knowing, all loving, and all wise. God is Father in truth to those who become children of God through faith in Jesus Christ. He is fatherly in His attitude toward all men.

Genesis 1:1; 2:7; Exodus 3:14; 6:2–3; 15:11ff.; 20:1ff.; Leviticus 22:2; Deuteronomy 6:4; 32:6; 1 Chronicles 29:10; Psalm 19:1–3; Isaiah 43:3,15; 64:8; Jeremiah 10:10; 17:13; Matthew 6:9ff.; 7:11; 23:9; 28:19; Mark 1:9–11; John 4:24; 5:26; 14:6-13; 17:1–8; Acts 1:7; Romans 8:14–15; 1 Corinthians 8:6; Galatians 4:6; Ephesians 4:6; Colossians 1:15; 1 Timothy 1:17; Hebrews 11:6; 12:9; 1 Peter 1:17; 1 John 5:7.

B. God the Son

Christ is the eternal Son of God. In His incarnation as Jesus Christ He was conceived of the Holy Spirit and born of the virgin Mary. Jesus perfectly revealed and did the will of God, taking upon Himself human nature with its demands and necessities and identifying Himself completely with mankind yet without sin. He honored the divine law by His personal obedience, and in His substitutionary death on the cross He made provision for the redemption of men from sin. He was raised from the dead with a glorified body and appeared to His disciples as the person who was with them before His crucifixion. He ascended into heaven and is now exalted at the right hand of God where He is the One Mediator, fully God, fully man, in whose Person is effected the reconciliation between God and man. He will return in power and glory to judge the world and to consummate His redemptive mission. He now dwells in all believers as the living and ever present Lord.

Genesis 18:1ff.; Psalms 2:7ff.; 110:1ff.; Isaiah 7:14; 53; Matthew 1:18–23; 3:17; 8:29; 11:27; 14:33; 16:16,27; 17:5; 27; 28:1–6,19; Mark 1:1; 3:11; Luke 1:35; 4:41; 22:70; 24:46; John 1:1–18,29; 10:30,38;

11:25–27; 12:44–50; 14:7–11; 16:15–16,28; 17:1–5,21–22; 20:1–20,28; Acts 1:9; 2:22–24; 7:55–56; 9:4-5,20; Romans 1:3–4; 3:23–26; 5:6–21; 8:1-3,34; 10:4; 1 Corinthians 1:30; 2:2; 8:6; 15:1–8,24-28; 2 Corinthians 5:19–21; 8:9; Galatians 4:4–5; Ephesians 1:20; 3:11; 4:7–10; Philippians 2:5–11; Colossians 1:13–22; 2:9; 1 Thessalonians 4:14–18; 1 Timothy 2:5–6; 3:16; Titus 2:13–14; Hebrews 1:1–3; 4:14–15; 7:14–28; 9:12–15,24–28; 12:2; 13:8; 1 Peter 2:21–25; 3:22; 1 John 1:7–9; 3:2; 4:14–15; 5:9; 2 John 7–9; Revelation 1:13–16; 5:9–14; 12:10–11; 13:8; 19:16.

C. God the Holy Spirit

The Holy Spirit is the Spirit of God, fully divine. He inspired holy men of old to write the Scriptures. Through illumination He enables men to understand truth. He exalts Christ. He convicts men of sin, of righteousness, and of judgment. He calls men to the Saviour, and effects regeneration. At the moment of regeneration He baptizes every believer into the Body of Christ. He cultivates Christian character, comforts believers, and bestows the spiritual gifts by which they serve God through His church. He seals the believer unto the day of final redemption. His presence in the Christian is the guarantee that God will bring the believer into the fullness of the stature of Christ. He enlightens and empowers the believer and the church in worship, evangelism, and service.

Genesis 1:2; Judges 14:6; Job 26:13; Psalms 51:11; 139:7ff.; Isaiah 61:1–3; Joel 2:28–32; Matthew 1:18; 3:16; 4:1; 12:28–32; 28:19; Mark 1:10,12; Luke 1:35; 4:1,18–19; 11:13; 12:12; 24:49; John 4:24; 14:16–17,26; 15:26; 16:7–14; Acts 1:8; 2:1–4,38; 4:31; 5:3; 6:3; 7:55; 8:17,39; 10:44; 13:2; 15:28; 16:6; 19:1–6; Romans 8:9–11,14–16,26–27; 1 Corinthians 2:10–14; 3:16; 12:3–11,13; Galatians 4:6; Ephesians 1:13–14; 4:30; 5:18; 1 Thessalonians 5:19; 1 Timothy 3:16; 4:1; 2 Timothy 1:14; 3:16; Hebrews 9:8,14; 2 Peter 1:21; 1 John 4:13; 5:6–7; Revelation 1:10; 22:17.

III. Man

Man is the special creation of God, made in His own image. He created them male and female as the crowning work of His creation.

The gift of gender is thus part of the goodness of God's creation. In the beginning man was innocent of sin and was endowed by his Creator with freedom of choice. By his free choice man sinned against God and brought sin into the human race. Through the temptation of Satan man transgressed the command of God, and fell from his original innocence whereby his posterity inherit a nature and an environment inclined toward sin. Therefore, as soon as they are capable of moral action, they become transgressors and are under condemnation.

Only the grace of God can bring man into His holy fellowship and enable man to fulfill the creative purpose of God. The sacredness of human personality is evident in that God created man in His own image, and in that Christ died for man; therefore, every person of every race possesses full dignity and is worthy of respect and Christian love. *Genesis 1:26–30; 2:5,7,18–22; 3; 9:6; Psalms 1; 8:3–6; 32:1–5; 51:5; Isaiah 6:5; Jeremiah 17:5; Matthew 16:26; Acts 17:26–31; Romans 1:19–32; 3:10–18,23; 5:6,12,19; 6:6; 7:14–25; 8:14–18,29; 1 Corinthians 1:21–31; 15:19,21–22; Ephesians 2:1–22; Colossians 1:21–22; 3:9–11.*

IV. Salvation

Salvation involves the redemption of the whole man, and is offered freely to all who accept Jesus Christ as Lord and Saviour, who by His own blood obtained eternal redemption for the believer. In its broadest sense salvation includes regeneration, justification, sanctification, and glorification. There is no salvation apart from personal faith in Jesus Christ as Lord.

A. Regeneration, or the new birth, is a work of God's grace whereby believers become new creatures in Christ Jesus. It is a change of heart wrought by the Holy Spirit through conviction of sin, to which the sinner responds in repentance toward God and faith in the Lord Jesus Christ. Repentance and faith are inseparable experiences of grace. Repentance is a genuine turning from sin toward God. Faith is the acceptance of Jesus Christ and commitment of the entire personality to Him as Lord and Saviour.

B. Justification is God's gracious and full acquittal upon principles of His righteousness of all sinners who repent and believe in Christ.

Justification brings the believer into a relationship of peace and favor with God.

C. Sanctification is the experience, beginning in regeneration, by which the believer is set apart to God's purposes, and is enabled to progress toward moral and spiritual maturity through the presence and power of the Holy Spirit dwelling in him. Growth in grace should continue throughout the regenerate person's life.

Genesis 3:15; Exodus 3:14–17; 6:2–8; Matthew 1:21; 4:17; 16:21–26; 27:22–28:6; Luke 1:68–69; 2:28–32; John 1:11–14,29; 3:3–21,36; 5:24; 10:9,28–29; 15:1–16; 17:17; Acts 2:21; 4:12; 15:11; 16:30–31; 17:30–31; 20:32; Romans 1:16–18; 2:4; 3:23–25; 4:3ff.; 5:8–10; 6:1–23; 8:1–18,29–39; 10:9–10,13; 13:11–14; 1 Corinthians 1:18,30; 6:19–20; 15:10; 2 Corinthians 5:17–20; Galatians 2:20; 3:13; 5:22–25; 6:15; Ephesians 1:7; 2:8–22; 4:11–16; Philippians 2:12–13; Colossians 1:9–22; 3:1ff.; 1 Thessalonians 5:23–24; 2 Timothy 1:12; Titus 2:11–14; Hebrews 2:1–3; 5:8–9; 9:24–28; 11:1–12:8,14; James 2:14–26; 1 Peter 1:2–23; 1 John 1:6–2:11; Revelation 3:20; 21:1–22:5.

V. God's Purpose of Grace

Election is the gracious purpose of God, according to which He regenerates, justifies, sanctifies, and glorifies sinners. It is consistent with the free agency of man, and comprehends all the means in connection with the end. It is the glorious display of God's sovereign goodness, and is infinitely wise, holy, and unchangeable. It excludes boasting and promotes humility. All true believers endure to the end. Those whom God has accepted in Christ, and sanctified by His Spirit, will never fall away from the state of grace, but shall persevere to the end. Believers may fall into sin through neglect and temptation, whereby they grieve the Spirit, impair their graces and comforts, and bring reproach on the cause of Christ and temporal judgments on themselves; yet they shall be kept by the power of God through faith unto salvation.

Genesis 12:1–3; Exodus 19:5–8; 1 Samuel 8:4–7,19–22; Isaiah 5:1–7; Jeremiah 31:31ff.; Matthew 16:18–19; 21:28–45; 24:22,31; 25:34; Luke 1:68–79; 2:29–32; 19:41–44; 24:44–48; John 1:12–14; 3:16; 5:24; 6:44–45,65; 10:27–29; 15:16; 17:6,12,17–18; Acts 20:32; Romans 5:9–10; 8:28–39; 10:12–15; 11:5–7,26–36; 1 Corinthians

1:1–2; 15:24–28; Ephesians 1:4–23; 2:1–10; 3:1–11; Colossians 1:12–
14; 2 Thessalonians 2:13–14; 2 Timothy 1:12; 2:10,19; Hebrews 11:39–
12:2; James 1:12; 1 Peter 1:2–5,13; 2:4–10; 1 John 1:7–9; 2:19; 3:2.

VI. The Church

A New Testament church of the Lord Jesus Christ is an autonomous local congregation of baptized believers, associated by covenant in the faith and fellowship of the gospel; observing the two ordinances of Christ, governed by His laws, exercising the gifts, rights, and privileges invested in them by His Word, and seeking to extend the gospel to the ends of the earth. Each congregation operates under the Lordship of Christ through democratic processes. In such a congregation each member is responsible and accountable to Christ as Lord. Its scriptural officers are pastors and deacons. While both men and women are gifted for service in the church, the office of pastor is limited to men as qualified by Scripture. The New Testament speaks also of the church as the Body of Christ which includes all of the redeemed of all the ages, believers from every tribe, and tongue, and people, and nation.
Matthew 16:15–19; 18:15–20; Acts 2:41–42,47; 5:11–14; 6:3–6; 13:1–3; 14:23,27; 15:1–30; 16:5; 20:28; Romans 1:7; 1 Corinthians 1:2; 3:16; 5:4–5; 7:17; 9:13–14; 12; Ephesians 1:22–23; 2:19–22; 3:8–11,21; 5:22–32; Philippians 1:1; Colossians 1:18; 1 Timothy 2:9–14; 3:1–15; 4:14; Hebrews 11:39–40; 1 Peter 5:1–4; Revelation 2–3; 21:2–3.

VII. Baptism and the Lord's Supper

Christian baptism is the immersion of a believer in water in the name of the Father, the Son, and the Holy Spirit. It is an act of obedience symbolizing the believer's faith in a crucified, buried, and risen Saviour, the believer's death to sin, the burial of the old life, and the resurrection to walk in newness of life in Christ Jesus. It is a testimony to his faith in the final resurrection of the dead. Being a church ordinance, it is prerequisite to the privileges of church membership and to the Lord's Supper. The Lord's Supper is a symbolic act of obedience whereby members of the church, through partaking of the bread and the fruit of the vine, memorialize the death of the Redeemer and anticipate His second coming.

Matthew 3:13–17; 26:26–30; 28:19–20; Mark 1:9–11; 14:22–26; Luke 3:21–22; 22:19–20; John 3:23; Acts 2:41–42; 8:35–39; 16:30–33; 20:7.

VIII. The Lord's Day

The first day of the week is the Lord's Day. It is a Christian institution for regular observance. It commemorates the resurrection of Christ from the dead and should include exercises of worship and spiritual devotion, both public and private. Activities on the Lord's Day should be commensurate with the Christian's conscience under the Lordship of Jesus Christ.

Exodus 20:8–11; Matthew 12:1–12; 28:1ff.; Mark 2:27–28; 16:1–7; Luke 24:1–3,33–36; John 4:21–24; 20:1,19–28; Acts 20:7; Romans 14:5–10; 1 Corinthians 16:1–2; Colossians 2:16; 3:16; Revelation 1:10.

IX. The Kingdom

The Kingdom of God includes both His general sovereignty over the universe and His particular kingship over men who willfully acknowledge Him as King. Particularly the Kingdom is the realm of salvation into which men enter by trustful, childlike commitment to Jesus Christ. Christians ought to pray and to labor that the Kingdom may come and God's will be done on earth. The full consummation of the Kingdom awaits the return of Jesus Christ and the end of this age.

Genesis 1:1; Isaiah 9:6–7; Jeremiah 23:5–6; Matthew 3:2; 4:8–10,23; 12:25–28; 13:1–52; 25:31–46; 26:29; Mark 1:14–15; 9:1; Luke 4:43; 8:1; 9:2; 12:31–32; 17:20–21; 23:42; John 3:3; 18:36; Acts 1:6–7; 17:22–31; Romans 5:17; 8:19; 1 Corinthians 15:24–28; Colossians 1:13; Hebrews 11:10,16; 12:28; 1 Peter 2:4–10; 4:13; Revelation 1:6,9; 5:10; 11:15; 21–22.

X. Last Things

God, in His own time and in His own way, will bring the world to its appropriate end. According to His promise, Jesus Christ will return personally and visibly in glory to the earth; the dead will be raised; and Christ will judge all men in righteousness. The unrighteous will be consigned to Hell, the place of everlasting punishment. The righteous in their resurrected and glorified bodies will receive their reward and will dwell forever in Heaven with the Lord.

Isaiah 2:4; 11:9; Matthew 16:27; 18:8–9; 19:28; 24:27,30,36,44; 25:31–46; 26:64; Mark 8:38; 9:43–48; Luke 12:40,48; 16:19–26; 17:22–37; 21:27–28; John 14:1–3; Acts 1:11; 17:31; Romans 14:10; 1 Corinthians 4:5; 15:24–28,35–58; 2 Corinthians 5:10; Philippians 3:20–21; Colossians 1:5; 3:4; 1 Thessalonians 4:14–18; 5:1ff.; 2 Thessalonians 1:7ff.; 2; 1 Timothy 6:14; 2 Timothy 4:1,8; Titus 2:13; Hebrews 9:27–28; James 5:8; 2 Peter 3:7ff.; 1 John 2:28; 3:2; Jude 14; Revelation 1:18; 3:11; 20:1–22:13.

XI. Evangelism and Missions

It is the duty and privilege of every follower of Christ and of every church of the Lord Jesus Christ to endeavor to make disciples of all nations. The new birth of man's spirit by God's Holy Spirit means the birth of love for others. Missionary effort on the part of all rests thus upon a spiritual necessity of the regenerate life, and is expressly and repeatedly commanded in the teachings of Christ. The Lord Jesus Christ has commanded the preaching of the gospel to all nations. It is the duty of every child of God to seek constantly to win the lost to Christ by verbal witness undergirded by a Christian lifestyle, and by other methods in harmony with the gospel of Christ.

Genesis 12:1–3; Exodus 19:5–6; Isaiah 6:1–8; Matthew 9:37–38; 10:5–15; 13:18–30,37–43; 16:19; 22:9–10; 24:14; 28:18–20; Luke 10:1–18; 24:46–53; John 14:11–12; 15:7–8,16; 17:15; 20:21; Acts 1:8; 2; 8:26–40; 10:42–48; 13:2–3; Romans 10:13–15; Ephesians 3:1–11; 1 Thessalonians 1:8; 2 Timothy 4:5; Hebrews 2:1–3; 11:39–12:2; 1 Peter 2:4–10; Revelation 22:17.

XII. Education

Christianity is the faith of enlightenment and intelligence. In Jesus Christ abide all the treasures of wisdom and knowledge. All sound learning is, therefore, a part of our Christian heritage. The new birth opens all human faculties and creates a thirst for knowledge. Moreover, the cause of education in the Kingdom of Christ is co-ordinate with the causes of missions and general benevolence, and should receive along with these the liberal support of the churches. An adequate system of Christian education is necessary to a complete spiritual program for Christ's people.

In Christian education there should be a proper balance between academic freedom and academic responsibility. Freedom in any orderly relationship of human life is always limited and never absolute. The freedom of a teacher in a Christian school, college, or seminary is limited by the pre-eminence of Jesus Christ, by the authoritative nature of the Scriptures, and by the distinct purpose for which the school exists. *Deuteronomy 4:1,5,9,14; 6:1–10; 31:12–13; Nehemiah 8:1–8; Job 28:28; Psalms 19:7ff.; 119:11; Proverbs 3:13ff.; 4:1–10; 8:1–7,11; 15:14; Ecclesiastes 7:19; Matthew 5:2; 7:24ff.; 28:19–20; Luke 2:40; 1 Corinthians 1:18–31; Ephesians 4:11–16; Philippians 4:8; Colossians 2:3,8–9; 1 Timothy 1:3–7; 2 Timothy 2:15; 3:14–17; Hebrews 5:12– 6:3; James 1:5; 3:17.*

XIII. Stewardship

God is the source of all blessings, temporal and spiritual; all that we have and are we owe to Him. Christians have a spiritual debtorship to the whole world, a holy trusteeship in the gospel, and a binding stewardship in their possessions. They are therefore under obligation to serve Him with their time, talents, and material possessions; and should recognize all these as entrusted to them to use for the glory of God and for helping others. According to the Scriptures, Christians should contribute of their means cheerfully, regularly, systematically, proportionately, and liberally for the advancement of the Redeemer's cause on earth.

Genesis 14:20; Leviticus 27:30–32; Deuteronomy 8:18; Malachi 3:8–12; Matthew 6:1–4,19–21; 19:21; 23:23; 25:14–29; Luke 12:16–21,42; 16:1–13; Acts 2:44–47; 5:1–11; 17:24–25; 20:35; Romans 6:6–22; 12:1–2; 1 Corinthians 4:1–2; 6:19–20; 12; 16:1–4; 2 Corinthians 8–9; 12:15; Philippians 4:10–19; 1 Peter 1:18–19.

XIV. Cooperation

Christ's people should, as occasion requires, organize such associations and conventions as may best secure cooperation for the great objects of the Kingdom of God. Such organizations have no authority over one another or over the churches. They are voluntary and advisory bodies designed to elicit, combine, and direct the energies of our people in the most effective manner. Members of New Testament churches should cooperate with one another in carrying forward the missionary, educational, and benevolent ministries for the extension of Christ's Kingdom.

Christian unity in the New Testament sense is spiritual harmony and voluntary cooperation for common ends by various groups of Christ's people. Cooperation is desirable between the various Christian denominations, when the end to be attained is itself justified, and when such cooperation involves no violation of conscience or compromise of loyalty to Christ and His Word as revealed in the New Testament. *Exodus 17:12; 18:17ff.; Judges 7:21; Ezra 1:3–4; 2:68–69; 5:14–15; Nehemiah 4; 8:1–5; Matthew 10:5–15; 20:1–16; 22:1–10; 28:19–20; Mark 2:3; Luke 10:1ff.; Acts 1:13–14; 2:1ff.; 4:31–37; 13:2–3; 15:1– 35; 1 Corinthians 1:10–17; 3:5–15; 12; 2 Corinthians 8–9; Galatians 1:6–10; Ephesians 4:1–16; Philippians 1:15–18.*

XV. The Christian and the Social Order

All Christians are under obligation to seek to make the will of Christ supreme in our own lives and in human society. Means and methods used for the improvement of society and the establishment of righteousness among men can be truly and permanently helpful only when they are rooted in the regeneration of the individual by the saving grace of God in Jesus Christ. In the spirit of Christ, Christians should oppose racism, every form of greed, selfishness, and vice, and all forms of sexual immorality, including adultery, homosexuality, and pornography. We should work to provide for the orphaned, the needy, the abused, the aged, the helpless, and the sick. We should speak on behalf of the unborn and contend for the sanctity of all human life from conception to natural death.

Every Christian should seek to bring industry, government, and society as a whole under the sway of the principles of righteousness, truth, and brotherly love. In order to promote these ends, Christians should be ready to work with all men of good will in any good cause, always being careful to act in the spirit of love without compromising their loyalty to Christ and His truth.
Exodus 20:3–17; Leviticus 6:2–5; Deuteronomy 10:12; 27:17; Psalm 101:5; Micah 6:8; Zechariah 8:16; Matthew 5:13–16,43–48; 22:36–40; 25:35; Mark 1:29–34; 2:3ff.; 10:21; Luke 4:18–21; 10:27–37; 20:25; John 15:12; 17:15; Romans 12–14; 1 Corinthians 5:9–10; 6:1–7; 7:20–24; 10:23–11:1; Galatians 3:26–28; Ephesians 6:5–9; Colossians 3:12–17; 1 Thessalonians 3:12; Philemon; James 1:27; 2:8.

XVI. Peace and War

It is the duty of Christians to seek peace with all men on principles of righteousness. In accordance with the spirit and teachings of Christ they should do all in their power to put an end to war. The true remedy for the war spirit is the gospel of our Lord. The supreme need of the world is the acceptance of His teachings in all the affairs of men and nations, and the practical application of His law of love. Christian people throughout the world should pray for the reign of the Prince of Peace.
Isaiah 2:4; Matthew 5:9,38–48; 6:33; 26:52; Luke 22:36,38; Romans 12:18–19; 13:1–7; 14:19; Hebrews 12:14; James 4:1–2.

XVII. Religious Liberty

God alone is Lord of the conscience, and He has left it free from the doctrines and commandments of men which are contrary to His Word or not contained in it. Church and state should be separate. The state owes to every church protection and full freedom in the pursuit of its spiritual ends. In providing for such freedom, no ecclesiastical group or denomination should be favored by the state more than others. Civil government being ordained of God, it is the duty of Christians to render loyal obedience thereto in all things not contrary to the revealed will of God.

The church should not resort to the civil power to carry on its work. The gospel of Christ contemplates spiritual means alone for the pursuit of its ends. The state has no right to impose penalties for religious opinions of any kind. The state has no right to impose taxes for the support of any form of religion. A free church in a free state is the Christian ideal, and this implies the right of free and unhindered access to God on the part of all men, and the right to form and propagate opinions in the sphere of religion without interference by the civil power.

Genesis 1:27; 2:7; Matthew 6:6–7,24; 16:26; 22:21; John 8:36; Acts 4:19–20; Romans 6:1–2; 13:1–7; Galatians 5:1,13; Philippians 3:20; 1 Timothy 2:1–2; James 4:12; 1 Peter 2:12–17; 3:11–17; 4:12–19.

XVIII. The Family

God has ordained the family as the foundational institution of human society. It is composed of persons related to one another by marriage, blood, or adoption. Marriage is the uniting of one man and one woman in covenant commitment for a lifetime. It is God's unique gift to reveal the union between Christ and His church and to provide for the man and the woman in marriage the framework for intimate companionship, the channel of sexual expression according to biblical standards, and the means for procreation of the human race. The husband and wife are of equal worth before God, since both are created in God's image. The marriage relationship models the way God relates to His people.

A husband is to love his wife as Christ loved the church. He has the God-given responsibility to provide for, to protect, and to lead his family. A wife is to submit herself graciously to the servant leadership of her husband even as the church willingly submits to the headship of Christ. She, being in the image of God as is her husband and thus equal to him, has the God-given responsibility to respect her husband and to serve as his helper in managing the household and nurturing the next generation.

Children, from the moment of conception, are a blessing and heritage from the Lord. Parents are to demonstrate to their children God's pattern for marriage. Parents are to teach their children spiritual and moral values and to lead them, through consistent lifestyle example and loving discipline, to make choices based on biblical truth. Children are to honor and obey their parents.

Genesis 1:26–28; 2:15–25; 3:1–20; Exodus 20:12; Deuteronomy 6:4–9; Joshua 24:15; 1 Samuel 1:26–28; Psalms 51:5; 78:1–8; 127; 128; 139:13–16; Proverbs 1:8; 5:15–20; 6:20–22; 12:4; 13:24; 14:1; 17:6; 18:22; 22:6,15; 23:13–14; 24:3; 29:15,17; 31:10–31; Ecclesiastes 4:9–12; 9:9; Malachi 2:14–16; Matthew 5:31–32; 18:2–5; 19:3–9; Mark 10:6–12; Romans 1:18–32; 1 Corinthians 7:1–16; Ephesians 5:21–33; 6:1–4; Colossians 3:18–21; 1 Timothy 5:8,14; 2 Timothy 1:3–5; Titus 2:3–5; Hebrews 13:4; 1 Peter 3:1–7.

APPENDIX 11
How to Conduct a Business Meeting

Depending on the denomination, the instructions about this topic may vary. Even in a denomination, such as Baptist, where congregational government is practiced, the instructions may vary. Some Baptist churches have adopted elder rule, which is basically presbyterian church polity. There is a form of elder rule that maintains congregational government. To ensure congregational government, the congregation must elect the elders. The major decisions of the church, such as calling a pastor, electing deacons, adopting a budget, a capital purchase, selling property, and admitting or dismissing members, should be brought to the congregation for approval.

Some Baptist churches elect a layman to be the moderator of the church and conduct business meetings. In most Southern Baptist churches, the pastor is the moderator. An incoming pastor should read carefully the constitution and bylaws of the church to which he has been called and carefully follow those documents.

If the pastor is the moderator, he should become very familiar with *Robert's Rules of Order*,[1] latest edition. While some pastors do not like the formality of following *Robert's Rules of Order*, doing so will head off many problems. If the congregation is not familiar with rules of order, they can be gently guided to proceed accordingly. A professional parlimentarian, Barry C. McCarty, has written an excellent book on how to use parliamentary rules effectively and appropriately in a church setting.[2]

While smaller churches have monthly business meetings, some larger churches have changed their bylaws to have quarterly business meetings. Churches affiliated with the American Baptist Convention sometimes have only one annual meeting, with called meetings in between as needed. It is best not to have a business meeting on Sunday morning, unless it is a called business meeting at the end of the service to take an important vote, such as calling a new pastor. Whenever it is scheduled, a business session should not replace a worship service but should follow it.

There are regular business meetings and called business meetings. The church's bylaws should explain how both are to be scheduled. It is good to have a printed agenda for every business meeting, regular or called. In a called business meeting, only the purpose for which the meeting was called can be discussed. In a regular business meeting, there is always a final item, "Other Business."

A Suggested Agenda

Call to Order
Motion to Adopt the Printed Agenda
Prayer
Reading of the Minutes of the Prior Business Meeting
Old Business
New Business
    1. Reports (should be written and distributed with the agenda)
    2. Recommendations from committees or deacons or elders
    3. Other
Motion to Adjourn
Prayer

Any motion must have a second in order to discuss it, unless the motion comes from a committee. If the item is controversial, the moderator should ask those who support the motion and those who are against it to alternate speaking. When there are no more expressions of dissent, the moderator asks, "Are you ready for the question?"

A voice vote is usually taken first. The moderator says, "All in favor please say 'aye.' Those opposed by the same sign." If the outcome is in doubt, the moderator can call for a show of hands. If that is in doubt, he can call for a standing vote. In either case, he should call on deacons to do the counting. On more important matters, it is best to use written ballots. Deacons should be asked to count the votes.

In a congregationally governed church, it is imperative that committees and other authoritative groups in the church be involved in items to bring before the church. If an item is brought up directly on the floor of the business meeting, the moderator can refer the item to a committee or to the deacons or elders to study and bring back a report at the next business meeting.

The pastor as moderator must be fair and impartial in presiding over the church's business meetings. Knowing Robert's Rules of Order will help him in that regard. There is a Reformation doctrinal reason for church business meetings. It is called the doctrine of the priesthood of believers. Churches that embrace that doctrine should give all believers the opportunity to express themselves. In congregational polity, that is the ultimate way a church determines God's will. But those expressions should be guided by the Holy Spirit and not by personal opinion.

There is no place in a church business meeting for a display of the flesh or power struggles. If conflict arises during a business meeting, the pastor should stop and exhort his people to be loving and kind and orderly as they do God's business. Paul said, "But everything must be done decently and in order" (1 Cor. 14:40). If conflict continues, he should contact his denomination for help and guidance in conflict resolution (see appendix 1).

Calendar Planning

First Corinthians 14:40 says, "Everything must be done decently and in order." While this verse is about worship, it also applies to the pastor's calendar.

The Weekly Calendar

Worship services are already set for the pastor, and these should be the apex of his week. Everything during the week should lead up to Sunday. It is the Lord's Day and the most important day in the pastor's weekly calendar. Although many churches want to have committee meetings and deacons meetings on Sunday afternoon, I would urge the pastor to ask them to schedule those meetings at other times. The pastor and the people need to focus on worship and not on business matters. The mid-week prayer service is the second most important day on the pastor's calendar. An evening for visitation is the third.

The rest of the week should include hospital visitation, counseling appointments, denominational meetings, staff meetings, and so forth. In the midst of all this, the pastor should set aside his mornings for study and prayer. He should have his sermons ready before Friday. That way he can reserve Friday as a day for his wife and family. No pastor can keep from working six days a week, but it is imperative that he not work seven days a week. He breaks the spirit of the fourth commandment if he does. "Six days you shall labor and do all your work" (Exod. 20:9 NKJV).

Sunday is a day of work for the pastor. He should take one day, other than Saturday or Sunday, as a day of rest from his work. Any pastor who tries to break God's fourth commandment will break himself or his family instead. Wise churches will write a weekly day off into the pastor's job description.

The Preaching Calendar

The wise pastor will plan his preaching a year in advance. This author, when a pastor, took the first week of his summer vacation to plan his preaching for the coming year. If a pastor preaches through books of the Bible, the planning is easy to do. Six months to a year before planning his preaching calendar, the pastor should be building his library and reading commentaries on the book of the Bible he plans to preach through next.

Take your family on vacation, get up early before them each morning the first week, and plan your preaching. With just an hour or two a day you should be able to divide the book you plan to preach through into logical sections or what I call "preaching paragraphs." Then capture the theme, the line of direction, give a title, and a brief major point outline. When you return from vacation, further research can be done, and the sermons can be developed and written week by week. But the planning should be done in advance.

If you are focusing on a long book of the Bible, you may want to preach Sundays morning and evening from the same book. Just take up on Sunday evening where you left off Sunday morning. If it is a short book, you may want to plan to preach from a different book on Sunday nights. Wednesday nights should be approached devotionally because this is primarily a church prayer meeting.

The Church Program Calendar

If the church is large enough to have a full-time staff, the pastor and staff should plan the annual church program calendar. If the church is small, the pastor should form a church council, consisting of the pastor, any part-time staff members, the chairman of deacons, the director of the Sunday school, the director of Church Training or Discipleship Training, and the leader of the women's ministry or the Women's Missionary Union. They can submit the program calendar to whatever body needs to approve it, such as the deacons, elders, or congregation. The wider the involvement in planning, the more participation there will be in those events.

The Pastor's Office Hours

The wise pastor needs to devote his mornings to Bible study and prayer. He may be able to do this best at home rather than at the church office. People tend to drop in for unscheduled visits with the pastor at the church. If space is available, he can prepare an "upper room" or hideaway at the church in a room other than his office. In other words, he can have an office in which he meets people and a different room where he meets God, studies, and prays. There will be times when his morning is interrupted by emergencies or funerals, but it is amazing how a church will leave a pastor alone in the mornings if they know from his preaching that he is meeting with God in Bible study and prayer.

W. A. Criswell, pastor of the First Baptist Church of Dallas, Texas, for nearly fifty years, said that he gave his mornings to God, his afternoons to the staff and people of the church, and his evenings to meetings of the church. That is not a bad plan. Church members can be trained to call and make appointments.

If that sounds too professional and cold, just tell your people that if they need to see you, they should call the church office and let you know when they want to come. That way you will be sure to be there, and their visit will not conflict with another appointment. Then they can be guided into specific times when you are available. Appointments are as much for the protection of the members' time as they are for the pastor's time.

Calendaring Church Business Meetings

Churches that practice congregational government will have a regularly scheduled church business meeting or church conference. Some churches have monthly business meetings, usually on Wednesday night. A growing trend is to have quarterly business meetings, usually on Sunday night. In some Baptist denominations there is only one business meeting a year, an annual church conference. Whatever the frequency, the church conferences should be scheduled and put on the church calendar a year in advance. If there is need to deviate from the regular schedule, an extra business meeting may be called at anytime as long as proper notice is given. This requirement should be stated in the church's bylaws.

Calendaring Time Away from the Church Field

In the pastor's job description should be a statement about pre-approved times when he can be away from the church field. This includes vacations, sick days, funeral leaves, leaves for jury duty, leaves to hold revivals at other churches, and professional development days. The last item should include time off to attend denominational conventions (at church expense), local, state, and nationwide.

If all of this is spelled out on the pastor's calendar, he can make adjustments in his preaching schedule and also monitor himself to make sure he is not taking advantage of the church by being gone too much. The wise pastor will always notify in writing the chairman of the personnel committee when he will be gone and how he can be reached in case of an emergency.

Calendaring Weddings and Funerals

The pastor should put weddings, rehearsals, and counseling appointments on his calendar when a wedding is scheduled by the couple planning to be married. This information can also be used to develop an anniversary calendar. Sending anniversary letters to those he has married will endear the pastor to his people. The same thing can be done with funerals. These sorts of entries in the pastor's annual calendar can be used by him to audit his ministry in the church at the end of the year. In his column in the church newsletter, he can share how many weddings and funerals he has officiated at during the previous year. Just adding it all up will amaze you.

APPENDIX 13 How to Give a Public Invitation in Church

The pastor needs to know how to give a public invitation during a worship service. Two books on this topic are included in the bibliography at the end of this book. Alan Streett has a book titled *The Effective Invitation*.[1] The other book, *Drawing the Net*,[2] is by O. S. Hawkins. Streett has taught evangelism at Criswell College in Dallas, Texas, for many years. Hawkins was pastor of the First Baptist Church of Dallas before becoming president and CEO of GuideStone Financial Services, a Southern Baptist agency.

I have heard both men preach. Both give superb invitations. With Hawkins's permission, I am copying here the typical public invitation that he extended at the close of a Sunday service. He always asked the people to bow their heads in prayer.

"In just a moment I am going to ask you to do something that is going to take courage. I am going to ask you to leave your seat, step into the aisle, make your way to the front, and join me here for prayer. Many of you are going to come to be included in this prayer this morning. Some of you have never opened your heart's door to receive the free gift of eternal life, Jesus Christ, as your very own personal Savior. You have a divine appointment with Him this morning, and you are not here by accident.

"Perhaps you sense God's Spirit knocking at the door of your heart but, quite honestly, just don't know what you would say if you were to respond and join me here at the front. I have good news for you. You do not have to worry about what to say. By your coming you will be saying, 'I am going to go God's way today!' When you get here, I am going to lead us all in a word of prayer. We have some Bible study

292

material to give you to help you, and if you come as an inquirer, we want the privilege of leading you to faith in the Lord Jesus.

"By trusting in Him alone this morning, it will mean God will forgive you of all your sin and make it just as if it never happened. It also means that Christ Himself will take up residence in your life and never leave you. It means He will give you a place in heaven and a heavenly time on the way. So, in just a moment, I am going to ask you to come and receive this free gift.

"There are others of you here this morning who have already opened your hearts to Christ—perhaps this week, last week, last month, or whenever. But you have never stood for Him publicly, openly, or unashamedly. In just a moment, I am going to ask you to join the others who are coming, and, by your coming to be included in this prayer, you will be saying, 'I am making a public pledge of my life to Jesus Christ.'

"There is something about standing for Christ publicly that helps seal the personal decision that has already been made in the heart. In fact, Jesus said, 'Whosoever therefore shall confess Me before men, him will I confess also before My Father which is in heaven.' How can you expect to stand for Christ in the marketplaces of the world, which are so hostile to Him, if you will not stand for Him by walking down a carpeted aisle of an air-conditioned church in front of a lot of Christians who will rejoice with you in your decision? Therefore, in a moment, when others come, I am going to ask you to lead the way to this altar.

"Still others of you are here who are Christians but you are not active in a local church in our city. Perhaps you have just moved here. You have moved everything you have—your furniture, your family, even your pets. Everything, that is, except your church membership. In a moment, I am going to ask you to join the others in coming and by doing so you will be saying, 'I am going to come out of the shadows today and put on the uniform of church membership and serve Christ in and through this local expression of His body.'

"You have been eating your spiritual food here for some time. You have been thinking about joining our team. You have even been planning on it and praying about it. The only thing left to do is to do it, right now. By your coming to join us this morning and being included in this prayer, you will also be serving as an escort for many here who need to know Jesus Christ personally.

"There are yet others of you here this morning with a friend who needs to know Jesus. It may be that the Spirit of God would have you reach out and take that friend by the hand and say, 'Let's go God's way this morning. I'll go with you. Let's go together.' Many in the Bible did that very thing. Andrew found Peter, took him by the hand, and brought him to Jesus. Philip brought Nathaniel. And on and on the church has grown. You can be confident that if the Spirit is leading you to encourage your friend, He is dealing with his heart at the same time. Take your friend by the hand this morning and say, 'Let's go together. I'll go with you.' And bring your friend to Jesus. You will be so glad you did.

"There are others of you here this morning who are honest enough to say, 'Preacher, I don't know what I need. But my life has no purpose or direction.' The something you have looked for to fill the void of life can be found this morning in someone, and His name is the Lord Jesus. I am going to ask you to join the others in coming to be included in this prayer. Don't worry about what to say when you get here. By your coming as an inquirer you will be saying, 'I want to go God's way today and trust in Him.' And when you come, 'Your sins He'll wash away, your night He'll turn to day, your life He'll make it over anew.' He has a brand-new life for you and a brand-new beginning.

"Whatever the decision may be in your heart—a desire to know Christ personally, a public pledge of your life to Him, to unite with our fellowship and join our team, to bring a friend to Jesus, or simply to come in honest inquiry—I am going to ask you to leave your seat, make your way to the front, and join me here. By your coming you are saying, 'I am going God's way today.' Don't wait for anyone else. If there is the slightest tugging at your heartstrings, it is the Spirit of God. Many are going to come, and it is the right thing to do. You lead the way, right now."[3]

Then the pastor can ask the congregation to remain seated and pray as the choir sings a hymn of invitation and people respond. Be sure to give the Holy Spirit time to work and the people time to come. This invitation takes about five minutes to give, but it is important. One of the things pastors may have to answer to God for is bringing people right up to the gates of the kingdom but not inviting them to come in.

APPENDIX 14
What Version of the Bible Should the Pastor Use?

When I (Bryant) was a new Christian in 1951, there were only two or three versions [the word *version* is Latin for "translation"] of the Bible available for Protestants: The original King James Version (1611), the old English Revised Version (1885), and the old American-Standard Version (1901). There were translations that had been done by individuals like Moffatt, but the three above were the only ones done by translation committees. I had the King James Version. And that is the Bible I began to commit to memory.

When the proliferation of new English translations began, I was flabbergasted. The Revised Standard Version was first. Then came The Living Bible. I liked The Living Bible, but I recognized that it was a paraphrase and not a translation. The Amplified Bible came out. I found all of them helpful for study, but I preached out of the King James Version because that was the translation most church people carried and that was the one I was memorizing.

When the New King James Version was published in 1982, I quickly adopted it both for a preaching Bible and for a pew Bible in three different churches I pastored over the years. W. A. Criswell used the New King James for his Criswell Study Bible, which is still in the pews at the First Baptist Church of Dallas, Texas, where he served for fifty years. It was close enough to the King James for people who still carried the original King James to follow when he preached.

Many young pastors turned to the New International Version. The New American Standard Bible also became a favorite. How does one go about choosing a Bible in the midst of so many options?

Read the introduction in each translation you are considering. There are two basic translation philosophies: formal equivalency and dynamic equivalency. Formal equivalency seeks to do a word-for-word translation. This is difficult if not impossible to do because the order of words in Greek and Hebrew is often different from the order of words in English. Dynamic equivalency seeks to do a thought-for-thought translation. Translators defend this approach by pointing out that exact word-for-word translations do not exist.

If you believe in the plenary, verbal inspiration of the Bible, there are theological implications for translations. I want a formal equivalency. I realize it is not exact, but if every word of the Bible is inspired, I think it is important to know what the words are. If you are going to do expository preaching, you need a Bible that uses a formal equivalency approach. If you are going to do topical preaching, it doesn't really matter. The authors of this book urge you to do expository preaching.

Until 2004, there were only two modern translations in English that used formal equivalency—the New King James Version and the New American Standard Bible. In 2004 Holman Bible Publishers produced a very fine translation done by a top-notch committee of scholars with excellent English editors. Known as the Holman Christian Standard Bible, it is one of the Bibles we quote from in this book.

The Christian Standard Bible introduction suggests there are three translation philosophies, not two. There is the formal equivalency that seeks a word-for-word translation. There is the dynamic equivalency that seeks a thought-for-thought translation. The CSB follows what they call optimal equivalency. Optimal equivalency uses formal equivalency as a default translation approach, but adjusts beautifully to good English when word-for-word just does not work. The result is a very readable Bible, but one committed to a plenary, verbal theory of inspiration. I have lost count of the number of these Bibles I have given away as presents. Everyone loves it.

I still preach from the New King James because people with other translations seem to be better able to follow in their Bibles, and it is closer to the Bible I memorized as a teenager, updated with "you" and "your" instead of "thee" and "thou." I study using a wide variety of translations, but I preach out of one Bible.

Whatever version you choose, I suggest you consider putting that version in the pews at your church and urge your people to buy that version. Then all of you can be on the same page as you read the Scriptures out loud together and as you preach the Word of God.

Notes

Preface and Acknowledgments

1. W. A. Criswell, *Criswell's Guidebook for Pastors* (Nashville: Broadman, 1980).

Introduction

1. See Andrew Blackwood, *Pastoral Work* (Philadelphia: Westminster Press, 1945) and *Pastoral Leadership* (New York: Abingdon, 1949).

2. Richard Baxter, *The Reformed Pastor*, revised and abridged (New York: American Tract Society, 1829).

3. See *Criswell's Guidebook for Pastors*.

4. Baxter, *The Reformed Pastor*, 89.

5. Ibid., 101.

6. Swank was pastor of Sagamore Hill Baptist Church in Fort Worth, Texas.

Chapter 1: The Pastor and His Call

1. See John Piper, *Brothers, We Are Not Professionals* (Nashville: Broadman & Holman, 2002), xiii.

Chapter 2: The Pastor and His Preparation

1. www.billgothard.com.

Chapter 3: The Pastor and His Preaching

1. John Albert Bengel, *Gnomon of the New Testament*, ed. Andrew R. Fausset, 5 vols. (Edinburgh: Clark, 1857–1858: 1:7), quoted in Walter C. Kaiser Jr., *Toward an Exegetical Theology* (Grand Rapids: Baker Book House, 1981), 7.

2. Kenton C. Anderson, *Choosing to Preach* (Grand Rapids: Zondervan, 2006).

3. John A. Broadus, *On the Preparation and Delivery of Sermons* (New York: HarperSanFrancisco, 1979), 7.

4. Ibid.

5. Walter C. Kaiser Jr., *The Uses of the Old Testament in the New* (Grand Rapids: Wm. B. Eerdmans Publishing Co., 1958), 17.

6. R. T. Kendall, "Expositional Preaching" in *Northcutt Lectures* (Fort Worth: Southwestern Baptist Theological Seminary, 1988), sound.

7. If you have not studied Greek and Hebrew extensively enough to do this, you can use an exhaustive concordance that has both Greek and Hebrew indexes in the back and trace the root meanings of the words. Exegetical commentaries can also be consulted to

give you information about tense of verbs and declension of nouns. Although not exhaustive, books such as A. T. Robertson, *Word Pictures in the New Testament*, 6 vols. (Nashville: Broadman & Holman, 1980) will do that in an alphabetical manner.

8. Fritz Rienecker and Cleon Rogers, *Linguistic Key to the Greek New Testament* (Grand Rapids: Zondervan, 1976), 627.

Chapter 4: The Pastor and His Prayer Life

1. E. M. Bounds lived from 1835–1913. He wrote eight classic volumes on prayer. Excerpts from all eight can be found in *The Best of E. M. Bounds on Prayer* (Grand Rapids: Baker Book House, 1981).

2. E. M. Bounds, *Power Through Prayer*, rev. ed. (Grand Rapids: Zondervan, 1962), 12.

3. G. Campbell Morgan, *The Practice of Prayer* (Alexandria: Lamplighter Publications, n.d.), 105–106.

4. Charles Spurgeon, *Only a Prayer Meeting* (Pasadena, Tex.: Pilgrims Publications, 1976).

5. Ibid., 23

6. Ibid., 25.

7. Ibid., 27–30.

8. Daniel Henderson, *Fresh Encounters* (Colorado Springs: NavPress, 2004).

9. Ibid., 26.

10. Charles Spurgeon, as quoted in Daniel Henderson, *Fresh Encounters*, 28.

Chapter 5: The Pastor and His Family

1. Dean R. Hage and Jacqueline E. Wenger, *Pastors in Transition* (Grand Rapids: Eerdmans, 2005), table of contents.

2. Andy Stanley, *Choosing to Cheat* (Sisters, Ore.: Multnomah, 2003).

Chapter 6: The Pastor and His First Church

1. Lyle Schaller, *The Pastor and the People* (Nashville: Abingdon, 1973), 32–44.

2. Blackwood, *Pastoral Work*, 35–40.

3. Ibid., 36.

Chapter 7: The Pastor and His Leadership

1. Fred Smith, *Learning to Lead* (Waco: Word, 1986), 22.

2. James Means, *Leadership in Christian Ministry* (Grand Rapids: Baker, 1989).

3. www.infoplease.com/ipa/A0004979.html

4. Myron Rush, *The New Leader* (Wheaton: Victor, 1987), 85.

5. Jim Collins, *Good to Great and the Social Sectors: A Monograph to Accompany Good to Great* (New York: Collins), 12.

6. Ibid., 12–13.

7. Leon McBeth, *The First Baptist Church of Dallas: Centennial History 1868–1968* (Grand Rapids: Zondervan Press, 1968), 118–19.

8. O. S. Hawkins, *The Pastor's Primer* (Dallas: GuideStone, 2006), 96.

9. Ken Blanchard, *One Minute Manager* (Berkley: Berkley Trade, 1983).

10. Ken Blanchard and Phil Hodges, *Lead Like Jesus* (Nashville: Thomas Nelson, 2005), 3.

11. Ibid., 4.

12. David Garland, *1 Corinthians*, in the Baker Exegetical Commentary (Grand Rapids: Baker Academic, 2003), 125.

Chapter 8: The Pastor and His Staff

1. Acts 6:1–7 does not use the word *deacon*, but most certainly these seven men were the first deacons. The traditional Baptist practice of having deacons handle business matters only misses the point of this passage. The business the first deacons handled was what is known today as pastoral visitation. As such, the first deacons were actually assistants to the apostles. By the way, they also preached and did evangelism.

2. See stephenministries.org. for an interdenominational program of training lay men and women to assist the pastor in meeting the pastoral needs of church members.

3. Chad Owen Brand and R. Stanton Norman, *Perspectives on Church Government: Five Views of Church Polity* (Nashville: Broadman & Holman, 2004.)

Chapter 9: The Pastor and Worship

1. George Barna and Michael D. Warren, eds., *Experience God in Worship* (Loveland, Colo.: Group Publishing, 2000), 16.

2. D. A. Carson, ed., *Worship by the Book* (Grand Rapids: Zondervan, 2002), 29.

3. Warren Wiersbe, *Real Worship* (Grand Rapids: Baker Book, 2000), 28.

4. In a study of Reformation architecture, one discovers that frequently the pulpit was bolted to the floor so it could not be moved to one side.

5. Carson, *Worship*, 167.

Chapter 10: The Pastor and Technology

1. George Barna, *Boiling Point: Monitoring Culture Shifts in the 21st Century* (Venture: Regal Books, 2003).

2. "A Science Odyssey: People and Discoveries: KDKA begins to broadcast." Accessed at www.pbs.org/wgbh/aso.databank/entries/dt20ra.html.

3. "KDKA Made Religious Waves," Christian History Institute, January 21, 1921.

4. Ibid.

5. The Baptist State Convention of North Carolina uses this term in an article at www.bscnc.org/churchministries/digitalministry/technologyresources.

6. Pew Internet & American Life: Faith Online at www.pewInternet.org.

Chapter 11: The Pastor, Missions, and Evangelism

1. Criswell, *Criswell's Guidebook for Pastors*, 229.

2. Roy J. Fish and J. E. Conant, *Every Member Evangelism* (New York: Harper & Row, 1992), 20.

3. Greg Laurie, *The Upside Down Church* (Wheaton: Tyndale House, 1999), 65–66.

Chapter 12: The Pastor and the Ordinances

1. By original sin, he meant the fallen, sinful, human nature that he saw being passed on genetically to the entire human race.

2. *Ana* is the Latin prefix that means "again." In English we would call them "rebaptizers." They had been baptized as infants in the Roman Catholic Church and then were baptized again.

3. In all fairness to those who practice infant baptism, they point to Acts 16:31, "Believe on the Lord Jesus, and you will be saved—you and your household." Also, Acts 16:33 says, "Right away he and all his family were baptized." Of course, they are assuming that the jailer had infants in his family.

4. Closed communion takes one of two forms. In some churches only the members of the local church are allowed to take communion. In other churches only members of that

denomination are allowed to take communion. Open communion usually allows anyone present to take communion as long as they are believers in Christ.

5.   There are now available serving cups with a lip on each to hold a piece of bread, serving both elements at once.

Chapter 13: The Pastor, Weddings, and Funerals

1.   For instance, see Chad O. Brand and R. Stanton Norman, *Perspectives on Church Government: Five Views on Church Polity* (Nashville: Broadman & Holman, 2004).

2.   After everyone had his say, James made the decision. This is single-elder rule.

3.   Guy Duty, *Divorce and Remarriage* (Bethany: Bethany Publishing House, 2002).

Chapter 14: The Pastor and His Counseling

1.   See www.maranathalife.com.

2.   C. W. Brister, *The Promise of Counseling* (San Francisco: Harper & Row, 1978).

3.   Wayne Oates, *Pastoral Counseling* (Philadelphia: Westminster Press, 1974), chapter 9.

4.   William E. Hulme, *How to Start Counseling* (New York: Abingdon, 1955).

5.   Wayne E. Oates, ed., *Protestant Pastoral Counseling* (Philadelphia: Westminster Press, 1962), 106.

6.   Ibid., 107.

7.   www.aacc.net.

8.   www.minirthclinic.com.

9.   John MacArthur and the Master's College Faculty, *Introduction to Biblical Counseling* (Dallas: Word, 1994), chapter 20. Please note that this book recommends only one approach to Christian counseling, the Nouthetic approach of Jay Adams.

10.   www.billgothard.com.

11.   MacArthur, *Introduction to Biblical Counseling*, 323.

12.   Jim Henry and Marilyn Jeffcoat, *The Two Shall Become One* (Nashville: Broadman & Holman, 2000).

13.   www.ccci.org.

14.   www.eeinternational.org.

15.   Howard John Clinebell, *Basic Types of Pastoral Counseling* (Nashville: Abingdon Press, 1966). It should be noted that this book is written for pastors with maximum counseling training, but it still outlines the basic types.

16.   Gary R. Collins, *Christian Counseling: A Comprehensive Guide.* (Waco: Word, 1988).

17.   Gail Sheehy, *New Passages* (New York: Random House, 1995), 10–11.

Chapter 15: The Pastor and Finances

1.   You may contact Bob Eklund at bkeklund@aol.com.

2.   One of the most thorough financial policies and procedures manuals I have ever seen has been adopted by the deacons of the First Baptist Church of Dallas, Texas. See www.firstdallas.org.

Chapter 16: The Pastor and His Ethics

1.   Billy Graham, *Just As I Am* (San Francisco: Harper, 1997), 127–29.

2.   Joe E. Trull and James E. Carter, *Ministerial Ethics* (Grand Rapids: Baker Academic, 2004), appendix E.

3.   Ibid., appendix A.

4. Ibid., 40–41.
5. Ibid., 54.

Chapter 17: The Pastor, Politics, and Moral Issues
1. James Sire, *Chris Chrisman Goes to College* (Downers Grove: InterVarsity, 1993), 123–26.
2. One of the best discussions of the proper interpretation of the First Amendment and its two clauses, prohibiting the establishment of a state church and prohibiting interference in church matters by the state, is The Williamsburg Charter. It was drafted and presented to the United States in Williamsburg, Virginia, July 25, 1988, the 200th anniversary of the call in Virginia for a United States Bill of Rights. President Jimmy Carter, President Gerald Ford, and Chief Justice William H. Rhenquist of the Supreme Court signed it, along with Chief Justice Warren E. Burger, retired from the Supreme Court, and more than two hundred other civic and religious leaders. See James D. Hunter and Os Guinness, eds., *Articles of Faith, Articles of Peace: The Religious Liberty Clauses and the American Public Philosophy* (Washington, D.C.: The Brookings Institution, 1990).
3. See www.aclj.org.
4. See www.Rutherford.org.
5. The Free Market Foundation Voters Guide for the 2006 general election presented these moral issues and the response of the various candidates to questions about them. See http://www.freemarket.org/votersguide.
6. See www.citizenlink.com.
7. www.family.org.
8. For example, the Free Market Foundation at www.freemarket.org/votersguide.
9. The following material comes from www.erlc.com.
10. www.billgothard.com.
11. John Bunyan, *Pilgrim's Progress* (London: Penguin Books, 1964).
12. Leon McBeth, *The Baptist Heritage* (Nashville: Broadman Press, 1987), 279–83.
13. John J. Pitney Jr. denies that de Tocqueville ever wrote these words even though presidents Eisenhower, Reagan, and Clinton gave de Tocqueville credit for the thought. For Pitney's full discussion, see www.tocqueville.org/pitney.htm.

Chapter 18: The Pastor Changing Churches
1. McBeth, *The Baptist Heritage*.
2. Schaller, *The Pastor and the People*.
3. Frank Peretti, *This Present Darkness* (Carol Stream, Ill.: Tyndale House, 2003).
4. Bunyan, *Pilgrim's Progress*.
5. See www.olford.org.

Chapter 19: The Pastor and His Denomination
1. See Alister McGrath, *Introduction to Christian Theology*, 4th ed. (London: Blackwell Publications, 2006).
2. See Jerry Sutton, *The Baptist Reformation* (Nashville: Broadman & Holman, 1999).

Chapter 20: The Pastor and His Retirement
1. Ministers have two years after their ordination to opt out of Social Security for their ministerial earnings. To do so, they must have a conscientious objection to receiving government funds for ministerial duties. Most denominational pension funds advise ministers to stay in Social Security.

2. Today it is called GuideStone Financial Services, which makes its services in retirement planning available to most evangelical ministers, not just Southern Baptists. See www.guidestone.org.

Chapter 21: The Pastor and His Reward

1. W. A. Criswell, *Standing on the Promises* (Dallas: Word Publishing, 1990), 248–50.
2. The author considers the words *pastor, elder,* and *bishop* to refer to the same office.
3. This alleged quote is not found in his writings, although he could have said it in an unrecorded speech.
4. See Harry Ironside's *Commentary on Ephesians* (Kregel Academic & Professional, 2007).
5. Since 1997 called the Southern Baptist International Mission Board.
6. John Bunyan identifies a seventh piece of armor, a secret weapon, "all prayer."
7. See Criswell's autobiography, *With a Bible in My Hand* (Nashville: Baptist Sunday School Board, 1978).

Appendix 2: Where Does a Pastor Go for Help When He Is Fired?

1. www.lifeway.com/leadercare, main page.

Appendix 3: How Does a Pastor Build His Personal Library?

1. Allen taught expository preaching at Criswell College in Dallas, Texas, for many years. He is now dean of the school of theology at Southwestern Baptist Theological Seminary in Fort Worth, Texas.

Appendix 6: Sample Staff Organization Charts

1. This chart comes from the First Baptist Church of Dallas, Texas.
2. The minister of music has a staff of four full-time, seven part-time, and one volunteer under him.
3. Community Life Fellowship pastor. Under him are Downtown Ministries, Family Life Ministries, Leadership Development, Discipleship Ministries, Counseling and Care Ministries, and an Associate of Worship. The CLF staff includes twenty-one full-time persons and three part-time persons.
4. Connection groups = the Sunday school. These ministries, involving twenty-four employees, are divided into preschool, children, students, and adults.
5. An alternative worship service meeting in Center Stage, the name for the church's dining hall.

Appendix 9: Journaling and Filing

1. Whitney is associate professor of biblical spirituality at Southern Baptist Theological Seminary.
2. Donald S. Whitney, *Spiritual Disciplines for the Christian Life* (Colorado Springs: NavPress, 1991).
3. Donald S. Whitney, *Simplify Your Spiritual Life* (Colorado Springs: NavPress, 2003).
4. Whitney, *Spiritual Disciplines for the Christian Life*, 206–17.
5. Whitney, *Simplify Your Spiritual Life*, 101.
6. Ibid., 153.
7. Ibid.

Appendix 11: How to Conduct a Business Meeting

1. Henry M. Robert, III, William J. Evans, Daniel H. Honemann, and Thomas J. Balch, eds., *Robert's Rules of Order* (London: Harper Collins, 2000).

2. Barry C. McCarty, *A Parliamentary Guide for Church Leaders* (Nashville: Broadman & Holman, 1987).

Appendix 13: How to Give a Public Invitation in Church

1. R. Alan Streett, *The Effective Invitation*, updated ed. (Grand Rapids: Kregel, 2004).

2. O. S. Hawkins, *Drawing the Net* (Dallas: GuideStone, 2002).

3. Ibid., 141–45.

Bibliography

Adam, Peter. *Speaking God's Words: A Practical Theology of Preaching*. Vancouver, British Columbia, Canada: Regent College Publishing, 2004.

Adams, Jay E. *Marriage, Divorce, and Remarriage in the Bible*. Grand Rapids: Zondervan, 1980.

———. *Pastoral Leadership*. Grand Rapids: Baker, 1975.

———. *Shepherding God's Flock*. Nutley, N.J.: Presbyterian and Reformed, 1974.

Anderson, Kenton C. *Choosing to Preach*. Grand Rapids: Zondervan, 2006.

Anderson, Robert C. *The Effective Pastor*. Chicago: Moody, 1995.

Andrewater, John M. [pen name for John Maxwell]. *Elder, Bishop, Pastor*. 1989.

Armerding, Hudson T. *The Heart of Godly Leadership*. Wheaton: Crossway, 1992.

Armstrong, John H. *Can Fallen Pastors Be Restored?* Chicago: Moody, 1995.

Arzurdia, Aturo. *Spirit Empowered Preaching*. Scotland: Christian Focus Publications, 2000.

Bailey, E. K. and Warren W. Wiersbe. *Preaching Black and White*. Grand Rapids: Zondervan, 2003.

Barna, George. *Boiling Point: Monitoring Culture Shifts in the 21st Century*. Ventura: Regal Books, 2003.

Barna, George and Michael D. Warden, eds. *Experience God in Worship*. Loveland, Colo.: Group Publishing, 2000.

Baxter, Richard. *The Reformed Pastor*. Carlisle, Pa.: Banner of Truth, 1979.

Beck, Karl. *Pastor Karl's Rookie Year*. Downers Grove: InterVarsity Press, 1993.

Bedell, Gregory Thurston. *The Pastor: Pastoral Theology*. New York: J. B. Lippincott, 1880.

Beecher, Henry Ward. *Yale Lectures on Preaching*. New York: J. B. Ford & Co., 1873.

Bengel, John Albert. *Gnomon of the New Testament*, edited by Andrew R. Fausset. 5 vols. Edinburgh: Clark, 1857–58: 1:7.

Bickers, Dennis W. *The Tent-Making Pastor*. Grand Rapids: Baker, 2000.

Bisagno, John R. *Letters to Timothy: A Handbook for Pastors*. Nashville: Broadman, 2001.

Blackaby, Henry T. and Richard Blackaby. *Spiritual Leadership*. Nashville: Broadman & Holman, 2001.

Blackaby, Henry T. and Henry Brandt. *The Power of the Call*. Nashville: Broadman & Holman, 1997.

Blackwood, Andrew W. *Pastoral Leadership*. New York: Abingdon, 1949.

———. *Pastoral Work*. Philadelphia: The Westminster Press, 1945.

Blanchard, Ken. *One Minute Manager.* Berkley: Berkley Trade, 1983.

Blanchard, Ken, and Phil Hodges. *Lead Like Jesus.* Nashville: Thomas Nelson, 2005.

Booth, Abraham. *Pastoral Cautions.* London: C. Whittingham, 1805.

Bounds, E. M. *Power Through Prayer.* Rev. ed. Grand Rapids: Zondervan, 1962.

———. *The Best of E. M. Bounds on Prayer.* Grand Rapids: Baker, 1981.

Brand, Chad Owen and R. Stanton Norman. *Perspectives on Church Government: Five Views of Church Polity.* Nashville: Broadman & Holman, 2004.

Brister, C. W. *Pastoral Care in the Church.* 3rd ed. San Francisco: HarperSanFrancisco, 1992.

———. *The Promise of Counseling.* San Francisco: Harper & Row, 1978.

Broadus, John Albert. *A Treatise on the Preparation and Delivery of Sermons.* New York: A. C. Armstrong & Son, 1870.

Brooks, Phillips. *Lectures on the History of Preaching.* New York: Sheldon, 1876.

———. *The Joy of Preaching.* Grand Rapids: Kregel, 1885, 1987.

Bryson, Harold T. *Expository Preaching.* Nashville: Broadman & Holman, 1995.

Bulkley, Ed. *Why Christians Can't Trust Psychology.* Eugene, Ore.: Harvest House, 1993.

Bunyan, John. *Pilgrim's Progress.* Signet Classics. London: Penguin Books, 1964.

Capill, Murray A. *Preaching with Spiritual Vigour: Lessons from the Life of Richard Baxter.* Fearn: Mentor, 2003.

Carson, D. A. *Worship by the Book.* Grand Rapids: Zondervan, 2002.

Chapell, Bryan. *Christ-Centered Preaching.* Grand Rapids: Baker, 1994.

———. *Each for the Other.* Grand Rapids: Baker, 1998.

———. *Using Illustrations to Preach with Power.* Grand Rapids: Zondervan, 1992.

Chapman, Thomas W., ed. *A Practical Handbook for Ministry.* Louisville: Westminster/ John Knox Press, 1992.

Click, E. Dale. *Evangelism by a Seasoned Pastor Experienced in Church-Wide Evangelism.* 1994.

Clinebell, Howard John. *Basic Types of Pastoral Counseling.* Nashville: Abingdon, 1966.

Clinton, J. Robert. *The Making of a Leader.* Colorado Springs: NavPress, 1988.

Collins, Gary R. *Christian Counseling: A Comprehensive Guide.* Waco: Word, 1988.

Collins, Jim. *Good to Great and the Social Sectors: A Monograph to Accompany Good to Great.* New York: Collins.

Cowan, Steven B., ed. *Who Runs the Church: 4 Views of Church Government.* Grand Rapids: Zondervan, 2004.

Criswell, W. A. *Criswell's Guidebook for Pastors.* Nashville: Broadman, 1980.

———. *Standing on the Promises.* Dallas: Word Publishing, 1990.

———. *With a Bible in My Hand.* Nashville: Baptist Sunday School Board, 1978.

Culbertson, Philip Leroy. *The Pastor: Readings from the Patristics.* Minneapolis: Fortress Press, 1990.

Dale, Robert D. *Pastoral Leadership.* Nashville: Abingdon, 1986.

Dallimore, Arnold. *George Whitefield: The Life and Times of the Great Evangelist of the Eighteenth-Century Revival.* Vol. I. Westchester, Ill.: Crossway Books, 1979.

Dargan, Edwin Charles. *A History of Preaching.* Vols. 1–3. Grand Rapids: Baker, 1954.

Davis, Ellen R. *The Art of Reading Scripture.* Grand Rapids: Erdmans, 2003.

Dever, Mark. *Nine Marks of a Healthy Church.* Wheaton: Crossway, 2000.

Draper, James T., Jr. *Preaching with Passion.* Nashville: Broadman & Holman, 2004.

Drummond, Lewis A. *Spurgeon: Prince of Preachers.* Grand Rapids: Kregel, 1992.

Duduit, Michael, ed. *Handbook of Contemporary Preaching.* Nashville: Broadman & Holman, 1993.

Duty, Guy. *Divorce and Remarriage.* Reprint ed. Bethany: Bethany Publishing House, 2002.

Eby, David. *Power Preaching for Church Growth.* Fearn, UK: Mentor, 1996.

Edwards, Jonathan. *The Works of Jonathan Edwards.* Vol. I. 1834; reprint. Edinburgh: The Banner of Truth Trust, 1974.

English, Donald. *An Evangelical Theology of Preaching.* Nashville: Abingdon, 1996.

Erdman, Charles R. *The Work of the Pastor.* Philadelphia: The Westminster Press, 1928.

Fish, J. Roy and J. E. Conant. *Every Member Evangelism.* New York: Harper & Row, 1992.

Foshee, Howard B. *Broadman Church Manual.* Nashville: Broadman, 1973.

Fabarez, Michael and John MacArthur. *Preaching That Changes Lives.* Eugene, Ore.: Wipf & Stock Publishers, 2005.

Fisher, David. *The 21st Century Pastor.* Grand Rapids: Zondervan, 1996.

Gali, Mark, and Craig Brian Larson. *Preaching That Connects.* Grand Rapids: Zondervan, 1994.

Garland, David. *1 Corinthians,* in the Baker Exegetical Commentary. Grand Rapids: Baker Academic, 2003.

Garvie, Alfred E. *A Guide to Preachers.* 4th ed. London: Hodder and Stoughton, 1911.

Glass, James D. *Profession: Minister.* Nashville: Abingdon, 1968.

Goldsworthy, Graeme. *Preaching the Whole Bible as Christian Scripture.* Grand Rapids: Eerdmans, 2000.

Graham, Billy. *Just As I Am.* Rev. ed. San Francisco: HarperSanFrancisco, 1999.

Greidenus, Sidney. *Preaching Christ from the Old Testament.* Grand Rapids: Eerdmans, 1999.

Grenz, Stanley and Roy D. Bell. *Betrayal of Trust: Sexual Misconduct in the Pastorate.* Downers Grove: InterVarsity, 1995.

Griffith Thomas, W. H. *Ministerial Life and Work.* Grand Rapids: Zondervan, 1996.

Gushee, David P. and Walter C. Jackson, eds. *Preparing for Christian Ministry: An Evangelical Approach.* Grand Rapids: Baker, 1998.

Hage, Dean R. and Jacqueline E. Wenger. *Pastors in Transition.* Grand Rapids: Eerdmans, 2005.

Hawkins, O. S. *Drawing the Net.* Dallas: GuideStone, 2002.

———. *The Pastor's Primer.* Dallas: GuideStone, 2006.

Henderson, Daniel. *Fresh Encounters: Experiencing Transformation Through United Worship-Based Prayer.* Colorado Springs: NavPress, 2004.

———. *Think Before You Look: Avoiding the Consequences of Secret Temptation.* Chattanooga: AMG Publishers, 2005.

Henderson, Daniel and Patricia Roberts. *The Seven Most Important Questions You Will Ever Answer.* Grand Rapids: Discovery House Publishers, 1998.

Henderson, David W. *Culture Shift: Communicating God's Truth to Our Changing World.* Grand Rapids: Baker, 1998.

Hendricks, Howard. *Teaching to Change Lives.* Portland: Multnomah, 1987.

Hall, Robert. *God's Approbation: The Study of Ministers.* Coventry: J. W. Piercy, 1717.

Harmon, Nolan B. *Ministerial Ethics and Etiquette.* 2nd ed. Nashville: Abingdon, 1978.

Henry, Jim and Marilyn Jeffcoat. *The Two Shall Become One.* Nashville: Broadman & Holman, 2000.

Hoge, Dean R. and Jacqueline E. Wenger. *Pastors in Transition.* Grand Rapids: Erdmans, 2005.

Hoppin, James M. *Pastoral Theology.* 5th ed. New York: Funk and Wagnall's, 1884.

Hobbs, Herschel H. *Preacher Talk.* Nashville: Broadman, 1979.

Hull, Bill. *The Disciple-Making Pastor*. Grand Rapids: Fleming H. Revell, 1988.

Hulme, William E. *How to Start Counseling*. Nashville: Abingdon, 1955.

Hunter, James D. and Os Guinness, eds. *Articles of Faith, Articles of Peace: The Religious Liberty Clauses and the American Public Philosophy*. Washington, D.C.: The Brookings Institution, 1990.

Hunter, Rodney A. *Dictionary of Pastoral Care and Counseling*. Nashville: Abingdon, 1990.

Hunter, Steve. *Make Believe*. Garland, Tex.: Hannibal Books, 2006.

Ingle, Rick, ed. *If I Had My Ministry to Live Over I Would . . .* Nashville: Broadman, 1977.

Ironside, Harry. *Commentary on Ephesians*. Kregel Academic & Professional, 2007.

James, Powhatan W. *George W. Truett: A Biography*. Nashville: Broadman, 1939.

Jefferson, Charles. *The Minister as Shepherd*. Manila, Philippines: Living Books, 1973.

Jowett, J. H. *The Preacher and His Life and Work*. Cincinnati: Jennings and Graham, 1912.

Kaiser, Walter C., Jr. *Preaching and Teaching from the Old Testament*. Grand Rapids: Baker, 2003.

————. *Toward an Exegetical Theology*. Grand Rapids: Baker, 1981.

————. *The Uses of the Old Testament in the New*. Grand Rapids: Wm. B. Eerdmans Publishing Co., 1958.

Keller, Timothy J. *Ministries of Mercy: The Call of the Jericho Road*. Phillipsburg, N.J.: P and R Publishing, 1997.

Kendall, R. T. "Expositional Preaching" in *Northcutt Lectures*, sound. Fort Worth: Southwestern Baptist Theological Seminary, 1988.

Kent, Homer A., Sr. *The Pastor and His Work*. Chicago: Moody, 1963.

Kirksey, Franklin L. *Sound Biblical Preaching*. Charleston: BookSurge Publishing, 2004.

Klug, Ronald. *How to Keep a Spiritual Journal*. Nashville: Thomas Nelson, 1982.

Kouzes, James M. and Mary Z. Posner. *The Leadership Challenge*. 3rd ed. San Francisco: Jossey-Bass, 2002.

Kruis, John. *Quick Scripture Reference for Counseling*. Grand Rapids: Baker, 1994.

LaHaye, Tim. *If Ministers Fall Can They Be Restored?* Grand Rapids: Zondervan, 1990.

Laney, J. Carl. *A Guide to Church Discipline*. Minneapolis: Bethany House, 1985.

Larson, David L. *The Company of the Preachers*. Grand Rapids: Kregel, 1998.

Laurie, Greg. *The Upside Down Church*. Wheaton: Tyndale House, 1999.

Lee, Harris W. *Effective Church Leadership*. Minneapolis: Augsburg, 1989.

Liefeld, Walter L. *New Testament Exposition*. Grand Rapids: Zondervan, 1984.

Lloyd-Jones, Martyn. *Preaching and Preachers*. Grand Rapids: Zondervan, 1972.

London, H. B., Jr., and Neil B. Wiseman. *Becoming Your Favorite Church*. Ventura, Calif.: Regal Books, 2002.

————. *It Takes a Church Within a Village*. Nashville: Thomas Nelson, 1996.

————. *Married to a Pastor*. Ventura, Calif.: Regal Books, 1999.

————. *The Heart of a Great Pastor*. Ventura, Calif.: Regal Books, 1994.

————. *They Call Me Pastor*. Ventura, Calif.: Regal Books, 2000.

————. *Pastors at Greater Risk*. Ventura, Calif.: Regal Books, 2003.

————. *Pastors at Risk*. Wheaton: Victor Books, 1993.

————. *Your Pastor Is an Endangered Species*. Wheaton: Victor Books, 1996.

MacArthur, John, Jr., Wayne A. Mack, and The Master's College Faculty. *Introduction to Biblical Counseling*. Dallas: Word, 1994.

MacArthur, John, Jr. *Being Leaders*. Grand Rapids: Baker, 2003.

————. *Pastoral Ministry: How to Shepherd Biblically.* Nashville: Thomas Nelson, 2005.

————. *Rediscovering Expository Preaching.* Dallas: Word, 1992.

————. *Rediscovering Pastoral Ministry.* Dallas: Word, 1995.

Malphurs, Aubrey. *The Dynamics of Church Leadership.* Grand Rapids: Baker, 1999.

————. *Values-Driven Leadership.* Grand Rapids: Baker, 1996.

Mann, Mark. *One Ministry of the Word.* Stanley, N.C.: Timeless Texts, 2004.

Mathewson, Steven D. *The Art of Preaching Old Testament Narrative.* Grand Rapids: Baker, 2002.

Mawhinney, Bruce. *Preaching with Freshness.* Grand Rapids: Kregel, 1997.

McBeth, H. Leon. *The Baptist Heritage.* Nashville: Broadman Press, 1987.

————. *The First Baptist Church of Dallas: Centennial History 1868–1968.* Grand Rapids: Zondervan Press, 1968.

McCarty, Barry C. *A Parliamentary Guide for Church Leaders.* Nashville: Broadman, 1987.

McDill, Wayne. *Moment of Truth.* Nashville: Broadman & Holman, 1999.

————. *The 12 Essentials for Great Preaching.* Nashville: Broadman & Holman, 1994.

McGrath, Alister E. *Introduction to Christian Theology.* 4th ed. London: Blackwell Publications, 2006.

Means, James E. *Leadership in Christian Ministry.* Grand Rapids: Baker, 1989.

Miles, Rebekah L. *The Pastor as Moral Guide.* Minneapolis: Augsburg Fortress, 1999.

Miller, Calvin. *The Empowered Leader.* Nashville: Broadman & Holman, 1995.

Milton, Joyce. *The Road to Malpsychia.* San Francisco: Encounter Books, 2002.

Mohler, Albert R. *Feed My Sheep.* Morgan, Pa.: Soli Deo Gloria, 2002.

Morgan, G. Campbell. *The Ministry of the Word.* New York: Fleming H. Revell, 1919.

————. *Preaching.* New York: Fleming H. Revell, 1937.

————. *The Practice of Prayer.* Alexandria: Lamplighter Publications, n.d.

Narramore, Clyde M. *Why a Christian Leader May Fall.* Westchester: Crossway, 1988.

Nelson's Minister's Manual. Nashville: Thomas Nelson, 2003.

Oates, Wayne E., ed. *An Introduction to Pastoral Counseling.* Nashville: Broadman Press, 1959.

————. *Pastoral Counseling.* Philadelphia: Westminster, 1974.

————. *Pastoral Counseling in Social Problems.* Philadelphia: Westminster, 1966.

————. *People in Pain.* Philadelphia: Westminster, 1985.

————. *Protestant Pastoral Counseling.* Philadelphia: Westminster, 1962.

————. *The Christian Pastor.* 3rd edition. Philadelphia: Westminster, 1982.

————. *The Religious Care of the Psychiatric Patient.* Philadelphia: Westminster, 1978.

————. *The Revelation of God in Human Suffering.* Philadelphia: Westminster, 1959.

————. *The Struggle to Be Free.* Philadelphia: Westminster, 1983.

————. *When Religion Gets Sick.* Philadelphia: Westminster, 1970.

Olford, Stephen F. and David L. Olford. *Anointed Expository Preaching.* Nashville: Broadman & Holman, 1998.

Pendleton, J. M. *Baptist Church Manual.* Rev. ed. Nashville: Broadman Press, 1966.

Peretti, Frank. *This Present Darkness.* Carol Stream, Ill.: Tyndale House, 2003.

Peterson, Eugene H. *The Contemplative Pastor.* Dallas: Word, 1989.

Piper, John. *Brothers, We Are Not Professionals.* Nashville: Broadman & Holman, 2002.

————. *The Supremacy of God in Preaching.* Grand Rapids: Baker, 2004.

Porter, Ebenezer. *The Young Preacher's Manual.* 1829

Powilson, David. *Power Encounters.* Grand Rapids: Baker, 1995.

Prime, Derek. *On Being a Pastor: Understanding Our Calling and Work.* Chicago: Moody, 2004.

Reid, Alvin. *His Heart, Our Hands.* Atlanta: SBC North American Mission Board, 2000.

Richmond, Kent D. *Preaching to Sufferers.* Nashville: Abingdon Press, 1988.

———. *The Pastor and the Patient.* Nashville: Abingdon Press, 1992.

———. *Time to Die: A Handbook for Funeral Sermons.* Nashville: Abingdon Press, 1990.

Rienecker, Fritz and Cleon Rogers. *Linguistic Key to the Greek New Testament.* Grand Rapids: Zondervan, 1976.

Robert, Henry M., III, William J. Evans, Daniel H. Honemann, and Thomas J. Balch, eds. *Robert's Rules of Order,* 10th ed. London: Harper Collins, 2000.

Robertson, A. T. *The Glory of the Ministry: Paul's Exultation in Preaching.* New York: Fleming Revell, 1911.

———. *Word Pictures in the New Testament,* 6 vols. Nashville: Broadman & Holman, 1980.

Robinson, Haddon W. *Biblical Preaching.* 2nd ed. Grand Rapids: Baker, 2001.

———. *Making a Difference in Preaching.* Grand Rapids: Baker, 1999.

Rush, Myron. *The New Leader.* Wheaton: Victor, 1987.

Sande, Ken. *The Peace Maker: A Biblical Guide to Resolving Personal Conflict.* Grand Rapids: Baker, 1991.

Sanders, J. Oswald. *Spiritual Leadership.* Chicago: Moody, 1967.

Schaller, Lyle. *Decision Makers: How to Improve the Quality of Decision-making in the Churches.* Nashville: Abingdon Press, 1974.

———. *Middle Sized Churches.* Nashville: Abingdon Press, 1985.

———. *Multiple Staff and the Larger Churches.* Nashville: Abingdon Press, 1980.

———. *Senior Minister.* Nashville: Abingdon Press, 1988.

———. *The Pastor and the People.* Nashville: Abingdon, 1973.

Shaddix, Jim. *The Passion Driven Sermon.* Nashville: Broadman & Holman, 2003.

Shawchuck, Norman and Roger Heuser. *Leading the Congregation.* Nashville: Abingdon, 1993.

Sheehy, Gail. *New Passages.* New York: Random House, 1995.

Sire, James W. *Chris Chrisman Goes to College.* Downers Grove: InterVarsity, 1993.

Smith, Charles Merrill. *How to Become a Bishop Without Being Religious.* Garden City: Doubleday, 1965.

Smith, Fred. *Learning to Lead.* Waco: Word, 1986.

Spurgeon, C. H. *Lectures to My Students.* Grand Rapids, Zondervan, 1977. Grand Rapids: Kregel, 2004.

———. *Only a Prayer Meeting.* Pasadena: Pilgrim Publishers, 1976.

Stanley, Andy. *Choosing to Cheat.* Sisters, Ore.: Multnomah, 2003.

Steer, Roger, ed. *The George Mueller Treasury.* Westchester, Ill.: Crossway Books, 1987.

Stewart, James S. *Heralds of God.* Vancouver, British Columbia, Canada: Regent College Publishing, 1946, 2001.

Stott, John R. W. *Between Two Worlds.* Grand Rapids: Eerdmans, 1982.

———. *I Believe in Preaching.* London: Hodder & Stoughton, 1982, 1986.

Streett, R. Alan. *The Effective Invitation.* Updated Ed. Grand Rapids: Kregel, 2004.

Sugden, Howard F., and Warren W. Wiersbe. *Answers to Pastors' FAQs.* Colorado Springs: NEXGEN, 2005.

Sutton, Jerry. *The Baptist Reformation.* Nashville: Broadman & Holman, 1999.

Swetland, Kenneth L. *The Hidden World of the Pastor.* Grand Rapids: Baker, 1995.

Taylor, Charles W. *The Skilled Pastor: Counseling as the Practice of Theology.* 1991.

Thomas, Gary. *Sacred Marriage.* Grand Rapids: Zondervan, 2000.

Trull, Joe E. and James E. Carter. *Ministerial Ethics*. 2nd ed. Grand Rapids: Baker Academic, 2004.

Unger, Merrill. *Principles of Expository Preaching*. Grand Rapids: Zondervan, 1955.

Vernick, Leslie. *How to Act Right When Your Spouse Acts Wrong*. Colorado Springs: Waterbrook Press, 2003.

Vines, Jerry and Jim Shaddix. *Power in the Pulpit*. Chicago: Moody Press, 1999.

Wagner, E. Glen. *Escape from Church, Inc.: The Return of the Pastor-Shepherd*. Grand Rapids: Zondervan, 1999.

Ward, Waylon D. *The Bible in Counseling*. Chicago: Moody Press, 1977.

Webber, F. R. *A History of Preaching in Britain and America*. Milwaukee: Northwest Publishers, 1952.

Webber, Robert, ed. *Biblical Foundations of Christian Worship*. Nashville: Star Song, 1993.

———. *Blended Worship*. Peabody: Hendrickson, 1996.

———. *Renewal of Sunday Worship*. Nashville: Star Song, 1993.

Weems, Lovett H., Jr. *Church Leadership*. Nashville: Abingdon, 1993.

Wells, C. Richard. *Inspired Preaching*. Nashville: Broadman & Holman, 2002.

Wemp, C. Sumner. *The Guide to Practical Pastoring*. Shelbyville, Tenn.: Bible and Literature Missionary Foundation, 1982.

Whitney, Donald S. *Simplify Your Spiritual Life*. Colorado Springs: NavPress, 2003.

———. *Spiritual Disciplines for the Christian Life*. Colorado Springs: NavPress, 1991.

Wiersbe, Warren W. *Developing a Christian Imagination*. Wheaton: Victor, 1995.

———. *Expository Outlines of the New Testament*. Wheaton: Victor, 1992.

———. *Expository Outlines of the Old Testament*. Wheaton: Victor, 1993.

———. *Listening to the Giants*. Grand Rapids: Baker, 1980.

———. *Making Sense of the Ministry*. Chicago: Moody Press, 1983.

———. *On Being a Servant of God*. Grand Rapids: Baker, 1993.

———. *Preaching and Teaching with Imagination*. Grand Rapids: Baker, 1994.

———. *Real Worship*. Grand Rapids: Baker Book, 2000.

———. *The Dynamics of Preaching*. Grand Rapids: Baker, 1999.

———. *Walking with the Giants*. Grand Rapids: Baker, 1976.

Wilkes, C. Gene. *Jesus on Leadership*. Nashville: LifeWay, 1996.

———. *Paul on Leadership*. Nashville: LifeWay, 2004.